MYTH AND ITS MAKING IN THE FRENCH THEATRE

Studies presented to W. D. Howarth

Edited by
**E. FREEMAN, H. MASON
M. O'REGAN, S. W. TAYLOR**

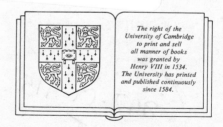

The right of the
University of Cambridge
to print and sell
all manner of books
was granted by
Henry VIII in 1534.
The University has printed
and published continuously
since 1584.

CAMBRIDGE UNIVERSITY PRESS

Cambridge

New York   New Rochelle   Melbourne   Sydney

Published by the Press Syndicate of the University of Cambridge
The Pitt Building, Trumpington Street, Cambridge CB2 1RP
32 East 57th Street, New York, NY 10022, USA
10 Stamford Road, Oakleigh, Melbourne 3166, Australia

First published 1988

Printed in Great Britain at
the University Press, Cambridge

British Library cataloguing in publication data
Myth and its making in the French theatre:
studies presented to W. D. Howarth.
1. French drama − History and criticism
2. Myth in literature
I. Howarth, W. D.   II. Freeman, E.
842′.00915   PQ591.M9

Library of Congress cataloguing in publication data
Myth and its making in the French theatre : studies presented to W. D.
Howarth / edited by E. Freeman . . . [et al.].
p.   cm.
Bibliography.
ISBN 0 521 32188 3
1. French drama − History and criticism. 2. Mythology in
literature. 3. Myth in literature. 4. Howarth, W. D. (William
Driver) I. Howarth, W. D. (William Driver) II. Freeman, E.
PQ518.M9   1988
842′.009 15 − dc 19   87−32992 CIP

ISBN 0 521 32188 3

GG

Contents

CONTENTS

vi

Illustrations

vii

W. D. Howarth: an appreciation

William Driver Howarth is of south Yorkshire stock, born in 1922 and educated at Silcoates School. In 1941 he went up to Queen's College, Oxford, to read French and Latin; but, in the manner of the time, after one session his undergraduate studies were cut short by war service. In his case, this meant Bomber Command of the Royal Air Force, in which he saw active service as a navigator in the European theatre. He took up his interrupted studies in 1945, graduating in 1947 and being awarded the college's Laming Travelling Fellowship. This enabled him to spend the 1947–8 session in Paris, where, as well as researching into the eighteenth-century novel, he continued his strenuous activities on the rugby field, playing for the local SNCF team and thereby becoming one of the few future professors of French to achieve the status of honorary *cheminot*. His cricketing prowess had to await his return to England to find continued outlet for its practice.

In 1948 he was elected Fellow and Tutor of Jesus College, Oxford, and there began the career of the probing and enthusiastic teaching of all aspects of modern French language and literature; this was to win him the gratitude and respect − as well as the friendship − of students over the next four decades. Meantime he devoted himself to research in an equally wholehearted manner, turning his attention now principally to the seventeenth century and also the French theatre over the whole of the modern period. His unremitting activity in the research field is clearly documented in the bibliography that Robin Slaughter, with characteristic care, has compiled for this volume. In addition to his publications, there has been a string of higher degrees supervised by him, whose recipients all testify to the thoroughgoing attention he devoted to their work. He also found time to act as general editor, over a period of many years, of Oxford University Press's Clarendon French Series.

In 1966, on William Stewart's retirement, Bill Howarth moved to Bristol where he was appointed Professor of Classical French Literature. He lost no time in fitting into the very different environment, and it was immediately evident that Bristol French Department's tradition of friendliness and hospitality was in no danger of going into decline. It was unfortunate that this move coincided with the onset of widespread student unrest, but within a year of his arrival in Bristol he was in the thick of the action, having accepted the chairmanship of the Union Management Committee just in time to be faced with a student occupation of Senate House. The fact that the university recovered from this painful experience fairly quickly and with a minimum of bitterness was due to the sense and cool judgement of a handful of people, and among them Bill played a decisive role, becoming Chairman of the newly created Joint Committee of Council, Senate and the Union – one of a number of reforming initiatives in which he was active. His departmental commitment remained unflagging, and on Ronald Grimsley's retirement in 1981 he became Head of the Department of French.

His willingness to take on a range of administrative tasks that most people would find daunting is almost legendary – perhaps in the present context it might even be considered to have a mythic quality. To rehearse the list of his committees strikes awe into the heart of an ordinary mortal: 1969, Publications Committee (under his chairmanship, 1973–81, the University Printing Unit was set up and the first works published under its imprint); 1970, Library Committee; 1975, Member of Council; 1976, Member of Finance Committee; 1978, Dean of the Faculty of Arts; 1983, Pro-Vice-Chancellor. That is a selection only. What has to be stressed is that – as all his departmental colleagues will testify – none of all this was allowed to affect either his research or his teaching: he was often forced to rearrange teaching commitments but he never abandoned them or sought to lighten his load.

His commitment to the development of his subject in its wider context within the university was illustrated when, in the mid-seventies he played an important role in establishing the School of Modern Languages inside the Faculty of Arts; what had before been a disparate set of autonomous departments and semi-autonomous sub-departments achieved a kind of federal union status that has worked to the benefit of all. It was appropriate that he should have been chosen to be its first Chairman. It was also thanks to him that the Subsidiary Subject 'European Literature in Translation' was set up: only his energy and friendly contacts could have made liaison with so many different departments possible, and he continued to organize the course until he became Dean. Similarly, but in a wider field, he was moving spirit and founding father of the Society for Seventeenth-Century French Studies, a notably successful development of the last decade; he served as its Chairman from 1981 to 1984.

Department, university, scholarship: enough to fill a life, one might suppose, but there is more. Where most people regard their civic duties as fulfilled when they record their vote, Bill Howarth insists on playing an active part in politics, having even stood for election as Liberal councillor (seldom can a family have prayed so fervently for the defeat of a loved one's ambitions). Shortly after coming to Bristol he was co-opted on to the Committee of the Bristol–Bordeaux Association − the first and one of the most active of Anglo-French town-twinnings, largely the brainchild of his predecessor as Head of the French Department, William Stewart; since 1976 he has been its Chairman, performing the duties with the enthusiasm and attention to detail that mark all he does, and presiding over its fortieth anniversary celebrations in 1987. Nor is his interest in the theatre just academic: since 1981 he has been Chairman of Bristol Opera Company, whose status is amateur but whose standards are professional; and in February 1987 he even emerged from an extended Thespian hibernation to play the part of Brid'oison in Beaumarchais's *Mariage de Figaro*.

Then there is the domestic man. There may be a score of student essays to be marked by Monday morning; the diary be full of meetings; a seminar or two to prepare; the proofs of an article to be read, and two or three dilatory contributors to the next volume to be chivvied. No matter, the cupboard in the spare bedroom will be completed by Sunday night, or the cottage in Wales reroofed. There are four children, and their families, dispersed over a fluctuating number of countries, to be kept in touch with. Barbara's life is no less animated than Bill's, yet not only does she unreservedly support him in his multifarious activities but they both give most generously of their time and concern to a wide circle of friends, among whom all the members, past and present, of the Bristol French Department are happy to be numbered.

S. W. T.

Bibliography of W. D. Howarth's writings

I. BOOKS

1 *Life and Letters in France: The Seventeenth Century*, London, Nelson (Life and Letters in France, I), 1965, xxvi + 237 pp. Paperback reprint, 1970.

2 (With C. L. Walton), *Explications: The Technique of French Literary Appreciation*, London, Oxford University Press, 1971, xlvii + 270 pp.

3 *Sublime and Grotesque: A Study of French Romantic Drama*, London, Harrap, 1975, 445 pp.

4 *Molière: A Playwright and his Audience*, Cambridge University Press (Major European Authors), 1982, xiii + 325 pp. Hardback and paperback. Several reprints by 1987.

4a *Molière: uno scrittore di teatro e il suo pubblico*, translation of no. 4 by Elisabetta Venturi & Vittorio Ricci, Bologna, Il Mulino, 1987.

5 *Anouilh: 'Antigone'*, London, Edward Arnold (Studies in French Literature, 33), 1983, 64 pp.

6 *Corneille: 'Le Cid'*, London, Grant & Cutler (Critical Guides to French texts) (to appear).

II. EDITIONS OF TEXTS

7 Henri Troyat, *La Neige en deuil*, with introduction and notes, London, Harrap, 1954, 143 pp. 16th reprint, 1985.

8 Molière, *Dom Juan, ou Le Festin de pierre* (based on the Amsterdam edition), with introduction and notes, Oxford, Basil Blackwell (Blackwell's French Texts), 1958, xliv + 100 pp. 5th impression, 1983.

9 Anouilh, *Pauvre Bitos*, with introduction and notes, London, Harrap, 1958, 151 pp. 7th reprint, 1983.

10 Anouilh, *Le Bal des Voleurs*, with introduction and notes, London, Harrap, 1960, 109 pp. 9th reprint, 1985.

11 Anouilh, *Becket ou l'Honneur de Dieu*, with introduction and notes, London, Harrap, 1962, 160 pp. 22nd reprint, 1986.

12 Molière, *L'Ecole des Femmes and La Critique de l'Ecole des Femmes*, with introduction and notes, Oxford, Basil Blackwell (Blackwell's French Texts), 1963, xxxiii + 142 pp. 5th reprint, 1983.

13 Nivelle de la Chaussée, *Mélanide, Comédie en cinq actes en vers*, with introduction and notes, Brighton, University of Sussex Library (Sussex Reprints), 1973, 102 pp.

14 Voltaire, *Le Droit du seigneur*, critical edition in *Complete Works*, 50 (1760, I), Oxford, Taylor Institution, The Voltaire Foundation, 1986, pp. 1–219.

III. BOOKS EDITED

15 (With Merlin Thomas), *Molière: Stage and Study. Essays in Honour of W. G. Moore*, Oxford, Clarendon Press, 1973, xvi + 293 pp.

16 *Comic Drama: The European Heritage*, with 'Introduction: Theoretical Considerations' (pp. 1–21), London, Methuen, 1978, ix + 194 pp.

17 (With Ian McFarlane and Margaret McGowan), *Form and Meaning: Aesthetic Coherence in Seventeenth-Century French Drama. Studies presented to Harry Barnwell*, Amersham, England, Avebury Press, 1982, vii + 203 pp.

IV. ARTICLES, CHAPTERS, CONTRIBUTIONS TO CONFERENCES AND FESTSCHRIFTEN, etc.

18 'The Theme of *Tartuffe* in Eighteenth-Century Comedy', *French Studies*, IV (1950), 113–27.

19 '*Dom Garcie de Navarre* or *Le Prince Jaloux*?', *French Studies*, V (1951), 140–8.

20 '*Dom Juan* Reconsidered: A Defence of the Amsterdam Edition', *French Studies*, XII (1958), 222–33.

21 'The Theme of the *Droit du seigneur* in the Eighteenth-Century Theatre', *French Studies*, XV (1961), 228–40.

22 'Cervantes and Fletcher: A Theme With Variations', *Modern Language Review*, LVI (1961), 563–6.

23 'The Sources of *L'Ecole des Femmes*', *Modern Language Review*, LVIII (1963), 10–14.

24 Contributions on Marie-Joseph Chénier, Crébillon Père & Fils, La Harpe, La Motte and Piron in *Encyclopaedia Britannica*, 1964.

25 'History in the Theatre: The French and English Traditions', *Trivium*, I (1966), 151–68.

26 'The Recognition Scene in *Le Mariage de Figaro*', *Modern Language Review*, LXIV (1969), 301–11.

27 '*Droit du seigneur*: Fact or Fantasy?', *Journal of European Studies*, I (1971), 291–312.

28 'French Literature from 1600 to 1750', *France: A Companion to French Studies*, ed. D. G. Charlton, London, Methuen, 1972, pp. 291–330. 2nd edition, 1979. University Paperback, 1983.

29 'Anouilh', *Forces in Modern French Drama, Studies in Variations on the Permitted Lie*, ed. John Fletcher, University of London Press, 1972, pp. 86–109.

30 'Anouilh and Molière', *Molière: Stage and Study* (no. 15 above), 1973, pp. 273–88.

31 *Molière, Man of Parts: Actor and Playwright*, pamphlet prepared in connection with a Molière Tercentenary Exhibition, University of Bristol, 1973, 24 pp.

32 'La Notion de la catharsis dans la comédie classique française', *Revue des Sciences Humaines*, CLII (1973), 521–39.

33 'Alceste, ou l'honnête homme imaginaire', *Revue d'Histoire du Théâtre*, 26e Année, I (Actes des journées internationales Molière) (1974), 93–8.

34   'French Literature from 1600 to 1750', republished in *French Literature from 1600 to the Present*, with Henri M. Peyre and John Cruickshank, London, Methuen (University Paperback), 1974, pp. 1–44 (same as no. 28 above).

35   'The Playwright as Hero: Biographical Plays with Molière as Protagonist, 1673–1972', *Molière and the Commonwealth of Letters: Patrimony and Posterity*, ed. Roger Johnson Jr, Editha S. Neumann and Guy T. Trail, Jackson, University Press of Mississippi, 1975, pp. 557–72.

36   'Victor Hugo and the "Failure" of French Romantic Drama', *L'Esprit Créateur*, XVI, 3 (1976), 247–56.

37   'Comedy in France', *Comic Drama: The European Heritage* (no. 16 above), 1978, pp. 102–21.

38   'Neo-Classicism in France; a Re-Assessment', *Studies in the French Eighteenth Century presented to John Lough*, ed. D. J. Mossop, G. E. Rodmell and D. B. Wilson, University of Durham, 1978, pp. 92–107.

39   'The Playwright as Preacher: Didacticism and Melodrama in the French Theatre of the Enlightenment', *Forum for Modern Language Studies*, XIV (1978), 97–115.

40   'Tragedy into Melodrama: the Fortunes of the Calas Affair on the Stage', *Studies on Voltaire and the Eighteenth Century*, CLXXIV (1978), 121–50.

41   'Word and Image in Pixerécourt's Melodramas: The Dramaturgy of the Strip-Cartoon', *Performance and Politics in Popular Drama: Aspects of Popular Entertainment in the Theatre, Film and Television 1800–1976* (arising from a conference held at the University of Kent, Canterbury, September 1977), ed. David Bradby, Louis James and Bernard Sharratt, Cambridge University Press, 1980, pp. 17–32.

42   'Portrait and Self-Portrait in French Classical Drama', *Newsletter of the Society for Seventeenth-Century French Studies*, II (1980), 52–9.

43   'Un Etranger devant le comique français', *Le Français dans le Monde*, CLI (1980), 31–5.

44   'Voltaire, Ninon de l'Enclos and the Evolution of a Dramatic

Genre', *Studies on Voltaire and the Eighteenth Century*, CXCIX (1981), 63–72.

45 'Molière at the "Maison de Molière", 1680–1715: The Taste of the *honnêtes gens*', *Newsletter of the Society for Seventeenth-Century French Studies*, III (1981), 21–9.

46 ' "Une pièce comique tout à fait achevée": Aesthetic Coherence in *Les Femmes savantes*', *Form and Meaning: Aesthetic Coherence in Seventeenth-Century French Drama* (no. 17 above), 1982, pp. 142–55.

47 'Some Thoughts on the Function of Rhyme in French Classical Tragedy', *The Equilibrium of Wit: Essays for Odette de Mourgues*, ed. Peter Bayley and Dorothy Gabe Coleman, Lexington, Kentucky, French Forum (French Forum Monographs, 36), 1982, pp. 150–65.

48 Contributions on Alexandre Dumas Fils and Victorien Sardou in *Makers of Nineteenth-Century Culture*, ed. J. Wintle, London, Routledge Kegan Paul, 1982.

49 'Drama', *The French Romantics*, ed. D. G. Charlton, Cambridge University Press, 1984, pp. 205–47.

50 'Mécénat et raison d'état: Richelieu, Corneille et la tragédie politique', *L'Age d'or du mécénat*, Paris, C.N.R.S., 1985, pp. 59–68.

51 'Corneille and Comedy', *Seventeenth-Century French Studies*, VII (1985), pp. 198–215.

52 'Une Peinture de la conversation des honnêtes gens: Corneille et la comédie de mœurs', *Pierre Corneille: Actes du colloque organisé par l'Université de Rouen tenu à Rouen du 2 au 6 octobre 1984*, ed. Alain Niderst, Paris, Presses Universitaires de France, 1985, pp. 343–56.

53 'Bonaparte on Stage: the Napoleonic Legend in Nineteenth-Century French Drama' (paper of which a draft was read at the *Themes in Drama* International Conference at the University of London, Westfield College, March 1984), *Historical Drama*, ed. James Redmond, Cambridge University Press (Themes in Drama, 8), 1986, pp. 139–61.

54 'L'Alexandrin classique, instrument du dialogue théâtral', *Dramaturgies, langages dramatiques: Mélanges pour Jacques Scherer*, Paris, Nizet, 1986, pp. 341–54.

55 'Comedy in the Theatre of Jean Anouilh: From a Rose-coloured to a Jaundiced View of Life', *Die Europäische Komödie*, ed. H. Mainusch (to appear).

56 'Assimilation and Adaptation of Existing Forms in the Drama of the Romantic Period', *Romantic Drama*, ed. G. Gillespie (to appear).

57 'French Literature: The Seventeenth Century', *Encyclopaedia Britannica* (to appear in next edition).

58 'From Satire to Comedy of Ideas: The Examples of Anouilh & Stoppard' (Lecture given at British Institute, Paris, 1982), to be published in *Franco-British Studies*, III.

59 'From *Le Roi s'amuse* to *Rigoletto*: More Sublime but Less Grotesque?' (Proceedings of Bristol 'Journée Victor Hugo', 1985), to be published in *Quinquereme*, X.

60 'From Classical Tragedy to Romantic Drama: The Monstrous Demythologised' (proceedings of Conference on Monsters and the Monstrous in French Literature, Durham, 1986), to appear in *Durham French Colloquies*, I.

61 'From Arlequin to Ubu: Farce as Anti-Theatre' (proceedings of *Themes in Drama* Conference at the University of London, Westfield College, 1986), to be published by Cambridge University Press (Themes in Drama, 10).

62 'English Humour and French *comique*: The Cases of Anouilh and Ayckbourn' (paper given at the British Comparative Literature Association Conference, Manchester, 1986), to be published in *New Comparison*, III, Summer 1987.

V. IN PREPARATION

63 (ed.), Voltaire, *Le Dépositaire*, critical edition in *Complete Works*, Oxford, Taylor Institution, The Voltaire Foundation.

64 (ed.), *A Documentary History of European Drama*, VIII, for Cambridge University Press.

65 'The Robespierre/Danton Theme in European Drama', for Colston Symposium, Bristol, 1988.

66 'A Hero Like Ourselves: A Theoretical Commonplace Re-examined', for *Kunstgriffe. Festschrift für Herbert Mainusch*, to be published by A. Narr, Tübingen, 1989.

In addition, Professor Howarth has contributed some 150 reviews to various scholarly journals from 1953 onwards.

H. R. Slaughter

Preface

'Le théâtre sera mythique ou il ne sera pas'
Antonin Artaud

'Tous les mythes sont vrais'　　Pierre Albouy

The authors of the fifteen essays that make up this volume were invited to interpret 'Myth and its Making' in the widest possible sense. They were encouraged to re-examine not only the time-honoured ancient themes that have been exploited in the French theatre from the Renaissance to the twentieth century, but other literary, historical or legendary subjects that have undergone a similar process of mythic enhancement and stylization. Thus they have explored the ways in which existing literary myths — those of Thebes, Troy and the erotic universe of Don Juan — renewed themselves, as well as the processes involved in creating new myths for the age in which we live. No culture has proved more richly innovative in its mythopoeia than the French from the time of the Revolution onwards. Indeed, in 1969 Pierre Albouy went so far (and further than the present editors would want to go) as to limit his *Mythes et mythologies dans la littérature française* more or less exclusively to the nineteenth and twentieth centuries.

However fruitful Albouy's study may be, we have not wished to restrict our contributors to a historical time-limit; rather, we have sought to transcend the great divide 1789–1815. Thus while some of the questions raised in the essays are specific to an age, many too touch on aesthetic or strategic dilemmas encountered by Racine *and* Montherlant, Voltaire *and* Sartre. How can myth serve as camouflage, a political expedient to ensure performance in a hostile climate? Do supernatural endings pose insuperable problems for a dramatist in a rationalistic age — that of *Iphigénie* for Racine in the seventeenth century, of *Don Juan* for Montherlant in the twentieth? What is the function of the various types of irony, parody and seemingly anti-mythic deflation in Musset, Giraudoux, Anouilh, and, once again, Montherlant? Cannot *place* — Rome in

xix

the sixteenth century, Troy in the imagination of Andromaque, sundry *grottes* and *palais* in the seventeenth and eighteenth centuries – attain a mythic status as significant as that of character? And is not the theatre itself, in its evolution from Aristotle to Artaud, as well as in its self-conscious, neo-baroque exploitation by Anouilh, the mythic place *par excellence*? What are the rhetorical devices and structures most suited to endowing a controversial political leader (who would have had the added disadvantage in the eyes of spectators of the 1840s of being small, ugly and black) with mythic grandeur? Toussaint Louverture's historical death was 'undramatic': how could it be replaced by a more heroic final curtain? Must myth in fact be grandiose? Is it not a delusion to look to myth for the meaning of life rather than for meanings? Is it not the case – as we see, appropriately, in the last essay in the volume – that myth can be everywhere in our daily life, polyvalent and all-pervasive?

These then are some of the subjects discussed in this collective examination of 'Myth and its Making in the French Theatre'. The questions raised are many, as are the types of play and mythic theme under scrutiny. It is by encouraging such an approach that the editors have sought to pay tribute to the eclectic critical taste, and unfailing personal curiosity and energy of the man who has been to so many a stimulating colleague and friend.

E. Freeman

1
Du texte à la représentation

MICHEL CORVIN

Texte et représentation, ces deux termes couvrent un champ conceptuel considérable; un champ historique également très vaste, si bien que l'on pourrait presque dire: du texte à la représentation ou: d'Aristote à Artaud! Aussi pour éviter de parler au hasard et avant d'aborder les rapports du texte et de la représentation, il n'est peut-être pas inutile de s'interroger sur leurs multiples sens, ce qui aboutit à rien de moins qu'à mettre en cause les fondements mêmes du phénomène théâtral.

Sur le texte on rappellera quelques truismes: qu'il est écrit et donc suppose une relation directe (même si elle n'est pas explicitée) entre un émetteur–auteur et un récepteur–lecteur; les personnages restent toujours prisonniers de la page où ils sont couchés noir sur blanc; les répliques sont toujours des phrases; la littérature n'est jamais bien loin, avec son arsenal de règles d'écriture (rhétoriques, syntaxiques, etc.), son jeu de références culturelles et le poids de son contenu (psychologique, idéologique, etc.). Le théâtre, à ce compte, est un genre littéraire : il est de la littérature qui 'se donne un genre', comme on le dit de quelqu'un qui cherche à toute force à manifester son originalité; mais ce qui fait le genre est de l'ordre de la manifestation, non du manifesté. Autrement dit, le texte de théâtre n'a rien à dire de spécifique; il le dit autrement, sans doute, mais cela ne suffit pas fondamentalement à changer le rapport du lecteur à l'œuvre. Rapport simple qui s'apparente à l'explication, c'est-à-dire étymologiquement, au dépliage soigneux, exhaustif et indiscutable d'une feuille (d'une page) fermée sur elle-même. Ce n'est pas un hasard si la tradition scolaire française veut que l'explication de texte soit la meilleure voie d'accès à la lecture.

Vision naïve, somme toute matérialiste, qui s'en tient à ce qu'on voit du texte, à ses marques scripturaires, alors que le mot de texte, dans son sens de texture, de tissage, dit assez que le tout n'est pas l'addition des parties, que les parties (trame et chaîne) changent de nature en se combinant et que décrire un tissu n'est certainement pas un moyen suffisant pour savoir comment il est fait. Les spec-

1

tateurs, peut-on dire déjà, qui attendent de la représentation qu'elle restitue, fidèlement comme on dit, le texte, veulent en fait assister à une lecture à haute voix, de type explicatif et tautologique, d'autant plus univoque et simplifiée qu'elle est rapide et brouillée par les conditions de l'émission (distance de la scène à la salle, occasions diverses de distraction, etc.). Si le sens est dans les mots, si le sens est déjà là (la notion de fidélité suppose à la fois permanence et immanence des valeurs) la représentation, rigoureusement, n'existe pas: elle n'est qu'un porte-parole.

Pourtant il semble qu'elle existe, et multiforme. Elle est d'abord un spectacle de mots, de sons, de gestes, de cris, de chants, de danse, et je le préfère alors dans une langue étrangère ou insaisissable, de telle sorte que je reste à la surface matérielle du théâtre, au niveau de ses signifiants: ce qu'avaient bien vu les Futuristes russes qui, en inventant le langage transmental (*zaoumny iazyk*) fait d'une 'succession informe de termes privés de sens, d'une suite confuse de sons à l'état brut et de combinaisons arbitraires' (A. M. Ripellino), manifestent brutalement leur rejet de la littérature et situent le contenu du message théâtral à un niveau autre que conceptuel. Représentation dès lors signifie prestation spectaculaire, performance au sens français, c'est-à-dire de tour de force qui se justifie de ce qu'il montre, non de ce qu'il veut dire. Car qu'est-ce que veut dire la performance d'un athlète? Echappant totalement au dire, cette représentation-là échappe également au lire.

Représenter a bien d'autres sens:

Représenter c'est remplacer quelqu'un, se substituer à lui. Le représentant est un valant-pour; l'individu alors ne compte plus, mais sa fonction. C'est sans doute encore une figure (puisque le représentant se manifeste sous les espèces d'un individu, homme ou femme), mais pour une fonction. Le théâtre est plein de représentants de cette sorte: ce sont les comédiens; ils sont les substituts des personnages; ils sont présents mais en fait ils représentent; leur être profond, leur vie privée importent peu. Compte seul l'ensemble de traits différentiels (jeune, riche, puissant, méchant ou l'inverse) grâce auquel ils mettent en marche un être imaginaire n'ayant d'existence que par eux et à qui les comédiens accordent leur présence physique pour nous donner l'impression que ces êtres, les personnages, vivent d'une vraie vie: représenter c'est bien remplacer, avec ce résultat ambigu qu'à force de remplacer quelqu'un qui ne se montrera jamais, on finit par vous prendre pour lui. C'est le mécanisme même de l'illusion scénique: à force de faire semblant,

2

de faire 'comme si', on finit par croire à la réalité de ce qu'on voit et à l'existence de ces 'caractères' d'imprimerie que sont les personnages.

Représenter c'est encore permettre la reconnaissance, faire que l'inconnu, la perception neuve s'inscrivent dans le cadre du connu, du déjà vu: on connaît la réaction habituelle en face de telle toile cubiste où la figurativité est dévoyée; on regarde avec stupeur ces taches désordonnées ou trop géométriques, ces zébrures incontrôlées et l'on dit, apitoyé ou méprisant: 'Qu'est-ce que cela représente?' On cherche alors un cadre de référence antérieur ou extérieur au tableau (guitare ou visage) qui en serait la forme organisatrice et, partant, la justification. En reconnaissant le sujet traité, je situerai la toile dans un univers familier et pré-artistique qui, paradoxalement, m'habilitera à donner au peintre le brevet d'artiste. Représenter c'est donc reproduire plus ou moins fidèlement (on accepte par exemple que Van Gogh, dans ses autoportraits, ait les cheveux verts) un modèle, physique quand il s'agit de peinture, mental, social, idéologique quand il s'agit de théâtre. Modèle, parce que la reproduction en elle-même n'intéresse pas; la fidélité de la copie ne vaut que si l'original s'inscrit dans un cadre de généralité assez vaste pour que je me reconnaisse à travers lui. On met ici le doigt sur l'ambiguïté de cette acception de la représentation: il s'agit sans doute de reproduire, mais de reproduire une réalité absente, non pas idéalisée mais au contraire 'médiocrisée' puisqu'elle résulte d'une sorte de moyenne établie à partir des traits individuels réduits au type; on dessine alors le portrait-robot de l'humanité. Et c'est bien ce que veut faire le théâtre dit psychologique, le théâtre qui, selon Aristote est 'l'imitation de la vie'. Certes, imitation n'est pas reproduction; imitation suppose différence (sinon c'est d'identité qu'il s'agit) pour la raison justement que la reproduction théâtrale ne peut être une restitution à l'identique; elle ne saurait être que la reconstitution, par une sorte de chirurgie esthétique, des traits essentiels de l'espèce.

On le voit: ici nous ne sommes plus dans le spectacle, dans la représentation théâtrale, mais dans le texte de théâtre, au moment même où il s'écrit et se demande de quoi il va bien pouvoir parler. Naturellement ce premier moment − de la transcription sur papier d'un modèle humain général connu et reconnaissable en histoire et personnages particuliers encore inconnus et non reconnaissables tant que par tel ou tel moyen l'écrivain n'aura pas réussi à faire percevoir aux spectateurs qu'ils ne sont que l'émanation du modèle

— cette transcription donc s'accompagne d'une autre transposition, elle sur la scène, et c'est derechef la représentation, au sens où elle rend présent ce qui était encore enfermé dans les pages intemporelles d'un livre. Autrement dit, le mouvement du théâtre — du théâtre occidental classique, s'entend, qui a connu quelques siècles de gloire, et quelques notables interruptions, du quatrième siècle avant Jésus-Christ à la fin du dix-neuvième siècle — est triple, en ce qui concerne la représentation: il part d'un univers de référence pré-existant, qu'il faut reconnaître et respecter; ensuite, par tout un jeu de substitutions, de réductions, de 'typisations', comme dirait Balzac, il procède à la réalisation livresque de cet univers; enfin, il parvient à l'incarnation en éléments scéniques (c'est-à-dire aussi bien en comédiens qu'en décors et lumières) de cet entrelacs de mots. Naturellement cette conception suppose et exige qu'il n'y ait pas de solution de continuité entre ces trois moments et mouvements, que le modèle soit intelligible, que l'écriture du réel soit fidèle (on ne se pose évidemment pas la question de savoir si elle a les moyens de l'être) et que la réalisation scénique n'ait qu'à se mettre à l'écoute et au service du texte sans que là non plus on se pose la question de savoir si, étant de nature différente du texte, la scène n'est pas, par principe, dans l'incapacité, le voudrait-elle, de représenter le texte.

C'est là ce qu'on peut appeler le théâtre aristotélicien, reconnaissable par tout ce qu'il a de mimétique.[1] Selon cette esthétique les gestes, la voix, la mimique des personnages doivent être en rapport de ressemblance étroit avec les gestes, la voix, la mimique d'un quelconque individu tiré de notre univers d'expérience et soumis aux mêmes états de conscience: la colère, dans la rue, ça se crie, la jalousie, ça se siffle, l'amour, ça se susurre, l'angoisse, ça se tremble: il en ira de même dans ce théâtre-là. Quant aux états de conscience eux-mêmes, ils seront identiques puisqu'ils s'expriment de la même façon et que le théâtre est un art du comportement — c'est sa limitation en même temps que la garantie de son caractère sensoriel, visuel et auditif. La fable et la situation, de même, répondront aux canons de l'expérience: généralement un conflit (et il suffit de mettre deux personnes l'une en face de l'autre pour qu'il y ait conflit) présente un début, un milieu et une fin, le milieu correspondant aux périodes de crise que toute relation humaine connaît. En ce qui concerne l'inscription de ce conflit et de ses personnages dans l'espace et le temps, il en ira de même: le lieu théâtral, en Grèce par exemple, est un morceau d'espace prélevé sur la

4

nature; il est à ciel ouvert, c'est-à-dire en communication directe avec l'environnement: le mur de la skènè qui le clôt, au fond, est assez bas (trois mètres environ) pour permettre aux spectateurs de voir, par-delà, la campagne ou la mer. Les deux entrées gauche et droite du théâtre s'appellent à cette époque côté ville et côté campagne, parce qu'effectivement, au Théâtre de Dionysos situé au pied de l'Acropole, l'on venait de la ville en entrant par la gauche et l'on s'en allait à la campagne en sortant par la droite. Pour le temps, il y va d'un même esprit de mimétisme car le temps fictif de la fable représentée doit correspondre autant que possible au temps réel de la représentation, de telle sorte que le spectateur ait l'impression que les personnages vivent vraiment devant lui, et au même rythme que lui, une aventure que lui-même pourrait vivre. Là-dessus, il est vrai, Aristote n'a pas dit grand-chose, mais ses successeurs ont beaucoup glosé et l'on sait combien les théoriciens classiques français du dix-septième siècle, par exemple, ont bataillé pour obtenir des écrivains de théâtre, de Corneille particulièrement, qu'ils respectent cet impératif.

Voilà donc les traits essentiels d'un théâtre 'naturaliste' avant la lettre, apte, par toutes ses caractéristiques mimétiques, à prendre le spectateur par la main, au niveau même de connaissances et de références où il se trouve, pour le mener à un élargissement de son expérience dans les domaines les plus divers: psychologique, social et idéologique. On voit que, selon cette conception, texte et représentation ne peuvent pas ne pas s'accorder et marcher du même pas, puisqu'ils sont mimétiques l'un et l'autre du même monde. Ce n'est pas que la représentation, par une sorte d'humilité forcée (où se lirait le dédain des cols blancs − les écrivains − pour les cols bleus − les techniciens de la scène) se mette au service du texte: texte et représentation regardent dans la même direction. La continuité est donc sans faille, même si le mimétisme textuel a un caractère plus subtil dans la mesure où le texte n'a pas, quoi qu'il fasse, de caractère directement figuratif, mais opère par transcription de l'invisible. Qu'à cela ne tienne: la représentation fera voir cet invisible, déjà presque révélé (comme une photographie) par le texte. C'est ce que pense et espère J. Copeau: 'La mise en scène est l'ensemble des opérations artistiques et techniques grâce auxquelles l'ouvrage conçu par un auteur passe d'une vie spirituelle et latente, celle du texte écrit, à une vie concrète et actuelle, celle de la scène.'

Naturellement un correctif s'impose d'emblée, mais qui ne modifie pas radicalement la nature de cette esthétique. 'L'art', comme l'ont dit les Anciens, 'c'est l'homme ajouté à la nature', c'est-à-dire une intervention délibérée de procédures techniques et intellectuelles propres à rendre la nature (la nature humaine évidemment) plus perceptible et consommable. Ce qui fait que, dans le théâtre classique, au nom de la concentration des effets — que j'appellerais volontiers 'dramatisation' — on a réduit le personnage à quelques traits différentiels nets et tranchés; on a exigé de lui qu'il soit stable, homogène et cohérent dans son être, d'un bout à l'autre de la pièce; on a voulu que la fable soit unitaire et très clairement centrée autour d'un conflit majeur; on a fait comme si ce conflit pouvait se régler dans un seul espace qui serait à lui seul le résumé de tous les espaces possibles; on a voulu que le temps soit ramassé en une crise rapide et décisive. Tout cela a constitué la convention théâtrale. Et dans le dosage de convention (arbitraire, artificielle et inventive, on le voit) et de reproduction (motivée, naturelle et passive) se situe le champ de l'esthétique théâtrale classique.

A ce théâtre psychologique-là Artaud réservera ses sarcasmes, estimant — laissons-en-lui la responsabilité — qu'il y a une liaison indissoluble entre théâtre psychologique et théâtre de texte: liaison qui aboutit, selon lui, à rejeter à la périphérie la représentation, c'est-à-dire la mise en jeu et en corps. Il écrira par exemple: 'Un théâtre qui soumet la mise en scène et la réalisation, c'est-à-dire tout ce qu'il y a en lui de spécifiquement théâtral, au texte, est un théâtre d'idiot, de fou, d'inverti, d'anti-poète et de positiviste, c'est-à-dire d'Occidental.' On voit déjà se profiler la conception que se fait Artaud de la représentation et, par elle, du théâtre: la représentation est sur la scène et elle n'est que sur la scène. On connaît sa phrase célèbre: 'Je dis que la scène est un lieu physique et concret qui demande qu'on le remplisse et qu'on lui fasse parler son langage concret'; ou: 'Et cela permet la substitution à la poésie du langage, d'une poésie dans l'espace qui se résoudra justement dans le domaine de ce qui n'appartient pas strictement aux mots.' Artaud oppose avec la dernière vigueur les signes (entendez tous les signifiants visuels et sonores de la scène) aux mots, oppose la Parole, dans la matérialité de ses vibrations incantatoires, aux mots puisqu'il s'agit pour lui de retrouver la 'Parole d'avant les mots'.

Est-ce simplement par revendication du spectaculaire, par désir de fonder un théâtre où se fondraient musique, sons et gestes, qu'Artaud mène cette bataille? Nullement: il y va en effet, pour lui, de l'efficacité du théâtre à atteindre son but qui ne saurait être, selon ses termes, que magique, symbolique, métaphysique, de toute

Du texte à la représentation

façon propre à faire sortir le spectateur de son fauteuil, à le 'despectatoriser', pour le mettre face à face avec des forces, des menaces, des impulsions jusque-là inconnues ou interdites. Le théâtre est comme la peste, a-t-il dit:

La peste prend des images qui dorment, un désordre latent et les pousse tout à coup jusqu'aux gestes les plus extrêmes; et le théâtre lui aussi prend des gestes et les pousse à bout: comme la peste il refait la chaîne entre ce qui est et ce qui n'est pas, entre la virtualité du possible et ce qui existe dans la nature matérialisée. Il retrouve la notion des figures et des symboles-types . . .

Ce texte, tout fondateur qu'il est, est difficile et paradoxal, car il propose comme un point de non-retour où le théâtre comme représentation s'annulerait lui-même dans ses possibilités de communication et de spectacle: l'image extrême qui élève la figuration à la Figure, c'est-à-dire la représentation–reproduction à la représentation–révélation meurt d'être monnayée en gestes et en sons: 'Il ne peut y avoir théâtre qu'à partir du moment où commence réellement l'impossible et où la poésie qui se passe sur la scène alimente et surchauffe des symboles réalisés.' Il n'y a pas de façon plus nette de dire que le théâtre sera mythique ou ne sera pas, de dire que le théâtre se refuse comme discours pour devenir un acte, acte unique, libérateur et dangereux.

Pourtant le théâtre continue à exister, moins ambitieux sans doute, mais néanmoins marqué par une interrogation sur le statut du texte face à la représentation, sur le statut de l'auteur face au metteur en scène. On peut citer, parmi cent autres, l'opinion de G. Pitoëff:

Le maître absolu dans l'art scénique c'est le metteur en scène; la pièce écrite existe dans le livre. Lorsqu'elle arrive sur le plateau, la mission de l'écrivain est terminée. Je ne diminue pas la place de l'auteur; je défends seulement l'indépendance de l'art scénique. Le metteur en scène est libre, absolument libre . . .

C'est là un acte de foi plutôt qu'un argument; il souligne cependant l'hétérogénéité profonde des deux modes de l'écriture théâtrale et de l'écriture scénique. M. Foucault le dit également en d'autres termes:

On a beau dire ce qu'on voit, ce qu'on voit ne loge jamais dans ce qu'on dit, et on a beau faire voir, par des images, des métaphores, des comparaisons, ce qu'on est en train de dire, le lieu où elles resplendissent n'est pas celui que déploient les yeux, mais celui que définissent les successions de la syntaxe.

7

L'écart entre le texte et la représentation est particulièrement sensible et indiscutable quand il s'agit de représentations actuelles de textes anciens: le sens des mots a changé (pensons au 'Il est bon à mettre au cabinet' d'Alceste à propos du sonnet d'Oronte, ce qui déclenche l'hilarité, à contre-sens, des spectateurs), les enjeux psychiques et idéologiques aussi et même la conception de l'espace et du temps. Mais l'écart entre tout texte et toute représentation est de droit, pourrait-on dire: la continuité du texte à la représentation n'est plus possible (ou plutôt on a pris conscience qu'elle n'était plus possible) à cause du texte lui-même; c'est lui qui porte la responsabilité du divorce: 'le langage a été donné à l'homme pour déguiser sa pensée', a-t-on dit. Depuis Freud et quelques autres l'on sait que le texte dit à côté, ment: le texte n'est plus la propriété d'un sujet d'énonciation, extérieur et antérieur à son langage; il n'est que le produit d'un sujet de l'énoncé qui n'existe que dans et par son langage. D'où le caractère totalement subjectif du point de vue du personnage; il n'y a plus au théâtre de point de vue global, privilégié. Dieu le père — c'est-à-dire le spectateur — qui voit tout du point de vue de Sirius n'a plus de pouvoir totalisateur, englobant: le texte lui échappe en toutes directions, se fracture en sous-texte, en non-dit: c'est le brouillage du sens ou plutôt le miroitement des sens; on s'imagine, comme Ulysse, croiser dans l'espace de la scène telle silhouette familière, mais c'est un dieu, peut-être, qui a pris la défroque d'un humain; on croit entendre des hommes débattre de leurs problèmes quotidiens, mais ce sont des mythes, peut-être, qui se dissimulent dans l'ordinaire de leurs propos. Comment penser alors que la représentation puisse, sans mutiler le texte lui-même, en proposer un sens univoque?

Sans parler du fait que le texte est infirme, à l'instant même où il échappe à la prise par la surabondance de ses significations: infirme et parcellaire au sens où il ne suffit pas pour boucher les trous de l'espace que la représentation, elle, est tenue de combler. Sur la scène il y a celui qui parle et il y a ceux que l'écoutent. Mais à partir du moment où celui qui parle et ceux qui l'écoutent se mettent à occuper l'espace, à faire, on a toutes chances d'assister au conflit du dire et du faire: c'est particulièrement sensible dans les mises en scène actuelles, de Planchon ou Vitez par exemple. Et l'un des meilleurs procédés pour exalter le faire — non pas en opposition directe avec le dire mais en parallèle avec lui — c'est de donner un rôle moteur aux muets, aux personnages secondaires, aux figurants. Ce que fait Vitez en construisant toute la dramaturgie de ses *Molière* sur les rôles du garde dans *Le Misanthrope*, de l'exempt et de Laurent dans *Tartuffe*: la dramaturgie est justement l'art de faire parler le texte scéniquement, d'établir la jonction entre le texte et la scène. Jonction qui n'est pas la recherche d'une coïncidence impossible, mais saut par-dessus une faille, celle de la discontinuité. On aboutit alors à des constatations de plusieurs ordres: texte et représentation sont antinomiques et non seulement conflictuels. C'était déjà l'opinion de G. Craig estimant que des textes de théâtre trop parfaits, trop pleins, comme *Hamlet*, interdisaient la représentation en la rendant dérisoire. 'Est-ce à dire, demande l'amateur dans *De l'art du théâtre*, qu'on ne devrait jamais jouer *Hamlet*? — A quoi bon l'affirmer, répond le régisseur. On continuera de le jouer d'ici quelque temps encore et le devoir de ses interprètes sera de faire de leur mieux. Mais viendra le jour où le théâtre n'aura plus de pièces à représenter et créera des œuvres propres à son art.' Texte et représentation ont chacun son champ d'application spécifique; chacun revendique son autonomie et, à l'exact opposé de Craig, Vinaver affirme:

La guérison passe d'abord par la reconnaissance de l'existence de deux formes théâtrales distinctes et puis par la dénonciation et le refus de la mixité, par la résistance qu'il faut opposer au traitement véhiculaire des œuvres — classiques ou contemporaines — dont la charge poétique demande qu'elles soient prises pour ce qu'elles sont.

Sans doute existe-t-il quelques écrivains comme Adamov qui, dans une vision idéaliste, conçoivent la représentation comme la promotion dans le visible de l'exécution scénique de l'invisible contenu dans le texte:

Je demande qu'on s'efforce de purger ce mot de représentation de tout ce qui s'attache à lui de mondanités, de cabotinage et surtout d'intellectualité abstraite, pour lui restituer son sens le plus simple . . . Je crois que la représentation n'est rien d'autre que la projection dans le monde sensible des états et des images qui en contiennent les ressorts cachés. Une pièce de théâtre doit être le lieu où le monde visible et le monde invisible se touchent et se heurtent, autrement dit, la mise en évidence, la manifestation du contenu caché, latent qui recèle les germes du drame. Ce que je veux au théâtre . . . c'est que la manifestation de ce contenu coïncide littéralement, corporellement, concrètement avec le contenu lui-même.

Cette proposition revient à annuler la dichotomie de l'écriture théâtrale et de l'écriture scénique en faisant que la seconde soit contenue dans la première. C'est sans doute l'élément le plus original

9

du théâtre qu'on dit nouveau que cette dramaturgie totalitaire qui fait l'économie d'un délégué à la représentation qu'on nommerait metteur en scène . . .

Le mouvement actuel de la mise en scène est autre: il ne se contente pas de mettre en cause le sens univoque du texte; l'éclatement du sens provoque aussi l'éclatement de la représentation. On retrouve là l'héritage d'Artaud, à un niveau esthétique chez Mesguich disant:

L'acteur n'est pas un personnage, ni une personne. Le personnage, c'est personne. Le personnage zéro. Ce personnage n'existe pas, ou plutôt il est une absence, un creux, une potentialité, une différence. Un acteur qui entre en scène fait du vide. C'est ce vide qui permettra le mouvement, les mouvements. On pourrait croire que l'acteur parle. Il n'en est rien; l'acteur se tait au contraire. Et c'est sur cette parole tue que l'écriture peut poindre, prendre voix. L'acteur ne parle pas; il dit de l'écriture. Il fait jouer le passé de la trace sur la page avec le présent de la voix (du corps) dans l'espace;

à un niveau philosophique et spiritualiste chez C. Régy:

A chaque moment de l'œuvre, et mêlé à lui, un ailleurs est là, invisible. C'est cet étranger-là que je monte. Un autre temps, un autre lieu sont là. Ceux de la mémoire, ceux de l'imaginaire. Ces auteurs nous donnent d'emblée un manque à voir, à lire, à entendre . . . Ce que l'on voit sur la scène ne doit pas se prendre pour l'objet du spectacle . . . On dirait qu'il faut que le spectacle enfin s'arrête, qu'il échoue, pour que quelque chose puisse commencer.

La représentation, c'est l'invisible du texte.

Par là le mythe ressurgit car le mythe (*muthos*) est récit; il est dans le texte et, en même temps, occulté par le texte: il est l'autre du récit premier qu'est la fable, sa face cachée. Travail de dédoublement, de mise en perspective que seule la représentation peut effectuer dans l'écart qu'elle instaure du texte au texte; le texte n'est plus contenu dans les mots mais dans les images et leur combinaison organique.

Plus ambitieuse encore la représentation peut faire parler les silences du texte et, en ce sens, elle se fait texte elle-même pour donner le chiffre de mythes dont la lettre n'est pas inscrite dans les mots sinon à l'état virtuel. L'osmose du texte et de la représentation ne serait-elle pas alors en passe de se réaliser, si l'on en croit cette déclaration d'E. Corman, un des plus talentueux parmi les dramaturges de la nouvelle génération:

C'est un peu aux auteurs de savoir écrire du silence et beaucoup de silence, et j'ai l'impression que c'est le plus difficile . . . Je sens que si les auteurs ne sont pas capables d'écrire de grands espaces de silence, donc en fait des images virtuelles, donc du vrai théâtre pas forcément bavard, ils ne sont pas du tout susceptibles de rencontrer les metteurs en scène.

'Une vraie pièce de théâtre', disait Artaud, 'pousse à une sorte de révolte virtuelle et qui d'ailleurs ne peut avoir tout son prix que si elle reste virtuelle.' Il ne s'agit plus aujourd'hui de révolte, mais d'images. La virtualité reste la constante, comme valeur propre à dynamiser, voir à dynamiter conjointement texte et représentation, promis l'un et l'autre à un au-delà d'eux-mêmes. Sur les décombres de l'un et de l'autre le mythe ne serait-il pas le phénix qui renaîtra de ces cendres?

NOTE

1 Je signale au passage que la 'véritable' traduction en français de la fameuse mimesis aristotélicienne n'est pas 'imitation', comme on l'a dit jusqu'ici, mais 'représentation', ce qui exigerait que l'on révise l'idée que l'on se fait d'ordinaire d'Aristote: car la représentation selon Aristote est beaucoup moins passive que l'on imagine: elle est production du sens. Voir à ce sujet l'édition annotée de *La poétique*, éd. et trad. par R. Dupont-Roc et J. Lallot (Paris, 1980).

2

The presence of Rome in some plays of Robert Garnier

MARGARET McGOWAN

It is customarily said that Joachim du Bellay started a fashion when he published his *Antiquitez de Rome* in 1558.[1] Perhaps he did; yet interest in the imperial city and its impact on French writing is more complex and wide-ranging than can be represented by a single strand of influence, however significant.

The vision of Rome that would have been available from the 1550s was many-layered, rich and kaleidoscopic. To have some idea of its many-sidedness one might look no further than the summary provided by Maurice de la Porte in his manual of prejudices, *Les Epithètes françoises*:

> ROME: Capitale du monde, orgueilleuse, triomphante, ancienne, glorieuse, romuléane, noble, puissante, fameuse, superbe, magnifique, ornement du monde, papale, grande, admirable, pompeuse, guerrière, immortelle.[2]

Here the city's lasting power, its age, its victorious magnificence, its artistic splendour and martial qualities are stressed, as is the identification of city and world (the *urbs/orbis* conflation accepted in ancient times and used by the papacy); there is no hint of its decadence, its downfall or its ruins. Information about these deleterious aspects was, however, readily to hand in the numerous histories of Rome, of its emperors and its wars; these flooded from the presses in translation from the Greek, and increasingly, from the Latin, and their relevance to current affairs and to the theatre was swiftly understood.[3] As Henri Estienne explained in 1581, perusal of these volumes

> peut apporter aux courtisans de notre temps beaucoup d'utilité et aussi de plaisir, car ils représentent comme en un miroir les princes de leur siècle et leur cour . . . Considère ces deux commentaires historiques comme deux Théâtres où se jouent les comédies, les tragicomédies, les tragédies d'alors . . . si l'on établit des rapprochements avec les cours de notre temps, on est obligé de croire à nos yeux et à nos oreilles sur les faits dont autrement l'étonnement aurait rendu suspecte dans de tels théâtres la véracité . . .[4]

Rome in some plays of Robert Garnier

In Estienne's view, history and theatre are alike since they both offer scenes and actions from which the spectator/reader can derive both pleasure and moral uplift. These feelings are aroused less from the contemplation of events long since gone than from the realization of their extraordinary relevance to present times.

This attitude was a common one in the sixteenth century, when writers sought to bolster their princes' own inflated images of themselves by comparing them to powerful Roman emperors; or when they tried to console their kings at moments of difficulty;[5] or, more particularly, when they exploited their knowledge of Roman history to draw more specific parallels (and often less complimentary ones) between the run of affairs in ancient Rome towards the end of the Republic and the civil wars in France. Thus, Gabriel Symeoni writes of the timeliness of his second issue of *César renouvellé* (Paris, 1570):

Et comme le livre a esté tiré des Commentaires de Caesar sur la Guerre civile des Romains: aussi viendra il mieux à propos qu'il [se] face voir au temps de la troisième Guerre civile des Françoys . . . que d'avoir pris un autre temps plus mal convenable, pour le publier et mettre en lumiere.[6]

Many writers (including Garnier) followed his example, drawing parallels between civil wars in Rome and those in France in the hope that Frenchmen might learn at best to mend their ways or, at worst, to understand their plight and thereby receive consolation. Louis le Roy (1567/70), Jean de la Madeleyne (1575), George Buchanan (1576), and later Jean Bodin (1580) are but four who dwelt positively on the similarities,[7] while others were more pessimistic. Cardanus, for example, had some cynical comments in his *Life* (completed 1575/6), and Etienne Pasquier actually told his son not to waste time on antiquities while he was in Rome.[8]

Such admonitions were unlikely to be effective at a time when princes vied with each other in amassing large collections of antiquities – Francois Ier, cardinal du Bellay, the duc de Montmorency and the Guise all assembled notable collections of marbles, statues and coins; when antiquarians fed this craze with learned publications such as those of Du Choul, Le Pois, Jacques de Strada or Rouillé;[9] and when knowledge about the buildings of classical Rome and the technical means of constructing similar designs was generally available. Serlio's careful descriptions and measurements of the principal Roman monuments were published in France in several volumes from 1545;[10] French architects – Philibert de l'Orme and Jean Bullant – went to Rome themselves and, on their return, were anxious to impress French clients with the accuracy of any project; they specified on each occasion, as did Bullant, '[œuvre] que j'ay mesurée à l'antique dedans Rome'.[11] For those who could not make the journey to Rome, engravings of the city and its monuments were produced in increasing quantities from the workshops of Antoine La Fréry and from the hand of Marcantonio Raimondi (among others).[12] It is not surprising, therefore, that, from the mid-century at least, visual evidence of classical influences could be seen in France: in the reconstructions modelled on ancient example attempted by Charles de Lorraine at Meudon, where he built galleries and a grotto to house his collection of antique marbles;[13] or in the royal entries made by Henri II into the towns of his realm, where he gazed on triumphal arches, obelisks, columns, statues and other monumental structures built explicitly as re-enactments of Roman Triumphs;[14] or again, in the idealizing poetic forms inspired by architectural styles which had been admired in Rome.[15]

Preoccupation with things Roman was not only intense and varied, providing artists and writers with rich material for reflection and reconstruction, but also widespread, as is apparent in the way Jacques de Vintemille promotes the cause of history:

Si nous sommes tant amateurs des ouvrages antiques que nous voulons en tout imiter leurs bastimens, si nous sommes tant curieux de leurs statues et medailles, que bien souvent une teste, une main, un fragment ou piece rompue, nous est si precieuse que nous l'honnorons à merveilles et mettons en tresor, combien devons nous estimer l'Histoire?[16]

Sixteenth-century Frenchmen had a well-stocked vision of Rome. It was made from the fictions of Vergil, from historical accounts and from technical treatises; it was a vision shaped from artefacts and ancient remains, conjured up by the narratives of travellers and engravings of actual monuments, and one which they made their own through appropriation, reconstruction and re-enactment. From their own responses to both the triumph and the fall of Rome, they invested their notion of the place with powers and effects more akin to myth and legend than to the realities of the imperial city – ancient or modern. In the literary and artistic works they produced, their concepts of Rome were infinitely elastic, stretching to include abstract notions of empire, liberty, sound government or abuse of power; to encompass nostalgic evocations of *La Patrie*, peace and plenty, the fecundity of a Golden Age; or, conversely, to represent slavery displayed in triumph and the prospect of serene magnificence changed into a sepulchre filled with suffering.

There was much, therefore, that Garnier could take for granted when, in his plays on Roman themes – *Porcie* (*c.* 1563/7), *Cornélie* (1574) and *Marc Antoine* (1578) – he focused the drama on the downfall of empire. Rarely did he linger long on evocations of Golden Ages, of prosperity and magnificence;[17] his reader's own knowledge would supply the vision of the grandeur that had gone, and his experience would make calamity familiar, as Garnier himself noted in his dedication of *La Troade*.[18] He was careful, however, to make clear the relevance of his tragedies to French affairs. The title of *Porcie* is explicit:

> PORCIE, Tragedie françoise representant la cruelle et sanglante saison des guerres Civiles de Rome: propre et convenable pour y voir depeincte la calamité de ce temps.

In *Cornélie*, he laments the fact that tragedy is 'trop propre aux malheurs de nostre siècle'; and, in his dedication of *Marc Antoine* to Guy de Pibrac, he expands on the parallel 'Rome ruinée/France ruineuse':

> Mais sur tout, à qui mieux qu'à vous se doivent addresser les représentations Tragiques des guerres civiles de Rome? qui avez en telle horreur nos dissentions domestiques, et les malheureux troubles de ce Royaume, aujourd'huy despouillé de son ancienne splendeur et de la révérable maiesté de nos Rois, prophanée par tumultueuses rebellions.

The moral, philosophical and political lessons that Garnier drew from the juxtaposition of Rome/France were similar to those which had attracted other contemporary writers.[19] War might sometimes be legitimate in defence (*Cornélie*, 1267ff.), but civil disorder (276, 1170) is to be abhorred; it throws citizen against citizen (1224ff.), brother against brother (842ff.), and brings low a great republic through the ambition and greed of its own

15

people.[20] In fact, inspired by the examples of Greece and Rome exposed by Garnier, Robert Estienne — the printer of *Porcie* — in a preliminary poem, appealed to France to avoid war altogether:

> La civile fureur et le meurtre intestin
> De Rome et de la Grèce avança le destin,
> Et de leurs citoyens les feit la triste proye.
> France, fuy donc la guerre . . .　　　　　　　(9–12)

Estienne's words are abstract; the playwright's task is to give power and presence to the pestilence of war.

At the centre of his study of civil strife, Garnier sets Rome as the supreme example. Both as city and as empire, Rome stood impregnable — apparently; its downfall, shown as abrupt and inevitable, provides ample opportunity for the moralist to meditate upon the inconstancy of human affairs (*Cornélie*, 117ff.), to ponder the vanity of human achievement (*Porcie*, 409ff.) and to counsel moderation and endurance; and, for the playwright, to explore the causes of such exceptional catastrophe.

In *Cornélie*, Rome is Caesar's stage, on which he trumpets their mutual power:

> O superbe Cité, qui va levant le front
> Sur toutes les citez de ce grand monde rond,
> Et dont l'honneur, gaigné par victoires fameuses,
> Espouvante du ciel les voûtes lumineuses!
> O sourcilleuses tours! ô coustaux décorez!
> O palais orgueilleux! ô temples honorez!
> O vous, murs que les dieux ont maçonnez eux-mesmes,
> Eux-mesmes étoffez de mille diadèmes,
> Ne ressentez-vous point de plaisir en vos cueurs,
> De voir vostre César, le vaincueur des vaincueurs . . .
> 　　　　　　　(1333–42)[21]

Caesar's excitement touches in sufficient elements of the city to bring Rome before us, inflating its beauty and its status with a series of apostrophes and his vision of walls decorated with a thousand crowns. The victor's flamboyance reaches greater heights as (in this same speech) he sees the world, and even Rome, tumbling to pay him homage: 'mesme ceste Cité . . ./ Ploye dessous ma force' (1381, 1383). Our knowledge of the parlous state of Rome's classical monuments, of the martial powers that its citizens lost, and (at the time portrayed in the tragedy) of its impending decay gives this extravagant claim a curious unreality. Against Caesar's enthusiasm, we are invited to measure the contrasting sentiments of Cassie:

> Misérable Cité, tu armes contre toy
> La fureur d'un tyran pour le faire ton roy;
> Tu armes tes enfans, injurieuse Romme,
> Encontre tes enfans pour le plaisir d'un homme . . . (1095–8)

and, more potently still, to reflect on the blunt questions of Cicéron placed at the beginning of the tragedy:

> Quel droict eurent jadis nos avares ancestres,
> Ignoblement issus de grands-pères champestres,
> Aux royaumes d'Asie?   (125–7)

And Cicéron continues: what right to Persia, to Africa, Gaul, Britain or to Spain? Such an empire, he concludes, is outrageous (146). Ironically, in *Cornélie* it is Rome itself that has nourished the seeds that will flourish and bring its downfall: 'Méchante Ambition . . . Mortelle Convoitise' (23–5). Through excess, Caesar is shown, in effect, as his own murderer and the destroyer of the city he coupled with his glory: 'C'est toy, Rome, qui l'as nourri trop indulgente' (809), exclaims Cornélie. Like Lucan in the *Pharsalia* and Du Bellay in *Antiquitez III, VI, XXII*, Garnier argues that the causes of so exceptional a disaster lay in Rome's self-destructive powers. The point is simply stated at the start of the play:

> Immortelle, immuable, et dont l'empire fort
> Ne peut estre atterré que de son propre effort.   (55–6)

Self-inflicted destruction also forms the central preoccupation in *Porcie*, where the awful fate of the city is predicted with glee by Mégère:

> Rome, il est ore temps que sur ton brave chef
> Il tombe foudroyeur quelque extrême méchef.   (91–2)[22]

The boomerang effect which brings back to Rome the sorrows she herself wrought upon others is made to seem horribly appropriate:

> Tu souffres, pauvre Rome, hélas! tu souffres ores
> Ce que tu fis souffrir à la cité des Mores,
> A la belle Carthage, où tes fiers empereurs
> Despouillez de pitié commirent tant d'horreurs.   (439–42)

The reference to Carthage and to the horrors perpetrated there by Romans intensifies the present suffering of Rome not only because

17

the affliction is deserved, but also because these former deeds are known, and because nothing has been learned and they are being repeated.

In such circumstances, complaint and consolation alone remain, and the cries of pain and the display of carnage are made worthy of the magnitude of the fall. The lyrical power of Cornélie's wails and curse (*Cornélie*, 885–910), and the almost unrelieved tone of complaint that accompanies Porcie everywhere (this is how she introduces herself: 'Sus, misérable, sus, sus, pauvre infortunée / Recommence tes pleurs avecques la journée', 203–4) are matched by the graphic description of Porcie's death (1899–1928) and of the battlefield (*Cornélie*, 1785–90).[23] Maurice Gras argued that these manifestations of grief purging itself with words are 'voices not characters'.[24] Yet Garnier, by making his spectator hear the sound of grief and the noises of the dead, and see the detailed spectacle of the dying, also seeks a fuller participation.

This process of visual and aural projection is adopted in Garnier's presentation of Rome either as a spectacle of evil or as a place of grandeur and of triumph. Under both aspects, the playwright relies on our knowledge of the city and its customs. Thus, the city whose collapse Mégère foretells with such ghoulish delight is depicted as a mechanism, a great machine, whose parts shatter with a noise that reverberates around the world which Rome once dominated:

> Rome, il faut qu'alentour de la ronde machine
> Lon entende aujourdhuy le son de ta ruine. (129–30)

Another devastating picture of the city is made by Scipion, who roused his men to battle by a vision of Rome emptied of bustle, its streets echoing and deserted – but for the decrepit senators who lift their feelings and tearful faces to his gaze:

> Je voy Rome en horreur, en triste solitude,
> Et les vieux sénateurs gémir leur servitude:
> Je les voy, ce me semble, et que tous larmoyeux
> Ils lèvent dessur nous et le cœur et les yeux. (1683–6)

Often, a few names or things suffice to bring forth the picture; for instance, the lost grandeur recalled with a list of great captains – 'Les Marcels, les Torquats et encore/Les Scipions vainqueurs' (*Porcie*, 1703–4), or victory underlined by reference to statues (*Cornélie*, 957–60), or trophies (*Porcie*, 428).[25] A similar effect of presence is achieved by the simple naming of Roman legions or their phalanxes (*Marc Antoine*, 557, 563, 952, 1729), or by the evoking of the sacrifice of oxen on the altars of the Capitol which Marc Antoine offers in *Porcie* (1329–32), and which the Chœur also evokes in *Cornélie* (825–30).

The most lyrical presentation of the city occurs in *Porcie*, where physical shapes and abstract notions are blended together. We see its peaked skyline with the seven hills, its lofty buildings, its fame, its fertility and the way it glows as a symbol of the native land:

> O beau séjour natal esmerveillable aux dieux,
> O terre florissante en peuple glorieux,
> Coustaux sept fois pointus, qui vostre teste aigue
> Portez noble en palais jusque aux pieds de la nue:
> Soit où flanquez de tours vous honorez Jupin
> Dans un temple basti du roc Capitolin,
> Soit où vous élevez en bosse Célienne,
> En pointe Vaticane ou en Esquilienne,
> Soit où vous recourbez sous le faix Quirinal,
> Sous l'orgueil Palatin ou sous le Viminal,
> Joyeux je vous salue.   (*Porcie*, 1013–23)

Marc Antoine's greeting is systematically organized, and a clear picture emerges although the hills are merely named, and the monuments and palaces simply mentioned.

The Capitol is not always used in ways which conjure up a building with columns and altars for sacrifice. Sometimes it is isolated and made to carry notions of Roman power approved by the gods. In like manner, the river Tiber acquires a parallel extension; thus, in the expression 'le Rhin germain . . . subjet à son Tybre romain' (*Porcie*, 916–17), the rivers stand for countries and for military dominance. Such abstract association was common in the sixteenth century, although it is noteworthy that Garnier (like Du Bellay in *Elegiae ad Ianum Avansonium*) often gives the river a more active role. For instance, on his victorious return to Rome, Caesar greets the Tiber as though it were a person:

> O beau Tybre, et tes flots de grand'aise ronflans
> Ne doublent-ils leur crespe à tes verdureux flancs,
> Joyeux de ma venue?   (*Cornélie*, 1345–7)

Du Bellay had visualized the river as it was represented in sculpture, a bearded giant stretched out at his ease;[26] Garnier, on the other hand, evokes the waters themselves, showing their flow and their shape, and sounding their noise just as he had done at the climax of *Porcie*, where they transport not praise or the spoils of victory, but the defeated Roman standards:

> Le Tybre qui souloit enorgueillir ses rives
> Du superbe appareil des despouilles captives,
> Que nos princes vaillans tiroyent de toutes pars,
> Ne charge plus ses flots que de nos estendars.

(Porcie, 1845–8)

Elements of Rome are thus given a living presence in Garnier's plays and are integrated into the drama − often symbolically, as in the example from *Porcie*.

A more thorough integration and a more graphic visualization of Rome occurs in the playwright's use of the Triumph.[27] The ceremony of the Triumphator entering Rome on his chariot preceded by the kings and princes of the vanquished nations walking in chains, by cartloads of spoils, and by images of the captured towns and countries held aloft, was familiar to sixteenth-century Frenchmen. Their kings had adopted the ceremony intended to communicate the idea of victory to their own use, and engraved pictures of their Triumphs were readily available, as were copies of Mantegna's *Triumphs of Caesar*. In Garnier's plays, the Triumph becomes the means *par excellence* by which defeat is made plain. Pompey's triple Triumph, for instance, is evoked after his death by Cornélie, as the measure of that hero's fall (*Cornélie*, 319–22). The Triumph sticks in her mind and grows there. Cornélie uses the same image of Pompey enthroned, at his feet 'les rois de gros cordeaux contre le dos liez' (682), to paint, by contrast, the pale ghost that had visited her in her dreams. She also transposes the image and action of Triumph to Rome and, in a powerful personification of the city, by this means transmits the completeness of its degradation. Each ingredient of a Triumph is dwelt upon, and a visual subjugation is created: Rome is transformed into a being with head bowed and hands tied behind; she is shown walking in front of the splendid chariot of her victors − her own children, who have left fellow-Romans dead, their bones to be sucked clean by fishes or picked bare by birds:

> Tu sers, superbe Rome . . .
> Tu iras désormais la main au dos liée,
> La teste contre bas de vergongne pliée,
> Devant le char vainqueur, et ton rebelle enfant,

Le diadème au front te suivra trionfant.

Tes chefs si courageux, et de qui la vaillance,
Jointe avec si bon droit, levoit nostre espérance,
Sont morts atterrassez, pasture des oiseaux,
Pasture des poissons qui rament sous les eaux.

(*Cornélie*, 781, 785–92)

There are echoes of the same scene in the indignant words with which, in Act IV, Cassie succeeds in moving Décime Brute to action:

Nous le voyons terrible en un char élevé,
Traîner l'honneur vaincu de son peuple esclavé;
Ainsi Rome à César donne un pouvoir suprême,
Et de Rome César trionfe en Rome mesme.

(*Cornélie*, 1127–30)

Caesar's triumph is Rome's enslavement, and abuse of power is captured in this vision of Caesar riding high and terrible above the people of Rome. This awesome picture, which increases Cassie's sense of outrage, serves also to remind us of the double-edged nature of the Roman Triumph as recorded by ancient historians. A Triumph had to be accorded by the Senate with the agreement of the people and was intended as an expression of gratitude towards the victorious captain. In the case of Caesar, who personally supervised the details of his own triumphal entries into Rome, even to the ornamentation of his chariot, there were murmurings among the people that this attentive preparation was a sign of *outrecuidance*, and that it changed celebration and thanksgiving into some kind of bid for domination of the city itself.[28]

In *Cornélie*, similar doubts and apprehensions had been planted by Cassie in the minds of the conspirators. Garnier works these new feelings into the dramatic texture of his play and, when in Act IV Caesar prepares for a Triumph declaring 'Or, trionfons, Antoine, . . . Allons au Capitole', the spectator is now conditioned to see not the benign emperor, but the overweening commander, and to regard the sentiments enthusiastically expressed by Marc Antoine as overdone:

Allons, brave César;
Couronnez-vous la teste et montez dans le char.
Le peuple impatient forcène par la rue,
Et avecque liesse à la porte se rue
Pour voir son empereur . . .

(*Cornélie*, 1401–5)

21

From these considerations of the role of the Roman Triumph, it can be said that Garnier thought of it as an important and recurring visual sign by which characters and spectators alike could measure the rise and fall of power.

Marc Antoine shows a further development in the integration of the Triumph into the drama. In this play it is interiorized, occupying the characters' thoughts and preying on their minds. From the beginning to the end of *Marc Antoine*, the Triumph provides a constant thread, a point of reference for the characters' fears which, at the same time, ensures that the city of Rome is always present before us. At the outset, Marc Antoine determines to cling to his weapons as a final defence against personal capture, in order to avoid the ignominy of appearing in Rome as part of Caesar's Triumph:

> Car tant qu'elles seront en ma main, que César
> Ne me pense mener trionfé dans un char.
>
> (*Marc Antoine*, 27–8)

The same fear of participating in the public spectacle of a Triumph preoccupies Cléopâtre, who (as Dircet reports) has taken drastic measures to avoid personal surrender. She has shut herself up in the monumental tomb built to house her remains, and the door stays closed – even to the dying Marc Antoine:

> Car la roine, craignant d'estre faitte captive
> Et à Romme menée en un trionfe vive,
> N'ouvrit la porte . . .   (*Marc Antoine*, 1622–4)

She has good reason to be afraid, since Caesar's wish is precisely to have Cléopâtre humbled and to have her wealth displayed in his triumph when he returns to Rome. He makes this clear at once:

> Envoyons Proculée,
> Qui appaste d'espoir son âme désolée,
> L'asseure de propos, si que puissions avoir
> Ses richesses et elle en nostre plein pouvoir.
> Car entre toute chose ardemment je souhaite
> La pouvoir conserver jusqu'à nostre retraite
> De ceste terre icy, à fin d'en décorer
> Le triomphe qu'à Romme on nous doit préparer.
>
> (*Marc Antoine*, 1698–1705)

What Caesar sees as splendid decoration Cléopâtre and her servants view with dread; and the extent of their anxiety is graphically recounted in their last exchanges at the climax of the play. Eufron uses the threat of Caesar's Triumph in an attempt to dissuade the Queen from suicide. As he presses the argument, the triumphal procession, the streets of Rome and the final sacrifice are detailed before us:

EUFRON	desjà me semble voir Ceste petite enfance en servitude cheoir Et portez en trionfe.
CLÉOPÂTRE	Ha! chose misérable!
EUFRON	Leurs tendres bras liez d'une corde exécrable Contre leur dos foiblet.
CLÉOPÂTRE	O dieux! quelle pitié!
EUFRON	Leur pauvre col d'ahan vers la terre plié.
CLÉOPÂTRE	Ne permettez, bons dieux, que ce malheur advienne!
EUFRON	Et au doigt les monstrer la tourbe citoyenne.
CLÉOPÂTRE	Hé! plutost mille morts.
EUFRON	Puis l'infâme bourreau Dans leur gorge enfantine enfoncer le cousteau.
CLÉOPÂTRE	Hélas, le cœur me fend. (*Marc Antoine* 1816–26)

Seen from the viewpoint of the victim, these scenes of triumph acquire a barbarous strength not dissimilar to the impact of that image of decollated heads which Porcie paints as part of the enforced ornamentation of Rome when the city is filled with mercenaries and with arms:

> Rome ne verroit pas un millier de proscrits,
> Sous l'appas d'un guerdon en tant de lieux meurtris;
> Ni par divers cantons tant de testes tranchées,
> Pour un espouvantail aux rostres attachées.   (*Porcie*, 541–4)

The intrusion of sights like these, which disturb any settled view of a city adorned with noble buildings, brave citizens and gorgeous ceremonies, gives Rome a strong presence, a presence such that even when a conventional image − Rome equals sepulchre − is used, the figure does not lose its materiality. While Du Bellay and Jacques Grévin, for instance, keep the image at a fairly abstract level (in *Antiquitez XXIX*, Rome, once great, is now 'le tombeau du monde'; in *César*, its name implies a sepulchre: 'Toy Rome . . . ton nom servira de tombeau') Garnier makes the matter more solid. In Mégère's closing phrases, the city/sepulchre is closely linked to the notion of a body:

> Rome n'est qu'un sépulchre à tant de funérailles,
> Qu'elle voit entasser en ses froides entrailles. (*Porcie*, 145–6)

On several occasions, indeed, Rome is referred to by Garnier as though it were a living person, capable of feeling, suffering, and performing gestures. 'Nostre pauvre cité' (*Cornélie*, 374), or 'Nostre dolente Rome' (*Porcie*, 564), just begin to give substance to the body/city, while the expression 'courber son dos' — a phrase used at this time to denote military collapse — sketches in the gesture and the person.[29] This process of personalization of the city is strengthened by Garnier's heavy reliance on active verbs associated with bodily functions, as for example in

> Tu nages dans le sang de tes pauvres enfans
> Que n'aguère on voyoit marcher si triomphans!
>
> (*Porcie*, 437–8)

and also by the general tendency to emphasize physicality by placing the suffering human body at the forefront of attention. There are many examples, the most prominent, perhaps, being Cornélie's anticipation of Caesar's murder:

> Non, je verray bien tost (Dieu m'en face la grâce)
> Son corps souillé de sang estendu dans la place,
> Ouvert de mille coups, et le peuple à l'entour
> Tressaillant d'allégresse en bénire le jour.
>
> (*Cornélie*, 933–6)

Caesar's corpse sprawling on the streets of Rome, mocked by the populace, is fittingly in context, in the larger body of the city. The latter's pain is strikingly set forth in Porcie's anguished apostrophe, 'Tu souffres, pauvre Rome, Hélas! . . .' (*Porcie*, 439ff.), where the ironic and detailed reference to Carthage provides greater density.[30]

This thickening is characteristic of Garnier's work. Following methods of construction more familiar to epic poems, he moves back and forth in time, bringing Troy and Carthage behind Rome to weave lessons of history and (for the purposes of drama) to intensify the sense of inevitability that accompanies Rome's fall.[31] Thus, at the end of Act II in *Marc Antoine*, the Chœur declares Rome

> Semblable à l'antique Troye,
> Le séjour de tes ayeux,
> Tu seras l'ardente proye
> D'un peuple victorieux.   (*Marc Antoine*, 848–51)

While philosophers like Cicéron (*Cornélie*) or Arée (*Porcie*) stand aside and above the turmoil of events and look across time, the Nourrice in *Porcie* nostalgically returns to thoughts on the foundation of Rome, seeing at that early period peace and plenty and fields filled with pastoral activity contrasting sharply with the present bloodbath to which she is witness and which has yet to run its course (409–19). As much emotion and the same sense of deterioration and loss are generated by Porcie herself when she sweeps back to Romulus and to the first stones of Rome which had provided homes for the refugees from Troy; she traces the progress of the power that seemed so solidly built into the marble and of the freedom that persisted for so long before coming to the slavery and impiety which have now taken hold of 'nous et nostre Cité' (1685–94). Through such surges across history, the rise and fall of Rome is kept before the spectator, and both city and empire are thereby given significance beyond their immediate place in space and time. They are made into exemplars.

Of course, Garnier has not engineered this result on his own. Petrarch had seen, tasted and recorded the paradox of Rome – at once great and desolate; so had Janus Vitalis and, later, Joachim du Bellay.[32] They, too, had stressed the role of time; and it is within their tradition that Garnier works when at different points in his plays he balances assured statements of domination such as

> Nostre Rome qui s'eslevoit
> Sur toutes les citez du monde,
> Et qui triomphante exclavoit
> A sa grandeur la terre et l'onde   (*Porcie*, 191–4)

against the incredible paradox of 'Rome asservie' (*Porcie*, 556). It is clear that Garnier liked to construct different formulations of the master/slave, grandeur/nothing paradox, although he never went as far as Du Bellay, who, in *Antiquitez XIII*, ends the sonnet on 'la grandeur du rien' which still had the power to 'esmerveiller le monde'. The juxtaposition of pride and servitude is powerfully made in Cornélie's discovery 'Tu sers, superbe Rome' (781), while the same thought is given a new twist with Cassie's 'Rome sera sujette!' – a sudden revelation which triggers all the subsequent action. In *Marc Antoine*, Caesar enjoys the spectacle when 'cette orgueilleuse Romme/Sans bien, sans liberté, ploye au vouloir d'un homme' (1351–2). Studying the fate of Rome at more than one point in time, observing its rise and its decay, offered many opportunities for composing paradoxes and unexpected phrases, although they could, occasionally, degenerate into questionable word-play. 'Ceste cité riche de violence' (*Cornélie*, 138) provides a splendid, concentrated summary of Cicéron's ruminations on the ills of Rome; yet, the play on words that provides the culmination to a series of incantations on Rome and calamity at the beginning of the last act of *Porcie* — 'adieu, Romme, / Qu'un renommé malheur pour tout jamais renomme' (1837–8) — fails to sustain the surging complaint.[33]

Confidently and reverently, Agrippe had dwelt on the lasting condition of Rome, a city built by the gods for all eternity: 'cette Cité / Bastie pour durer en toute éternité' (*Marc Antoine*, 1453–4). He was right; to use Collingwood's words, 'Rome is a substance, changeless and eternal.'[34] Whatever the fate of the imperial city, its name and its face were known in the Renaissance; and, in making Rome a central character in his drama,[35] Garnier could be sure that his spectators would enter emotionally and intellectually into the vision he had drawn and, through these feelings, appreciate the moral and political lessons he had sought to impart.

NOTES

1 For the influence of Du Bellay, see Dorothy Gabe Coleman, *The Gallo-Roman Muse: Aspects of Roman Literary Tradition in Sixteenth-Century France* (Cambridge, 1979), p. 109, and Roland Mortier, *La Poétique des ruines en France* (Geneva, 1974), *passim*.

2 I quote from the Lyons edition of 1593 (first edition Paris, 1571), which appends the following: 'Rome, ville capitale d'Italie, et jadis le chef de tout le monde, a été ainsi appelée de Romule son fondateur. On dit, qu'anciennement elle a eu en ses murailles 634 tours et 37 portes: même que l'entour de la ville était de 20,000 pas.'

3 R. R. Bolgar, *The Classical Heritage and its Beneficiaries* (Cambridge, 1954).

4 These lines come from Estienne's dedication to Sir Philip Sidney of his two books of Zozime; they are cited in Jean Jehasse, *La Renaissance de la critique* (Saint-Etienne, 1976), p. 234.

5 Guillaume Budé was among the first, in his *Institution du prince* (Paris, 1547). His comparisons seem remarkably sober beside those of Béranger de la Tour d'Albenas in *Le Siècle d'or* (Lyons, 1551); a typical comment is 'Depuis aussi que la France Ha cest heur de l'avoir recouvert [i.e. the Golden Age] par le moyen de son César Auguste, non moins que l'autre heureux, causant la paix universelle' (p. 5). For later parallels, see A. Thevet, *Les Vrais Pourtraits et vies des*

26

hommes illustres grecs, latins et payens recuillez de leurs tableaux, livres, medalles antiques et modernes (Paris, 1584), and F. de Belleforest, *L'Histoire des neuf roys Charles de France* (Paris, 1568), who wrote history as an antidote to civil strife.

6 Sig. A. 4.

7 Le Roy, *Considération sur l'histoire françoise* (Paris, 1567), ff. 9ᵛff., *De la vicissitude . . . des choses en l'vniuers* (Paris, 1579), and *Exhortation aux François* (Paris, 1570), ff. 2ᵛ, 6ʳ–11ᵛ; De la Madeleyne, *De l'Estat et office d'un bon roy* (Paris, 1575), ff. 50ᵛff.; Bodin, *La République* (Paris, 1580), book 5, ch. 5, p. 587; Buchanan, *Baptistes* – see Ian McFarlane, *Buchanan* (London, 1981), p. 386. The political context of Garnier's plays has been set by Gillian Jondorf, *Robert Garnier and the Themes of Political Tragedy in the Sixteenth Century* (Cambridge, 1969): see especially ch. 5 (pp. 76–99).

8 Cardanus, *Ma Vie*, published by Gabriel Naudé (Paris, 1643), p. 41: 'Où est maintenant l'empire des Romains? chose ridicule et inoüie: en Allemagne.' Pasquier's request was made in a letter to the French ambassador, Paul de Foix: see *Lettres familières*, ed. D. Thickett, (Geneva, 1974), book 7, p. 91.

9 Guillaume du Choul, *Discours de la religion des anciens romains illustré* (Lyons, 1556); Antoine Le Pois, *Discours sur les medalles et graveures antiques, principalement Romaines* (Paris, 1579); Jacques de Strada, *Epitome du trésor des antiquités* (Lyons, 1553); and Guillaume Rouillé, *Le Promptuaire des medalles* (Lyons, 1576).

10 For a discussion of Serlio's influence in France, see my *Ideal Forms in the Age of Ronsard* (Berkeley, 1985).

11 Bullant, *Reigle generale d'architecture* (Ecouen, 1568), sig. Aii.

12 See McGowan, *Ideal Forms*, pp. 138–9.

13 The castle and grotto at Meudon immediately became tourist attractions: see F. de Belleforest, *Cosmographie* (Paris, 1575), p. 278, col. 1, and Arnold van Buchel, *Description de Paris* [1585–6], published by L. A. van Langeraad and A. Vidier, in *Mémoires de la Société de l'Histoire de Paris* (Paris, 1899), pp. 59–195; the description of Meudon is at pp. 92–3.

14 Notably, Henri II's entries into Lyons (1548), Paris (1549) and Rouen (1550).

15 See McGowan, *Ideal Forms*, pp. 121–58.

16 Dedication of De Vintemille's translation of Herodian to Anne de Montmorency (Lyons, 1554), sig. *2ᵛ.

17 Garnier did make an exception in Arée's monologue at the beginning of Act III in *Porcie* (725–90).

18 Dedicating his play to the archbishop of Bourges, Garnier writes: 'les passions de tels sujets nous sont jà si ordinaires, que les exemples anciens nous devront doresnavant servir de consolation en nos particuliers et domestiques encombres'.

19 Jondorf, *Robert Garnier*, pp. 26–46, discusses these; she also makes plain Garnier's horror of war, the violence of his descriptions and the emotional force of his laments (pp. 85–6, 99).

20 Du Bellay had lamented civil disorder and its dreadful consequences, in *Antiquitez XXIII, XXIV*.

21 Garnier may have been inspired by the equivalence that Jacques Grévin gave Rome and Caesar in *César* (1561), 125–6:

> Heureuse Rome, heureuse ores d'avoir receu
> L'heur du Ciel qu'un César en tes bras fut conceu.

22 The self-infliction theme forms the principal matter of the Chœur's speech, in *Porcie* 985–1012.

23 The following passage gives a fair idea of Garnier's passionate abhorrence of the consequences of war:

> On ne voyoit qu'horreur, que soldars encombrez
> Sous le faix des chevaux, que des corps démembrez
> Nageans dans leur sang propre, et des piles dressées
> D'hommes qui gémissoyent, sous les armes pressées,
> Coulant comme un esponge, ou l'amas raisineux
> Qu'un pesant fust escache en un pressouer vineux.
>
> (*Cornélie*, 1785–90)

24 Maurice Gras, *Robert Garnier, son art et sa méthode* (Geneva, 1965), p. 81: 'c'est le concert des différentes voix qui forme l'essentiel de ces premières tragédies de Garnier'.

25 For other examples, see *Cornélie*, 17–18; *Marc Antoine*, 1079–81.

26 Joachim du Bellay, *Oeuvres poétiques, VII: Oeuvres latines, Poemata*, ed. G. Demerson (Paris, 1984), p. 47, ll. 31–4:

> At pater ipse iacens immani corpore Tybris,
> Muscosoque fouens hispida membra toro,
> Vestibulo in thalami cubito subnixus et urnae,
> Subiectis senior iura dabat populis.

27 Du Bellay incorporates the Triumph into his elegy addressed to Jean Avanson (*Oeuvres poétiques*, ed. Demerson, p. 53, ll. 122–36). A good account of the Triumph is provided by Robert Payne, *The Roman Triumph* (London, 1962).

28 See Payne, *Roman Triumph*, pp. 110–28.

29 See *Porcie*, 811; *Cornélie*, 779–80.

> Tu es assujettie, et portes à ce coup,
> Sur ton col orgueilleux un misérable joug!

30 See discussion above, pp. 17–18.

31 Obvious ancient examples are the *Aeneid* and the *Pharsalia*; Garnier also uses the technique in *Marc Antoine*, where Charmion recalls Troy (490–502).

32 See the discussion in Mortier, *Poétique des ruines*, pp. 22–59.
33 Compare also the expostulations of Mégère in *Porcie*, 85–6, and *Marc Antoine*, 1349–50.
34 R. G. Collingwood, *The Idea of History* (London, 1956), pp. 42–3; Collingwood is commenting on Livy, and the passage reads: 'Rome is the heroine of his narrative. Rome is the agent whose actions he is describing. Therefore Rome is a substance, changeless and eternal. From the beginning of the narrative Rome is ready-made and complete: Rome is described as "the eternal city". Why is Rome so called? Because people still think of Rome, as Livy thought of her, substantialistically, non-historically.'
35 Jondorf, *Robert Garnier*, pp. 137–8, thus describes *Porcie* and *Cornélie*.

3
Bradamante: de l'épique au burlesque

MICHELINE CUÉNIN

L'on sait à quel point l'*Orlando furioso* de l'Arioste, traduit en
français dès 1543 à Lyon, passionna lecteurs et lectrices de la
France des Valois. Cette épopée, qui conservait tant de traits des
romans de chevalerie, se distinguait cependant d'eux par la résur-
rection de deux figures de Guerrières, Marphise et Bradamante, qui
rejoignaient, par dessus la littérature médiévale, le mythe des
Amazones antiques. La restauration des lettres anciennes, dans un
contexte de guerres historiques, guerres d'Italie puis guerres civiles,
dirigeait les imaginations vers ces filles d'Arès qui voulurent se
mesurer aux plus grands: Penthésilée défiant Achille, Hippolyte défiant Hercule; Virgile, dans l'*Enéide*, dressera de même Camille
contre le fondateur de Rome.

Cependant, cette reviviscence du mythe de la Guerrière aux
seizième et dix-septième siècles connut une étrange destinée. Lorsque Christine de Suède, fuyant la peste romaine, se fit recevoir en
France, la cour et la ville de Paris lui réservèrent une entrée
mémorable. Le 8 septembre 1656, on vit la Reine prendre le chemin
de Notre-Dame montée sur un cheval blanc, en vêtements de
voyage peu soignés, et les pistolets à l'arçon de sa selle. Présenta-
tion 'extraordinaire' et qui, pour comble d'étrangeté, s'accom-
pagnait d'un train fort médiocre. 'Notre Amazone suédoise', écrit
Mme de Motteville très perplexe, 'voyageait sans dames, ni officiers, ni argent . . . Je pense même, vu son équipage et sa
pauvreté, qu'elle ne faisait pas plus de repos et ne dormait pas
mieux que Marphise ou Bradamante, et qu'à moins d'arriver par
hasard chez quelque grand Roi comme le nôtre, elle ne faisait pas
souvent bonne chère.'[1] Le trait est dur, mais fort instructif: il
permet de mesurer à quel point la grandiose figure de l'Arioste
s'était dégradée en un siècle.

Ce n'est pas à dire que tout le personnel féminin de l'*Orlando* ait
subi le même sort. Au contraire: l'on verra, pendant des généra-
tions et jusqu'au cœur du dix-huitième siècle, les femmes–objets

Bradamante: de l'épique au burlesque

(Angélique), les victimes malheureuses (Genèvre, Isabelle) et surtout les somptueuses magiciennes comme Armide ou Alcine, renaître sans cesse sous les formes littéraires, artistiques et lyriques les plus variées. Et pourtant dès avant les premières traductions lyonnaises de l'épopée italienne, l'enchanteresse, ce fut bien Bradamante.

En ces temps où la monte, la chasse, le tir à l'arbalète et au pistolet constituait le sport aristocratique obligé pour les femmes comme pour les hommes, qui suivaient les leçons des mêmes maîtres, le maniement des armes, la maîtrise d'un coursier nerveux s'inscrivait dans les usages: Louise Labbé, connue pour d'autres talents, évoquera fièrement son éducation martiale.[2] Mais le succès vint aussi de la cour. La maréchale de Retz, gouvernante des filles de France, était née Claude-Catherine de Clermont, et voyait dans les Claramonte de l'Arioste la tige illustre d'où sortait cette Pucelle de Dordogne, sa légendaire parente. Toutefois, la tradition gréco-latine offrait le choix entre maintes Amazones: Penthésilée, Camille, Reine des Volsques, Thomyris, Reine des Messagètes et vainqueur de Pyrrhus. Mais Bradamante se détachait vigoureusement de ces femmes chefs de guerre; elle se distinguait encore mieux de Marphise, sœur jumelle de Roger, allaitée comme lui par une lionne. Ayant dû défendre sa vie et son honneur contre des Barbares dès ses plus jeunes ans, elle en avait gardé un goût de la violence tel qu'elle s'éjouissait à faire voler têtes, bras et jambes à l'occasion, et consacrait sa jeunesse, comme un homme, à éprouver sa valeur contre tous les concurrents possibles.

Bradamante n'a pas reçu cette féroce formation sarrasine. Mais son épée redoutable lui a valu le commandement de la place de Marseille sur commission de Charlemagne, et la défense de tout le pays d'entre Rhône et Var contre les incursions barbaresques. Elle protège contre les prédateurs masculins les 'pèlerines' de la Provence. Bien incarnée dans la société imaginaire des lecteurs, elle est de plus fille du duc Aimon et de la duchesse Béatrix, hauts dignitaires de la cour impériale. Mais surtout, le personnage de Bradamante attachera tous les cœurs par son aptitude aussi grande à l'amour qu'à la vaillance. Conquis par leurs exploits respectifs, Roger et l'illustre guerrière ont spontanément décidé de combattre côte à côte, se promettant union et assistance. Et voici que le destin épargne l'amante pour s'acharner sur Roger, trahi par des sortilèges, prisonnier, disparu sans laisser de traces. Chaque fois, elle le délivre, mais non sans être passée par les affres de la jalousie, les affirmations pathétiques et déployées d'une fidélité qui ne trouve pour mesure que celle des grands éléments de la Nature, et des constellations célestes. Plus que celle de Didon, tragique et passive dans sa sensualité déchirée, la plainte de Bradamante se nourrit des échauffements de son imagination, de ses retours de foi, et d'appel à l'action. Eperonnant follement le cher Rabican, elle fonce droit sur la rivale prétendue, cette Marphise qui peut lui disputer et le prix de la vaillance et le cœur de Roger, elle l'abat sans les sommations d'usage, puis apercevant l'écu au champ d'azur, celui du bien-aimé, 'elle s'arrête, et, avec les yeux et le penser, elle considère son corsage, sa taille, sa bonne mine et son mouvement tout plein de grâce, . . . la fureur l'emporte: "Donc une autre baisera ces belles et douces lèvres, et je n'en aurai point ma part? Non, non, autre ne te possède jamais . . . Je veux que nous mourrions tous deux de ma main, avant que je meure toute seule de rage . . ."'[3] Est-il besoin de dire que ce chant XXXII suscita l'admiration générale, des dames en particulier, qui l'imitèrent et le firent imiter à l'envi,[4] en France et en Italie.[5] Les chants XLI et suivants de l'*Orlando* comportent aussi les plaintes superbes sur l'absence inexpliquée de Roger, sa défaillance poignante lors de la défaite, avec l'ardent appel au secours: 'Reviens, mon Roger, reviens!'

On pourrait imaginer deux Bradamantes juxtaposées: l'Amoureuse, et la Guerrière en fonction, celle qui renverse Sacripant et fait 'vider les arçons' à Rodomont, avec ou sans l'aide de sa lance enchantée. Il n'en est rien. Les contemporains ont fort bien perçu, et Brantôme en fait foi,[6] l'interaction permanente de la vaillance et de l'amour. De fait, une femme qui, en ces temps de violence, est capable d'assurer sa proper défense, de se préserver du rapt et du viol, de se dispenser des ruses dangereuses (ou avilissantes) pour échapper à un sort cruel, cette femme-là incarne le mythe de la liberté dans un monde féminin qui ne la connaît guère. Avec elle, le rapport n'est plus de fort à faible, mais d'équivalence et de stimulation: elle est l'épreuve de vérité. C'est pourquoi, malgré sa beauté, sa naissance, la noblesse de son maintien, les prétendants sont rares: la candidature de Léon, sur simple exhibition de la magnificence de son rang, a été ressentie par elle comme une provocation, comme une mésalliance. Roger seul a su respirer à la hauteur de Bradamante. Aussi sera-t-il récompensé par une félicité totale à sa mesure, un amour actif et inlassable, une passion aussi exaltante qu'exaltée, enrichie de toutes les harmoniques de la tendresse et de l'imagination.

Bradamante: de l'épique au burlesque

Une telle femme est un défi vivant, et l'on s'explique que, lorsqu'à la demande de Diane de Foix, Montaigne brosse un programme d'éducation qui inclut l'éducation sentimentale, c'est Bradamante qu'il propose à son élève, à l'exclusion d'Angélique:

Mon gouverneur . . . lui saura dire que les poètes suivent les humeurs communes . . . et, quand il commencera de se sentir, lui présentant Bradamante ou Angélique pour maîtresse à jouir, et d'une naïve, active, généreuse, non hommasse, au prix d'une beauté molle, affétée, délicate, artificielle; l'une travestie en garçon, coiffée d'un morion luisant, l'autre vêtue en garce, coiffée d'un attifet emperlé, il jugera mâle son amour même, s'il choisit tout diversement à cet efféminé pasteur de Phrygie.[7]

Montaigne se montre ici l'interprète de la seconde génération des lecteurs de l'Arioste: celle qui a vu en Bradamante moins l'héroïne d'aventures chevaleresques que le symbole, teinté de platonisme, d'un style de vie: opter pour la jouissance rare mais sûre au mépris des plaisirs éphémères et sans consistance.

Nous sommes en 1581, date qui marque comme l'apothéose du mythe, et où Robert Garnier compose sa tragi-comédie de même titre. En raison des lois du genre, il faut s'attendre à une chute de potentiel, et à l'intrusion dégrisante du réalisme social au sein d'un univers épique en expansion. Le dramaturge français s'est limité aux derniers chants de l'Arioste, qui voient se conclure le mariage de Bradamante. Sans falsifier les données, il réussit à créer une atmosphère originale qui ne sacrifiera ni la grandeur requise du caractère, ni le buttoir des intérêts familiaux: d'où la réussite humoristique de l'œuvre, dont l'effet sera durable.

Rappelons les faits. Durant une trève d'avec les Infidèles, Bradamante est demandée en mariage par les ambassadeurs de Léon, prince héritier de Byzance: alliance flatteuse, qui ravit les parents, et même Charlemagne. Confrontée à un type de difficulté inattendu, l'héroïne est d'abord paralysée: elle avait oublié que pour être Guerrière, elle n'en était pas moins fille, avec tout ce que cet état comporte de dépendance. Roger, qui assiste à l'affaire aussi impuissant que son amante, a pris sa décision: aller occire sur place le prétendant, seule manière juridique de rompre l'engagement conclu; mais le caractère radical de la démarche impose qu'il 'ne découvre pas son dessein'. Bradamante se voit donc seule, et apparemment abandonnée. Dans un premier temps, elle se désespère; puis, 'animant son courage et rappelant sa valeur accoutumée',[8] elle s'avise d'un expédient imparable, qui lui permettra de gagner du temps, et de mettre l'Empereur dans ses intérêts. Elle jouit en effet d'un double statut: chevalier de fait, grand officier de la couronne à titre personnel, elle exige l'application d'une incontestable coutume féodale qui prime le droit parental: la publication d'un cartel pour la possession de sa personne. Ainsi, par cette 'demande juste et digne d'elle', comme le reconnaît Charlemagne, elle récupère l'éclatante liberté que lui a conférée sa vaillance; ainsi Roger pourra-t-il recevoir ce cartel imaginé pour l'amour de lui, et qui, répercuté par toute la terre, sera compris par lui, où qu'il soit, comme un appel à venir vaincre et posséder son amante.

La longue exposition de Garnier (récit de Charlemagne) ne souffle mot du défi de Bradamante, supposé connu, et, dans le contexte délibérément bourgeois de cette tragi-comédie, il paraît une extravagance presque comique. Comme le dit gaillardement la mère à la fille pour la dissuader de son idée fixe,

> Les combats de l'amour ne sont guère sanglants;
> Ils se font en champ clos entre des linceuls blancs.

(627–8)

Bradamante, 'du monde la merveille' et qui ne voit point arriver Roger, tente, comme une simple fille, de choisir le couvent, et comme à la Marianne de Tartuffe, à qui Orgon lançait le fameux 'Ah! Voilà bien de mes religieuses . . .', elle s'entend répliquer:

> Comment, religieuse? Etes-vous bien si folle
> De m'avoir voulu dire une telle parole? (677–8)

Après cette excursion savoureuse dans la vie quotidienne, Garnier retourne à l'épopée. Le délai fixé par le cartel est expiré: seul se présente le chevalier aux armes impériales, le prétendu Léon. Outrée de désespoir, mais non de colère contre Roger, Bradamante exhale les beaux lamentos qu'attend le public (III, iii et IV, iii), puis Garnier rajoute de son cru un étonnant morceau de bravoure, plein de souffle et de mépris, où la Guerrière (et la femme) rassemble ses énergies pour donner à ce beau fils de Grèce la leçon de 'furia francese' qu'il mérite.[9] Elle le fera trop bien. Frappant inconsidérément, violemment, elle s'use, s'épuise, et perd aux points.

C'est Marphise qui va prendre la relève, et dénouer, comme dans l'Arioste, une situation sans issue apparente. Bradamante a buté sur l'incontournable lien de l'*obligation*: Roger, précipité dans un cul de basse fosse après une bataille où sa valeur lui avait fait des ennemis, ne pouvait entendre le 'cri' de son amante: bien au contraire, il était devenu l'homme-lige de Léon, qui, séduit par sa vaillance, l'avait rendu à la vie, et pouvait donc, suivant les usages féodaux, la lui redemander à sa convenance. Toutefois le mythe de la Guerrière est sauvé par l'adresse et l'intrépidité de Marphise, qui va opposer le droit canon au droit de l'épée: Bradamante n'était pas libre. En réalité, elle avait contracté une promesse de mariage avec Roger, en présence de Marphise elle-même, qui jetait le gant pour garantir le témoignage requis en pareille occasion. L'affaire prenait un tour juridique inattendu mais où la vaillance, dans ce climat féodal, imposait son verdict. Comme dans l'*Orlando*, Léon ne peut demander deux fois le même service à Roger, obligé de se découvrir. On observera donc que l'initiative appartient aux deux Guerrières, mais que la seconde, qui n'est pas amoureuse, est venue à la rescousse de celle qui l'est. Bradamante, pour sa part, a perdu sur tous les tableaux: déshonorée comme combattante, elle allait être 'gagnée' comme un butin − situation dégradante en soi, mais surtout pour elle, qui avait été prise à son propre piège. Mais l'Arioste donnait sa revanche à la Pucelle de Dordogne, en lui faisant défaire, aux côtés de Roger, le redoutable Rodomont, bien décidé à troubler les noces de celle qui l'avait autrefois fait rouler dans la poussière. La suppression de cet épisode ampute le mythe de Bradamante de sa vérité glorieuse, et prépare l'affadissement et même l'abaissement de la haute figure, en dépit des vers bouillants et nationalistes que Garnier met dans sa bouche.

On sait la faveur de cette tragi-comédie à la Cour de Marie de Médicis, où à deux reprises au moins, le Journal d'Héroard nous apprend que les enfants de France et leur petite cour ont représenté l'œuvre de Garnier.[10] Les troupes de campagne en régaleront le public provincial plus d'un demi-siècle après la création de l'œuvre, devenue un 'classique'. On la rehausse de beaux costumes d'Amazones qui mettent en valeur les comédiennes.[11] En 1615, Bradamante et Marphise sont cependant déjà 'rhabillées' en dames de cour: un admirable frontispice portant l'excudit de L. Gaultier et gravé pour orner, à la demande de la Reine, la traduction de Fr de Rosset, nous montre Bradamante tenant un luth (pour accompagner ses plaintes?) et Marphise se regardant dans un miroir! Dans la *Suite* de *Roland le furieux*, due au même Rosset et imprimée sous le même privilège, on voit Charlemagne déplorer le départ de ces Amazones, qui prive sa cour 'de la lumière de ces beaux astres'. Vers 1630, Pierre Ier Mariette grave un séduisant portrait de Bradamante avec une légende en vers louant son irrésistible beauté: de fait, l'héroïne apparaît coiffée d'une légère

et luxueuse toque de velours, dégageant des 'cheveux noués' abon-
dants dont une partie se déploie sur un col de cygne; les grands yeux
fendus en amande sont d'une vie étonnante; la jeune femme est
sûre d'elle: c'est apparemment tout ce qu'elle a gardé, au milieu de
ses 'attifets', de l'ancienne Guerrière, et de la mâle beauté dont
rêvait Michel de Montaigne.[12]

Mais le mythe n'est pas mort. L'année du *Cid*, un auteur
dramatique qui est peut-être La Calprenède composa une tragi-
comédie de *Bradamante*. Si l'œuvre est de lui, ce n'est pas la
meilleure, observe H. C. Lancaster.[13] Qu'est devenue notre
héroïne? On peut affirmer que, jusqu'à la tragédie de Thomas
Corneille en 1695, l'évolution se fait dans le sens d'une passivité de
plus en plus grande du personnage. Ainsi, dans un roman intitulé
Les Amours de Philocaste (Paris 1601, 1615), signé d'un certain
Jean Corbin, Philocaste–Bradamante ne participe pas au combat:
elle s'est bornée à se promettre au vainqueur dans le duel qu'elle
exige. Au fond d'elle-même, elle sait que le meilleur est celui qu'elle
aime: Pirame–Roger. En revanche, elle ignore l'identité des adver-
saires, et la fameuse obligation qui fausse les données du combat,
et son déroulement. En effet, Pirame se laisse vaincre exprès par
celui à qui il doit la vie, geste si extraordinaire, surtout à cette
époque, que le vainqueur ému de tant d'abnégation laisse
Philocaste à celui qui l'aime d'affection partagée.

La tragi-comédie de 1637 ne va pas jusque-là mais il est certain
que le nœud de l'action s'est déplacé: le conflit cornélien à la mode
ne peut valablement s'installer que dans le cœur de Roger, et l'action se développer entre les deux amis rivaux. Ajoutons que
l'auteur a prévu sur scène le spectacle commenté du combat, après
que Roger ait débité des stances consciencieusement imitées de
celles de Rodrigue. Par ailleurs, le combat de Bradamante et du
faux-Léon a été précédé d'une entrevue entre le vrai Léon et sa
'maîtresse'. Cette innovation est d'autant plus discutable que le
prétendant ose faire sa cour en déclarant vouloir mourir des mains
de celle qu'il adore! La Guerrière n'a pas le moral et l'arrogance
qui conviennent. Une fois seule elle redoute d'être vaincue, se
réconforte à la pensée que son frère Renaud se substituera à elle en
cas de défaite, ce qui constitue une notable entorse aux sources. Le
dénouement par Marphise, arguant d'un mariage clandestin, correspond sans doute à un sujet d'actualité; il nuit cependant à la
cohérence psychologique, dès lors qu'il ne s'agit plus d'un
stratagème (même reposant sur quelque promesse), mais d'une

réalité autrement grave. Ainsi non seulement cette œuvre a perdu l'unité d'action, mais l'unité de caractère indispensable, sans parler de scènes d'un franc mauvais goût: Léon, admirant la prestance de Roger qui se prépare à entrer en lice (II, i). Bradamante, aux mains d'un méchant auteur, ne pouvait guère sortir grandie de l'épreuve: il est sûr que le personnage n'est plus compris. L'aurait-il été par le public? Nous l'ignorons. La pièce ne semble pas avoir été représentée.

L'héroïne de l'Arioste avait donc perdu assez de substance pour faire bientôt les frais de divertissements comiques. L'impulsion vient, une fois de plus, de l'Italie: on présente un profil de Bradamante en virago avec menton en galoche.[14] Bientôt, quand, pour célébrer le premier carnaval de paix parisienne qui suit la Fronde, l'intendant du duc de Nemours prépare l'étonnant *Ballet de la Nuit*,[15] 'incessant passage de la mythologie noble à la verve burlesque', il ne manque pas de faire appel au couple Roger–Bradamante, dans la seconde partie de cet ample et 'inimitable ballet'. Vers neuf heures du soir, deux pages préparent la salle de bal où des courantes et des branles à la vieille mode vont être dansés, précisément par ces deux personnages antiques, représentés par d'excellents danseurs professionnels, deux hommes, Lalun fils et Bonnart. Leur numéro prélude à une pantomine moderne, le *Mariage de Thétis*, avec laquelle ils forment un contraste voulu, le tout emporté par une exubérance d'inspiration, une débauche de luxe et des costumes demeurés célèbres. Les personnages de l'Arioste figurent donc toute une population archaïque destinée à mettre en valeur la galanterie de la génération montante.

Le doute n'est plus permis lorsque nous abordons la *Bradamante ridicule*, dont l'existence scénique nous est connue par le Registre de La Grange, avec des mentions qui font sentir la pression dont la Troupe a été l'objet. Pour le début du carnaval 1664, le duc de Saint-Aignan, intendant des plaisirs de la cour, décida d'une folle mascarade, et réquisitionna à cet effet la salle du Palais-Royal:

Le jeudi 10 janvier 1664, joué dans notre salle . . . pour le Roi la Bradamante Ridicule, qui nous avait été donnée et commandée de la jouer par M. le duc de Saint-Aignan, Premier Gentilhomme de la Chambre, qui avait donné 100 louis à la troupe pour la dépense des habits qui avaient été extraordinaires.

Seule la cour ayant pu se divertir du spectacle, les Parisiens furent admis le lendemain, qui versèrent 1400 livres, et encore le dimanche (1014 livres). Mais La Grange note en marge qu'il a dû acquitter 616 livres 'pour lesdits habits et autres frais', sans compter 17 pistoles (170 livres), 'déjà remises la veille aux costumiers'. Mauvaise affaire financière: le succès de curiosité s'est vite épuisé. La mascarade est encore à l'affiche le mardi 15 (560 livres), puis le jeudi 18, mais soutenue par une farce troussée à la hâte par l'acteur Brécourt. C'est elle, *Le Grand Benêt de fils aussi fort que son père* (dont nous ne savons rien) qui fera monter le recette à 1176 livres. Apparemment, le duc académicien et poète sera mieux inspiré quelques mois plus tard en composant une partie du livret des *Plaisirs de l'Isle enchantée*, également tiré de l'*Orlando*, mais côté magiciennes.

Il est fort possible que nous disposions d'une trace du fastueux divertissement burlesque imposé à Molière. Il s'agit d'une gravure de forme circulaire, appartenant au Cabinet des Estampes de la Bibliothèque Nationale, selon A. Cioranescu qui la reproduit (vol. II, planche XII). On voit Roger monté sur un porc de grande taille somptueusement caparaçonné; le cavalier disparaît sous une quantité d'armures protectrices (parodie de l'armement lourd du seizième siècle) à énormes ergots saillants, tandis que Bradamante se tient fièrement debout sur des jambes recouverts de molletières, cuissots et genouillères, le tronc recouvert de ces cuirasses d'Amazones qui épousaient les seins et le ventre, mais agrémentée ici d'un pagne à longs triangles ajourés comme des haillons. Elle n'en tient que plus fièrement la fameuse lance, non point d'or, mais de grossier bois, terminée en boule comme un assommoir. Le plus significatif est le visage long, anguleux, pourvu d'une moustache et d'un petit bouc. La 'salade' (casque à l'ancienne) est sans panache, mais porte une visière longue d'une aune, à tête d'animal. Le 'train' est réduit à la suivante Hippalque, qui singe sa maîtresse en arborant un bonnet à plumes, et une jupe empesée d'Amazone. Pour sa part, Léon est revêtu du traditionnel costume de fou, avec panneaux à grelots. Les Bulgares, bien évidemment, participent à la fête: leur Roi est monté sur un animal qui tient du dindon et du chameau, les Grecs sont estropiés et couverts d'antiques oripeaux militaires. Dernier adieu, pourrait-on croire, non à l'Arioste, exploité sans limite pour les autres épisodes, mais à la Guerrière asexuée, symbole d'un temps révolu.

Croirait-on que ce phénix dénaturé allait revivre? Il est pourtant vrai que de nos jours encore, l'on s'en étonne: 'Bradamante est une querelleuse qui aime être vaincue au combat par celui qu'elle veut se donner pour mari.' Pourquoi cette 'opiniâtreté des écrivains'?[16] Parmi eux, il y eut pourtant un homme de métier, et qui, à la fin de sa vie, voulut se faire le plaisir de ressusciter l'héroïne de l'Arioste. C'était cette fois au moyen d'une tragédie, qui fut sifflée. Dans son avis *au lecteur*, le dramaturge reconnaît sans peine que 'le sujet s'est éloigné de nos mœurs', que la femme guerrière est passée de mode, et qu'il était bien difficile de faire admettre 'au parterre' qu'on pût être, comme Roger, 'si religieux observateur de sa parole' même envers un homme à qui on doit la vie. Mais le frère du grand Corneille ajoute aussitôt: 'C'est ce que ce sujet a d'extraordinaire qui m'a obligé de le choisir par les situations heureuses qu'il m'a fait trouver pour beaucoup de scènes. Si j'ai pu chercher à me satisfaire en composant cet ouvrage, j'ai peut-être eu tort de l'exposer.'[17] L'aveu est si émouvant, et si instructif, que cette *Bradamante* mérite, en dépit ou à cause de son insuccès, un examen attentif.

En ce qui concerne les données, l'esprit du défi est parfaitement restitué, mais il revêt une radicalité supplémentaire du fait que Léon, qui a l'audace de vivre encore alors que Roger a disparu, sera soumis à un duel à mort. En effet, si Roger n'est plus, l'amante combattra pour deux, et s'il est quelque part en vie la laissant seule pour échapper 'à une injuste flamme', elle combattra pour elle-même, pour sa 'gloire', en défendant sa haute réputation. Léon, qui n'avait pas encore songé à se faire remplacer par le chevalier valeureux que l'on sait, y pense cette fois, car il ne s'attendait pas à risquer sa vie. 'J'avais cru', avoue-t-il ingénument, 's'agissant de gagner votre cœur . . ./ Que ce serait assez pour avoir cette gloire/ Que sur vous, par l'adresse, on cherchât la victoire.' Pourtant, Léon n'est plus ici le 'débile Grégeois' de la tradition; il a à son actif un passé de vaillance non négligeable; mais comme il aime Bradamante, qu'il refuse de retirer son projet, et qu'il a devant lui une femme inexorable qui préfère la mort, s'il le faut, à la violence faite à son cœur, il va chercher Hippalque. L'intérêt de la situation de Bradamante, et son aspect tragique, c'est sa solitude. Thomas Corneille a en effet, pour obtenir ce résultat, modifié le caractère de Marphise, qui pousse sa compagne à accepter Léon et la couronne de Byzance: on perçoit ici l'influence d'un demi-siècle de tragédies politiques où la 'gloire du diadème' vaut bien celle des armes, surtout pour une femme. La fidélité de Bradamante qui, de plus, a famille et souverain contre elle, n'en est que plus héroïque, plus 'extraordinaire'. De sorte que, lorsqu'elle aura perdu le combat contre le faux Léon, Marphise répandra le bruit qu'elle s'est mal défendue par ambition réelle, n'ayant imaginé son bizarre défi que pour sauver la face. Un seul être pourrait la défendre et la sauver: Roger, avouant la vérité. Mais il ne le fait pas, s'abritant, pour cacher l'inviolable secret du combat, derrière le caractère légal du résultat: n'est-ce pas Bradamante elle-même 'qui a rendu cet hymen nécessaire'? 'Que puis-je faire?', déclare-t-il dans sa douloureuse impuissance. Il s'attire cette réponse sublime: 'Tout, si vous savez aimer.' Mais Roger, incapable de soutenir son personnage, quitte la scène. Bradamante aussi. Après avoir mené l'action seule, sans désemparer, jusqu'au milieu du troisième acte, elle n'a plus qu'à disparaître pour dissimuler, dans une dignité toute cornélienne, déception, soupçons, et infortune.

Le dénouement, cette fois, ne viendra pas d'un stratagème, promesse ou mariage dirimant, mais de la colère de Marphise contre celle qui, croit-elle, a faibli devant un adversaire qui ne la valait pas. Nous retrouvons alors les données de l'Arioste mais avec cette complication logique que la Guerrière demande un combat à quatre: elle contre Bradamante l'infidèle, et Léon contre Roger qui, dans l'œuvre de Thomas Corneille, s'est montré dès son arrivée (acte II). Le second affrontement étant impossible, le prince de Byzance apprend donc la vérité. On pourrait alors croire que, suivant ses sources, le dramaturge proposera finalement aux spectateurs cette émotion devant le dévouement et le silence héroïques de son ami qui pousse Léon à rendre Bradamante à Roger, d'autant qu'il l'a gagnée. Mais ici encore l'influence du grand aîné va se faire sentir, et particulièrement le trop célèbre dénouement de *Cinna*. D'abord, furieux de la 'défiance' de Roger qui lui a caché son identité, Léon, se muant soudainement en prince magnanime, rend le bien pour l'offense, et cède orgueilleusement la place. Il ne reste plus au frère de Marphise qu'à se racheter auprès de Bradamante, non par le truchement de la couronne bulgare, qui ne fait que lever un obstacle secondaire et sans valeur pour notre héroïne, mais par une vie de soins et de soumissions.

On voit donc que pour faire de Bradamante une grande figure cornélienne, les données étant ce qu'elles étaient, il a fallu affaiblir de façon presque insoutenable le caractère de Roger, et rendre Léon encore plus antipathique qu'ailleurs; d'où les critiques. 'Les spectateurs auraient été plus satisfaits' de voir Léon combattre contre Roger, n'étant plus admissible 'que les combats des femmes contre les hommes soient de notre goût'.[18]

La tragédie lyrique, créée à l'Académie royale de Musique le 2 mai 1707, et tirée apparemment de l'œuvre de Thomas Corneille par le librettiste Charles Roy, n'eut aucun succès. Seul le *Mercure galant* défend, il fallait s'y attendre, l'ouvrage de son principal rédacteur.[19] L'auteur du compte-rendu, après avoir résumé l'argument, emploie ce mot significatif: 'Voilà bien du *merveilleux*, qui aurait pu dégoûter les auditeurs s'il n'était si bien conduit.' Et de souligner ensuite la 'netteté des vers' et la 'justesse des pensées', visiblement appréciées 'lorsque cette pièce a été représentée à Versailles': bien du talent en somme, dépensé pour un sujet indéfendable.

Le dix-huitième siècle, qui verra régner les femmes par l'esprit ou l'adresse libertine, et les aimera parées d'une beauté de plus en plus sophistiquée, se gaussera de ces pucelles casquées. L'Agnès Sorel de la *Pucelle* voltairienne, toisant Jeanne d'Arc, lui décoche ce trait:

> Ciel, que je hais ces créatures fières,
> Soldats en jupe, hommasses chevalières,
> Du sexe mâle affectant la valeur
> Sans posséder les agréments du nôtre!

L'éditeur de 1762[20] ajoute en note: 'Il y a grande apparence que l'auteur a ici en vue les héroïnes de l'Arioste et du Tasse. Elles devaient être un peu malpropres, mais les chevaliers n'y regardaient pas de si près.'

N'est-ce pas là, en plus brutal, l'opinion de Mme de Motteville? Mais il y a plus explicite:

Quelque effort que je fasse, dira Fréron quelques années plus tard, je ne peux guère me représenter ces vigoureuses paladines qu'avec un teint un peu hâlé, des voix de basse taille, des membres musculeux et endurcis, et de la barbe au menton.[21]

Ainsi, un jour de mascarade, la jeune cour trépidante avait-elle déjà moqué l'immense figure épique de Bradamante. Mais depuis l'image éphémère et carnavalesque du monde à l'envers, parenthèse folle dans la durée du respect, un siècle s'était écoulé, qui avait remplacé les turbulents défoulements, ou les sentiments mitigés, par le sarcasme désinvolte et délibéré. Toutefois, en dépit de cette sensible différence, il n'en est pas moins vrai que le mythe de la Guerrière avait définitivement sombré dans le ridicule qui tue. Une fois vaincues les Frondeuses, ces dernières des Amazones historiques, le mythe avait comme perdu son support. Par ailleurs, un mouvement irréversible, issu de l'*Astrée*, s'était produit dans l'idéal féminin: la beauté physique, rehaussée de la modestie comme de la parure, puis le charme insinuant des grâces mondaines éliminaient la noble lance, faisant la preuve de leur pouvoir.

NOTES

1 *Mémoires*, éd. Michaud-Poujoulat (Paris, 1836), II, 10 (p. 452).

2 'Qui m'eût vu lors en armes fière aller/Porter la lance et bois faire voler/ Le devoir faire en l'estour furieux/Piquer, volter le cheval glorieux/Pour Bradamante ou la haute Marphise/Sœur de Roger, il m'eût, possible, prise' (Elégie III, *Oeuvres*, éd. Charles Boy (Paris, 1887), I, 89–90; cité A. Cioranescu, *Arioste en France* (Paris, 1938), I, 19).

3 Traduction de Francois de Rosset (Paris, 1615), fol. 334 r–v.

4 Toute la cour des Valois et des poètes officiels ou non: le plus abondant ayant été Desportes. La Reine Marguerite restera toujours fidèle à Bradamante. Voir Cioranescu, *Arioste en France*, pp. 50–4. N'oublions pas non plus l'un des premiers inspirés, à la demande de sa maîtresse Marguerite de Carle: Etienne de La Boétie, qui composa 240 vers sur les *Plaintes de Bradamante* (*Oeuvres complètes*, éd. P. Bonnefon (Bordeaux, 1892), p. 257).

5 Ces grandes plaintes lyriques donnèrent naissance au récitatif musical dont l'un des plus beaux exemples est le *Lamento della Nympha* de Claudio Monteverdi.

6 *Dames galantes*, Classiques Garnier (Paris, 1965), Cinquième Discours (p. 257).

7 *Essais*, I, 26.

8 Trad. de Rosset, p. 414.

9 IV, 6, dont voici les six derniers vers:

> Or vienne ce musqué, qui ne fit jamais rien
> Et qui n'est renommé que pour l'empire sien.
> A son dam apprendra qu'il n'est pas de vaillance
> Qu'on doive comparer à la valeur de France,
> Et qu'acquérir ne faut, par importunité,
> D'une fille l'amour qu'on n'a point mérité.

10 Voir *Les Juifves, Bradamante, poésies diverses*, éd. R. Lebègue, Belles-Lettres (Paris, 1949), p. 286.

11 Célèbre page de Scarron dans le *Roman comique*, Classiques Garnier (Paris, 1955), p. 169.

12 B. N. Estampes, OA 46. P.3484. Reproduit par Cioranescu, avec le seul nom de Mariette (pl. V).

13 Voir H. C. Lancaster, *La Calprenède dramatist* (Chicago, 1920), p. 10. L'auteur fait justement remarquer que l'œuvre a été publiée anonymement, le privilège étant donné au libraire Sommaville. Il n'y a pas trace non plus de représentation.

14 'La Bella Bradamanta', vers 1630, B. N. Estampes, Tf1 Rés. Fol. Pl. 03.

15 *Ballet Royal de la Nuit*, en VI parties et 45 entrées, dansé par Sa Majesté le 23 février 1643. Vers de Benserade. Voir M.-F. Christout, *Le Ballet de Cour en France (1643–1672)* (Paris, 1967), pp. 68–9.

Bradamante: de l'épique au burlesque

16 Cioranescu, *Arioste en France*, II, 85.

17 Thomas Corneille, *Bradamante*: voir Cioranescu, *Arioste en France*, II, 78, n. 91, et avis au lecteur: 'Le parterre est présentement toujours rempli de censeurs impitoyables qui éclatent avec violence dès la moindre chose qui ne leur plaît pas.' L'œuvre fut créée au Théâtre-Français le 18 novembre 1695, et à Versailles le 25 du même mois, mais elle était écrite, déclare-t-il, depuis quinze ans.

18 L. Bordelon, *Diversités curieuses en plusieurs lettres* (Amsterdam, 1699), I, 146–7; cité Cioranescu, *Arioste en France*, II, 80.

19 *Mercure galant*, novembre 1695, p. 330.

20 *La Pucelle*, III, 271–4, *Les Oeuvres complètes de Voltaire*, éd. T. Besterman (Geneva, 1970), p. 311. Cet éditeur de 1762 est évidemment Voltaire lui-même, qui feint de ne pas être l'auteur de ce poème mal reçu des admirateurs de Jeanne.

21 *Année littéraire*, IV, 299; cité Cioranescu, *Arioste en France*, p. 86.

4
Corneille's *Oedipe*[1]

I. D. McFARLANE

Oedipe was well received at court and by the King; its author also had a high regard for it: 'Je n'ai fait aucune pièce de théâtre où il se trouve tant d'art qu'en celle-ci' (*Examen*). But it has not really stood the test of time. It is by far the longest of Corneille's plays, running to some 1000 lines beyond his norm, though this in itself world not militate against its success. Comparatively few critics have paid close attention to it: Corneille's treatment of the myth has perhaps caused perplexity, or his lack of feeling for the Greek world has told against it, in which case he would not be alone – only Racine and Claudel among French dramatists show a special affinity.[2] It is nevertheless an important play: it brings together a cluster of concerns that were assuming increased relevance in the author's eyes, it renews an established myth, and it is shorn of the more eccentric notes of melodrama that show themselves in his plays both before and after his period of silence.

I

I am not sure that Corneille's 'explanations' of the play's origins take us all that far: one should always be suspicious of what writers tell us of their work. It is known that his patron Fouquet gave him a choice of three subjects: one which was soon to be treated by his brother Thomas (*Camma*, 1661), a second of which we know nothing, and *Oedipe*. Corneille says he thought at first of following Sophocles closely – he talks of being a 'traducteur', which surprises in view of his known absence of sympathy with aspects of Greek tragedy, as well as of his own dramatic practice and attitude to 'sources' ('Au lecteur'). He soon realized the problems with which he was faced. He feared that aspects of the myth might jar on a modern audience and that its violent elements would prejudice its success, though earlier in the century it had been treated in plays that had not shocked – plays of which, incidentally, Corneille seems to have been ignorant. The lack of a love-interest would be a more telling factor, but above all Corneille saw little point in following in such august steps: 'La différente route que j'ai prise m'a empêché de me rencontrer avec eux (Sophocles and other ancient dramatists) et de me parer de leur travail' (*Examen*). Two other points come to mind: he would wish to avoid another failure like *Pertharite*, and he certainly had no difficulty in writing *Oedipe*, which was produced rapidly and contains very few later variants; there were some alterations, including two long speeches excised between the first performance and the printed version (owing in part to remarks made by d'Aubignac). The despatch with which he polished it off could be explained less by his desire to have it performed before the end of the carnival − a suggestion favoured by some − than by the fact that many central concerns were picked up or developed from the dramatist's previous plays.

Other factors may be taken into account. Politically, the turmoil of the Frondes had died down, though Corneille's ideas had probably been affected by these events.[3] Whether his religious writings and meditations during the 1650s left their mark on the composition of the play is less clear.[4] More important is that Corneille was bringing together his views on the theatre for the edition of his plays which he was preparing.[5] This would allow an up-to-date *prise de position* on his earlier output, on the idea expressed by the abbé d'Aubignac[6] and, predictably, on theoretical sources, notably Aristotle (and/or his commentators) and examples from classical drama. The choice of Oedipus makes more sense if Corneille had been re-reading the *Poetics*, where the *Oedipus rex* appears as a primary illustration of dramatic practice − and Aristotle, as interpreted at that time, is an essential point of reference in discussions on the nature of drama.[7]

The modifications introduced into *Oedipe* by Corneille stem in part from awareness of what contemporary taste found acceptable; they also reflect the distance that shows up between himself and classical sources (especially Aristotle and Sophocles). The reduction of stage violence − for instance Oedipe's self-mutilation occurs off-stage − is in tune with public response; the number of oracles is diminished so that Oedipe's growing awareness of the truth is conveyed to a French audience (as well as to himself) in a manner it would find more 'vraisemblable'. The major novelty is the appearance of Dircé and Thésée: they were both known in classical times (especially Thésée), but their characters here are substantially invented by Corneille. He refers to what his audience might expect to find in a tragedy, but he is also following a model which runs through his 'tragic' career: he has normally opted for a linking of the political and love elements in his plots. Dircé opens and closes the play: Oedipe is in a sense framed within her presence; and Thésée is seen chiefly to act through his love for Dircé. Her prominence affects Jocaste, who, though essential to the myth, does not rise on stage much above the role of a superior confidante: she is a link with the past,[8] a passive witness to the unfolding of the present, a person in whom various characters confide; she initiates the theme of the 'voix du sang' — though this is not developed very far — and she sheds light on others' thoughts and actions: all this is dramatically useful, but it does not make her a major figure.

Contemporary concerns and Corneille's re-reading of Aristotle show the playwright's interest in various matters discussed by the philosopher: the treatment of a 'mythical' subject, the nature of the 'tragic' hero, and *agnitio*. On the first point, Corneille thinks that the essential must not be tampered with; in any case time will have domesticated elements that otherwise might be unacceptable. What can be invented are 'les moyens de parvenir à l'action'.[9] While the subject would preferably be 'invraisemblable', the manner of its treatment should follow 'verisimilitude'. With regard to the 'tragic' hero, Corneille strikes out on his own:[10] he considers Oedipe to be of tragic dimension, though virtuous (cf. Polyeucte), but then Cléopâtre (in *Rodogune*) will, for very different reasons, qualify.[11] And Corneille can point to tragic heroes who are persecuted by wicked persons, but finally escape the dangers into which they have fallen. Nor does he fully approve Aristotle's assessment of various types of tragedy arising between kinsmen of royal rank.[12] In any case, the modern ideas of the 'tragic' hero do not belong to Aristotle's world. One might add that, so far as Corneille's practice is concerned, French critics tend to emphasize the central role of a 'tragic hero' to a greater extent than do Anglophone spectators: for instance, apropos of *Horace* one notices a division between those who stress Horace, *the* tragic hero, and those who give more weight to the tragic situation within which *several* protagonists play out their roles. The theme of 'reconnaissance',[13] — allowance being made for the terminological difficulties that *agnitio* engenders for Corneille's contemporaries — does occur in his writings, but his views do not coincide even with what Aristotle was thought to mean: one may indeed wonder to what extent Corneille talks about real *agnitio* in genuine tragedy. Aristotle's remarks deal with actions of a complicated nature which reach their turning-point through reversal of fortune, or recognition, or both. Recognition can be of inanimate things or, especially, of persons, singly or mutually, and therefore, like reversal of fortune, it depends on surprises.[14] On the earlier assumption that *agnitio* was caused or sparked off by an event unattached to the action, and therefore shown not to be 'necessary' or 'vraisemblable', Corneille was more in tune with seventeenth-century sensibility; in any case, he takes the view that the device 'a ses incommodités'. On other matters such as *catharsis* or *hamartia*, it is likely that he was influenced by contemporary moralism. All in all, his views were very different from those of the Greeks; but Aristotle serves, at an opportune time, to refine his ideas. These divergences do not, however, explain why Corneille chose Oedipus from among the subjects offered by Fouquet.

Nor do the departures from the myth, in some measure pointed out by Corneille himself; in any case, we should be careful not to 'fix' the tale too rigidly, for it has varied quite a lot over the centuries in its emphases and interpretation.[15] There was a time in the Occident when the enigma and the sphinx were not understood, so that Oedipus was converted into a general.[16] Early on, until the seventeenth century (and beyond), the Greek dramatists were comparatively little known at first hand; even in the Renaissance they were more accessible through translations and adaptations (Latin or vernacular); then there was what one might call the Senecan interference — Seneca's textual influence on *Oedipe* has been clearly established — and no doubt other literary sources have been in action at various moments. In more modern times, critics have been far from unanimous on the sense of certain key themes in the *Oedipus rex*: the nature of Oedipus' *hamartia*, the matter of *hubris*, Oedipus' self-mutilation, the role of the gods.[17] Very often myths have tended to form a thematic cluster: thus Oedipus is associated chiefly with incest, prophecy and parricide. More recently, a greater familiarity with anthropological findings and the explorations of psychology (particularly of Freud) has opened up important avenues. We must be careful, however, not to fall into anachronistic temptation; and we must ask ourselves how a given myth fits in with an author's own evolution. In *Oedipe* Corneille is undoubtedly developing themes and concerns that have surfaced in previous plays; but what strikes me as a dominant here, over and above such themes, is the pervasive irony of the text. I wonder if we have not underplayed the role of irony in Corneille's drama, and here it may be associated with a moment of deep-seated scepticism and doubt. We are dealing not only with dramatic irony, but with the ironic presentation of concerns through situations and characters that undermine their validity, and with a familiar contrast between Cornelian 'principles' and Cornelian rhetoric. One should avoid the easy indulgence of linking an author's — and particularly a dramatist's — ideas and what his characters affirm; but in *Oedipe* so prominent is the irony informing the text that the tone of the play is as important as the themes it develops.

II

Dircé and Thésée are the most prominent innovations so far as the cast is concerned: they enhance the political aspects of the play and they provide the required love element — a double thread that reduces the early legendary presence of Oedipe and Jocaste. Oedipe's views are expressed quite soon: his intention to marry off Dircé to a man unlikely to threaten him politically is quickly shown to be motivated by self-interest — especially when Dircé's attitude to Thésée is disclosed.[18] The situation is based on a misconception, as Dircé is seen as Oedipe's stepdaughter. (Historically, Dircé was the wife of Lycus, a Theban prince, and was known for her cruelty to Antiope; the link with the Oedipus tale seems to have been invented by Corneille.) Over the first two acts, we are given information on the previous history of the family and on the political viewpoints of the King and of Dircé, who considers her 'stepfather' a usurper. We have here a good example of the ironic mould into which the plot is poured.

Oedipe's defence of his position rests on three main arguments. First, he married Jocaste: the claim of legitimacy by marriage is one which re-appears in *Pulchérie*, where Martian has no royal blood in his veins; but such an argument will find no favour with Dircé, even when the whole truth is known. Secondly, Oedipe's marriage has received the general approval of the people, another point that is taken seriously in some later plays,[19] but even if Oedipe's claims apparently have the backing of the gods, he remains a usurper to Dircé, who maintains a royal contempt for such democratic feelings and finds all this irrelevant to the issue of authority. In fact, later Oedipe admits that the people cannot choose a ruler (v, i) but may give support and backing: the matter remains in the hands of the gods. Thirdly, Oedipe claims that the original situation arose from necessity, a 'dernier besoin' (II, i) and that, had he not stepped in, chaos would have ensued. Once he is King, he is convinced that he can do as he pleases, for he is sure that he must follow the needs of 'politique partout'.[20] Here we are concerned with expediency, not principle. Predictably, Dircé has no more time for this line of argument than she has for the principle associated in later history with the Salic law: Oedipe doubts whether women have much blood-right to the succession, belonging as they do to the 'sexe imbecile' (I, iii). He winds up his views by stating that 'la parole des rois doit être inviolable' and that he cannot break his promise to Aemon, but this is yet another example of the masks adopted by self-interest. Two important points have emerged and contribute to the ironic colour of the play: first, principles of general validity (in the world of politics) are seen to be founded on self-interest and emotional involvement. Secondly, the whole discussion between Oedipe and Dircé rests on a fundamental misunderstanding: neither fully realizes yet what is the true family predicament: this will take time to come out, but retrospectively it will cast doubt on human assumption and insight.

Thésée, as an historical character, is remoulded to suit Corneille's requirements. By reputation he is the stereotype of the good ruler, a just and fearless warrior, one who is 'généreux' (as Oedipe recognizes, I, ii) and easily earns the respect of those around; but his own words prove that his love for Dircé determines his every thought and action: 'Le héros ne peut vivre où l'amour doit mourir' (II, iv). He considers some deceit to be forgivable, indeed justifiable, in a lover: 'Et l'amour/Peut faire vanité d'un peu de tromperie' (IV, ii). He accepts that a king has the right to go back on his word, but this is something in the context that would benefit Dircé. If anything appears to threaten her safety, he is eager to reach the conclusion most likely to spare her distress or danger. He is willing to believe uncritically the not very reliable testimony of the now dead Phaedime concerning his own parentage. His rather eccentric remarks about the 'normal' relationship between love and incestuous friendship bear all the signs of thinking muddied by feeling. Not surprisingly he is an easy prey to self-deception, though he can show insight, as when he suspects that Dircé's declarations in Act I do not correspond to her real attitudes. So far, Thésée strikes us as a ruler whose external image hardly coincides with his inner feelings; his behaviour stems not from political ideals, but from the needs of his heart. We can pass over the quasi-

Machiavellian ideas he expresses in order to support Dircé in her opposition to Oedipe; but the well-known oration he makes on behalf of free will (III, v) requires more attention. I am not sure that it is wise to follow critics who see this as a statement of Corneille's own views; nor should too much be made of the comparisons with contemporary debates on Molinism and Jansenism. It is true that French audiences of all centuries can read into a text relevance of which the author had no inkling: one thinks of Népomucène Lemercier and the way his plays fared at the hands of Napoleon and his censors. In the words Thésée utters to Jocaste, one may see as it were a sort of dramatic weight lent to Oedipe's later remarks; both men, in different ways, make a strong defence for free will. But it is in keeping with the ironic nature of the play that the character least fitted to speak in this fashion becomes the spokesman: Thésée is patently the prisoner of his feelings, and therefore of Dircé, whose emotional puppet he is, and it is he who speaks for free will!

Dircé is rather more complex: she has a broader range of roles to play and reacts more vigorously to the forces that surround her. She stands out against Oedipe as a sort of counter-heroine, especially in view of Jocaste's somewhat effaced part; Oedipe needs a firm personality to act as foil to himself. Thésée is marginal in this respect, so that the burden falls on Dircé. She resents Oedipe's usurpation of what she believes to be her legitimate claims; even his kindnesses are, in her eyes, prompted by self-interest. When circumstances favour her love for Thésée, she behaves as one would expect an 'amoureuse' to act; but as soon as this love is thwarted (by Oedipe), she changes her tune. Having first taken the view that women are made for love (I, i), she talks of the need for 'grandes actions', which Thésée understandably says appear to him to be skin-deep. Later on she holds that 'le trône a d'autres droits que ceux de la nature' (III, iii) and that this represents the will of the gods; she sees in public sacrifice on her part a surrogate for her thwarted feelings. Her attempts to 'save' Thésée, a scene based on misinformation and assumption, reflect strangely her love. Jocaste sees, in Dircé's talk of the need to sacrifice herself, the workings of 'orgueil' — to what extent is she concerned with the public weal? Earlier, she and Thésée think in terms of 'gloire' and 'générosité'; but are these 'Cornelian' attitudes and principles not more than a little carious? Much of this is mere talk; R. J. Nelson saw this long ago when he asserted that 'the stern implications of "générosité" are invoked finally to be denied'.[21] These values seem to be a form of posturing, displayed in situations which themselves turn out to be illusory. They are elements of a *persona* and do not belong to the inner being. In the relation between Dircé, Oedipe and Thésée the play of irony is all-pervasive.

III

The play, by tradition, centres on enigma and hidden truth, but Corneille seeks to broaden this theme, perhaps at the expense of others associated with the myth. What is truth, and how can it be attained? The epistemological problem seems to me to lie close to the centre of the play; situations and characters raise many doubts on this score; there are probably three main obstacles. In the first place, searching for the truth depends on outside factors that themselves are uncertain: truth so often appears in the form of enigma or of half-truth. Very rarely does it come before us in an unambiguous way – and the gods have their responsibility here; but truth is further communicated in unfavourable circumstances: we may learn things after a lapse of *time* – as the Oedipus myth makes only too evident. Even in the present, rumour is more rife than accurate report. So often, language is double-edged – not only, say, the words of Laius (III, iv) or oracles, but also the direct speech of living characters; the action of Oedipe is often propelled by unreliable speech. We depend more than we probably intend on intermediaries: even when information is more or less to hand, our reasoning powers may not be able to cope with the evidence, because they are limited (in an age of reason!); this is sometimes due to faulty mechanisms, but that is not the whole story.

Secondly, man is very rarely able to disentangle truth and fact from his emotional involvement(s). In *Oedipe* the characters more likely to grasp a truth are those who stand aside from the action, but Corneille does not simplify unduly; he knows that persons of genuine feeling can put their finger on some aspect of truth, yet he realizes that emotion can endanger comprehension or insight more than it can help. I mentioned intermediaries a moment ago: truth suffers not simply from the snares of communication, but by the fact that human emotion will warp what is conveyed. It is worth remembering that in *Oedipe* we have three (or four, if one includes Jocaste) *principal characters*; there are seven others, often in an intermediate capacity, not to speak of rumours, demons and oracles.

The principal characters are rarely free of emotional involvement; the play is riddled with the invasion of sentiment, prejudice, *amour-propre* (and *orgueil*). This does not mean that purely selfish interest is always at the root. The situation at the beginning of the play no doubt came about partly by fortune and the workings of the gods; it is further clouded by the activities of two old men: Iphicrate realizes that he is in some measure responsible for the King of Corinth assuming Oedipe to be his son and therefore his lawful heir (v, iii), but he acts out of a laudable desire to spare people suffering. Phorbas, on the other hand, is prompted by unworthy motives: 'reputation' and the desire to save his own skin. Cases naturally arise when evil urges are in play or thought to be so: in Delphi, possible falsity has been suspected (III, v), and rumours have suggested that Oedipe may have used a devious soothsayer, so that the information elicited would suit his book (v). Yet it is often self-deception rather than intentional trickery that lies at the heart: nothing is black and white, for the murky links between faulty epistemology, unsound principles and behaviour that belies professed ideals are plain for all to see.[22] Oedipe's deceit is patent; Dircé and Thésée, so keen to protect each other, are eager to jump to conclusions on the flimsiest of evidence. What emerges is a general impression of uncertainty on the shifting sands of doubt.

In these circumstances, truth is difficult, if not impossible, to handle; the reader (or spectator) may well ask himself whether principles (political ideals, ethical codes, etc.) have any objective validity of which we can be sure. This question also arises in less exalted realms: thus the notorious 'voix du sang', on which so much of later drama relied happily, is found wanting. The topic comes to the forefront when Thésée thinks, albeit for a brief period, that he might be related to the Oedipe family.[23] His fantasies are soon blown away, but the theme of blood-recognition is viewed with some scepticism, especially when it is mentioned in connection with Oedipe and Jocaste: at a crucial time, Jocaste was deaf to the 'voix du sang' and thus married Oedipe without a qualm.[24] Truth, or what passes for such, is seen to be flawed, unreliable, perhaps unattainable; values and attitudes based on such meagre evidence are too subjective, too coloured with emotional involvement to enjoy a wider validity.

There is a third and more important point: the gods who traditionally play a cardinal role in the myth. To begin with, they are seen through the various characters, whose views are neither consistent nor similar. It never becomes clear to what extent free-will or determinism can assert itself; overall a sense of claustrophobia is created so that everybody is englobed by the presence and activity of the gods. The reactions of the characters are limited by the constraints we mentioned earlier. Some are fearful that the gods are enigmatic (IV, ii), unpredictable, wayward even − Dircé thinks that they have allowed Oedipe to usurp her throne: they are amoral and often remain silent. Moreover they can be 'interpreted' by third parties whose reliability leaves plenty to be desired. Yet others − and one thinks above all of Oedipe − incline to the view that human beings have some independence and may have at least a say in the shaping of their fate (III, v). His final gesture is seen as a sign of this self-assertion; he goes so far as to hope that the gods will endorse his actions and destiny. His views are shaped by his needs and feelings: so when he puts his eyes out he declares: 'prévenons l'injustice des dieux', a cry that is echoed by those around him: 'Il s'est rendu maître de tout son sort.' He likes to think that his qualities are such that he 'ne les tien[t] pas d'eux' and that he is 'maître de [s]a fortune'; but this sounds more like conviction than reasoned demonstration; indeed, once again we suspect that irony lies behind his statements, or at least that they can be understood, in a framework of irony.

Quite apart from the self-deceiving attitude of so many of the cast and the problems that attend the unveiling of truth, there remain unexplained elements in the behaviour of the gods. Originally, it seems, they had demanded a 'pure' sacrificial victim to avenge Laius' murder (II, iii), but when Oedipe is discovered to be the character in question, he is hardly 'pure' − though Corneille alters the traditional tale by Oedipe's believing that he has killed not the King, but the latter's assassins; on the other hand he is certainly not 'guilty' or to be blamed for Laius' death. Oedipe's fate is not absolutely clear and critics seem divided on that score. Is he condemned to permanent exile? Or will he be exonerated, his self-mutilation being a form of purification or blood-sacrifice? Or will that act be seen as a form of *hubris*, since Oedipe defies the gods thereby, and how will they finally react? Or will the audience go home, reasonably satisfied by the various remarks of the characters at the end? Thésée believes that the gods' secret ways will in time show favour (IV, i); we are assured that 'un autre ordre peut demain nous être donné', Cléante talks of 'la bonté de nos Dieux' (V, ix), and Dircé sounds the final note, telling us to 'remettre aux

Dieux à disposer du reste' — a comment that echoes the closing sentiments of several later plays: time will work things out satisfactorily, for the gods will take the proper decisions. Corneille's denouements do not always bring a clear-cut solution, except in their dramatic effect. From one angle, with her future safe and sure, Dircé may not be the ideal character to utter the closure; and the recognition of Oedipe's predicament does not necessarily conclude the play. The gods remain as enigmatic as ever. In some ways, they have become a symbol rather than the architects of our destiny: they are capricious, they cannot or will not communicate fully, they come over often as the projections of our own desires and prejudices.

Corneille has stuck by the points he expressed on the treatment of an accepted legend, if his Dircé and Thésée are felt not to interrupt the pattern: respect the bones, but have discretion in the clothing of the skeleton. This has allowed him to introduce shifts of emphasis, to diminish considerably some topics (and characters) and to add substantially to the original story. But one might feel that, by taking these liberties, he has done more than reshape the myth: he has invested it with new significance. It has become a vehicle for his own concerns and anxieties. His preoccupation centres on the nature and possibility of knowledge. The play is a questioning about existence, anxiety about the barriers that stand between ourselves and others. Finally a suspicion lurks that these matters will remain unsolved: a gap between ourselves and reality will not be bridged. What gives the play its curious vitality is precisely this irony, which crops up at all moments; and we may wonder whether we can ever reach beyond the world of illusion — the play seems to prefigure themes we would associate with Bishop Berkeley. What is very patent is the human propensity to create, consciously or not, a web of appearance and disguise which is exposed in *Oedipe* with no great credit to mortals. We must live in a world of *feinte*, warping and falsifying whatever grip we hope to acquire upon reality and confining us within the sphere of appearance. Are we likely ever to reach reasonable clarity or certainty on matters of fundamental importance; 'Quelle énigme?'[25]

NOTES

1 Pending the completion of the new Pléiade edition of Corneille's works, I refer on the one hand to the Marty-Laveaux edition in the

Grands Ecrivains series, as it contains the variants of *Oedipe*, and on the other to the Intégrale edition (ed. Stegmann) with its numbering of the lines.

2 Among modern studies, one can mention: R. J. Nelson, *Corneille: His Heroes and their Worlds* (Philadelphia, 1963); Jacques Scherer, *Le Théâtre de Corneille* (Paris, 1984); Christian Delmas, 'Corneille et le mythe: le cas d'*Oedipe*', *Revue de la Société d'Histoire du Théâtre* XXXVII (1984), 132–52. The latter considers the play from a psycho-analytical angle.

3 See, for example, G. Couton, *La Vieillesse de Corneille* (Paris, 1948).

4 The play shows awareness of contemporary religious concerns (and climate). The translation of *L'Imitation de Jésus-Christ* belongs to the years 1651–6 (complete edn 1665).

5 The three *Discours* appeared in the 1600 edition of the plays: I use the edition by H. T. Barnwell, *Pierre Corneille: Writings on the Theatre* (Oxford, 1965).

6 D'Aubignac's treatise, *La Pratique du théâtre*, appeared in 1657: see the modern edition by P. Martino (Algiers, 1927).

7 I use S. H. Butcher's edition (with translation) of the *Poetics* (Oxford, 1895).

8 Generally speaking the original incest theme is played down or shifted (to the dialogue between Dircé and Thésée): the shadow of the past cannot be totally eliminated, but there is mitigation. Creon and Tiresias have no part as in Sophocles; kinships are altered with the insertion of Dircé. The usurpation theme occupies more space than does that of incest.

9 Here one may feel that the 'moyens' do rather more than Corneille admits. Though he makes changes that concern the narrative or plot aspects, he does not seek much technical innovation. The major characters all appear in the first act; every scene ending an act contains one character who will open the following act – though, as d'Aubignac observed, Corneille is not in line with strict principle here. There is only one monologue (beginning of Act III), if one may so call a series of *stances*. Act V contains far more scenes than the other acts; this is something becoming frequent enough in the contemporary theatre, but Corneille seems to be alone in justifying this practice on theoretical grounds. One notable feature is the high number of secondary characters (confidants, messengers, shades from the past, and so forth) and Jocaste can be counted among these; there may be thematic justification for this as well.

10 See also H. T. Barnwell, *The Tragic Drama of Corneille and Racine: An Old Parallel Revisited* (Oxford, 1982).

11 *Discours II*, ed. Barnwell, pp. 36ff.

12 *Ibid.*, pp. 37ff.

13 *Ibid.*, pp. 42ff.

14 Aristotle, *Poetics*, ch. 11.

15 Among older authorities, see C. Robert, *Oidipus*, 2 vols. (Berlin, 1915).

16 A. H. Krappe, *The Science of Folklore* (London, 1930), p. 130.

17 For discussion of various theories current up to the date of publication, see C. M. Bowra, *Sophoclean Tragedy* (Oxford, 1944).

18 Aemon is son of Creon, and therefore nephew of Jocaste. Though Oedipe points to the kinship with Jocaste in I, iii, his emphasis has been rather on Aemon's weaker character than Thésée's (Oedipe refers to 'quelque faiblesse').

19 In *Oedipe* various attitudes to the people are expressed, and often reveal the private interests of the speakers concerned. In II, i, Oedipe doubts whether the people would approve Dircé's marriage to Thésée; towards the end (v, i), rumours suggest that the people are beginning to turn against Oedipe; but in the same scene Dymas is more aware of the dangers presented by the people. In some of Corneille's plays, the people are seen to be 'on the right side'.

20 The charge is made by Dircé, who may be biased but is not devoid of insight.

21 Nelson, *Corneille*, p. 206.

22 The gap between 'Cornelian values' and Cornelian rhetoric has been examined in recent years, hence I have given the matter little space here: cf. M. Margitič, *Essai sur la mythologie du 'Cid'* (New York, 1976).

23 The theme of pseudo-incest had already interested Corneille, but treatment varies: whereas Léonor's instinct in *Don Sanche d'Aragon* turns out correct, this is not the case in *Héraclius*, where Phorbas' attitude works out otherwise.

24 It may be argued that Dircé's more compassionate view of Oedipe at the end (v, v) owes something to her true kinship. Of course, one finds traces of a different theme, that of the 'frères ennemis', which is not developed here.

25 I am grateful to Professor Barnwell for his helpful advice.

5
Racine's *Andromaque*: new myth for old

H. T. BARNWELL

Is it possible to discuss Racine's first masterpiece in terms of myth? Modern theories of myth, based on anthropological and archaeological evidence, and offering examples and explanations of universal psychological or social phenomena, seem scarcely appropriate tools for study of a play which so clearly belongs to its own rationalist age.[1] Yet the story and characters are in large measure derived from models in antiquity — literary models, for no others were known to Racine and his contemporaries — whose subject-matter was drawn from episodes of the Trojan war and its aftermath. Do those episodes belong to myth? If they do, does myth play a significant part in the play? For many modern theorists, myth is distinguished by the intervention of divine or supernatural powers in human affairs.

I do not propose to re-open the question of the reality of the gods in *Andromaque*. The word 'dieux' (never in the singular) occurs twenty-four times, on nineteen occasions simply as a rhetorical exclamation, and on half of those uttered by Oreste, with a predictable cluster (1613, 1628, 1635) in the mad scene at the end. The remaining cases equate the gods with a hostile fate (776) or the source of justice (1382–3), or invoke them as witnesses (487) or barbarous foreign agents of cruelty (492). They are not individualized or given proper names: they form part of the conventional rhetoric of tragedy drawn from ancient literary sources, and for whose audiences polytheism may already have been virtually dead as a system of actual belief.[2] Significantly enough, the gods are not mentioned at all until the beginning of Act II (401), when the exposition is complete: the action of the play is not set in a divine or divinely-ordered context, whereas the opening of the *Iliad*, for example, like the prologues of many Greek tragedies, immediately establishes such a context. The use of the words 'destin', 'destinée' (twelve occurrences in all) and 'fatal' (four occurrences) is in this respect similarly neutral. Of the principal characters, neither Pyrrhus nor Andromaque (except one instance, 904) utters these words at all, and it is on these two that I propose to concentrate.

Within that framework may we analyse the mythic (or mythological) aspects of *Andromaque*? In modern myth theory, no consensus emerges as to what myth really means or implies. As a general concept it is completely vague, signifying no more than a traditional story; a necessary association with sacred tales and rituals is misleading: '. . . myths are not connected with religion any more by a universal emotional intensity than they are by their subject-matter − for whereas some myths are about gods, others are not'. Myth and religion are not 'twin aspects of the same subject'. On this view, the *Iliad*, Racine's ultimate and historically remotest source, recounts heroic events which 'actually resulted in the capture and burning of Troy': their protagonists, entirely human, even the gods and goddesses being presented as 'supermen and superwomen with special powers', do, however, belong to the mythology of ancient Greece. Legend, rather than myth? Yes, but the characters 'have become mythical paradigms', not directly, but through literature, tragedy in particular, and the events in which they play a part have little in common with the 'spontaneous myths of the preliterate past' or 'their transitional descendants'.[3]

On this basis we may proceed. Nevertheless, some historical justification seems called for, the word myth not being attested in French before the beginning of the nineteenth century, nor in English before 1830. One of its uses is pejorative, suggesting fictions or false belief. The seventeenth-century equivalent, *fable* (from Latin rather than Greek), had existed in the language since the twelfth century, to denote a narrative with an imaginary basis. (From the fourteenth century *fabuleux* is attested, linking such narrative with the 'marvellous' of pagan antiquity.) These usages are not entirely unconnected with those which form a specific part of the critical vocabulary stemming from Aristotle by way of Latin translations. Racine was in a better position than most to be aware of the connection with μῦθος, which he himself translates as 'fable', following Vettori's 'fabula'. But the word has more than one meaning in the *Poetics*. In chapter 6, the instance universally remembered, we have, in Racine's version: 'La fable est proprement l'imitation de l'action. J'entends par le mot de fable le tissu ou le contexte des affaires.'[4] 'Fable' is plot. But it is also the 'traditional stories' on which dramatists draw for their subject-matter (chapter 14): 'On ne peut changer et démentir les fables qui sont reçues' (Vettori, 'fabulas'; Aristotle, μυθους).[5]

These uses of the word *fable* in themselves contain no suggestion either of falsehood or of the marvellous, any more than does Racine's version of the comment of a Greek scholiast on Sophocles' *Electra* at the end of his second preface to *Andromaque*.[6] There, as in his annotation of his copy of the Henri Estienne edition of the Greek play,[7] he is concerned with legitimate alterations to the traditional stories and with the 'excellent usage que [les poètes] ont fait de ces changements, et la manière dont ils ont su accommoder la fable à leur sujet'. The 'fable' may of course be used and modified on grounds either of dramatic necessity or of *vraisemblance* and *bienséance*.[8]

Fables in this general sense, whether actually historical or simply fictional,[9] provided the raw materials for the tragic playwright. They were undifferentiated, as Corneille among others points out.[10] Certainly, he and all his contemporaries would regard Homer's account of the Trojan war as history, even though that involved putting the activities of the gods in the category of what Racine was to call, in the preface to *Phèdre*, 'les ornements de la fable'. Corneille,[11] Boileau,[12] Rapin[13] and Bouhours,[14] like many others, all adopt the same attitude, never attributing to those 'ornements' or 'beautés' more than an aesthetic and possibly allegorical function. Does the 'fable' then in *Andromaque* constitute no more than a 'décor verbal', a literary embellishment for what is in fact Racine's new 'fable' or μυθος understood as plot? This question has given rise to controversy, which it is not my purpose here to pursue.[15] Instead, I shall attempt a fresh analysis of the precise function of the myth of the Trojan war − a traditional story − in the working out of that new 'fable', at whose centre lies the conflict between Andromaque and Pyrrhus.

The title of the play would hardly lead the audience to expect the dramatic situation and its development as invented by Racine on the basis of plays by Corneille and others and of seventeenth-century novels,[16] but this was of course nothing unusual. Although suggestions for some of the changes wrought in the character and role of Andromaque and Pyrrhus did exist in Racine's sources − not all of them acknowledged to be such − his play would not be what it is without the radical alterations to the traditional story which enable Andromaque to resist the advances of Pyrrhus, and Pyrrhus to behave in a courtly manner in attempting to persuade her, even if such behaviour does not exclude cruelty and blackmail. The developments of the first three acts of the tragedy revolve around the struggle thus created, and the fates of Hermione and Oreste, likewise oscillating, depend entirely upon its outcome. The first preface, while not denying Pyrrhus' courtliness, is largely devoted to replying to those who found him too violent and cruel, the second to justifying the prolongation of the life of Astyanax, which is the cause of Andromaque's dilemma and so of the dramatic uncertainties, and the possibility of the heroine's remaining a chaste and faithful widow. Both kinds of argument depend upon aspects of *bienséance*. Whether, in the actual creation of the play, they were of primary importance may be questioned.

In spite of all the changes – more numerous of course than Racine admits – he is justified in pointing to the features which attach these two characters to their ancient counterparts, features which are also more extensive than he claims. From the outset, the exposition carefully integrates the new situation with the myth of Troy – allusively, for spectators familiar with it. The departures from it would naturally give rise to dramatic curiosity as early as Pylade's reference to Pyrrhus' vacillations (119–22). Dependent upon his apparent success or real failure in his courtship (if it can be so called) of Andromaque, those vacillations shape the development of the dramatic action, a development which, through its effect on the characters, is also the source of pathos.[17] In its turn, the action, the plot as conceived by Racine, based not on the ancient myth, but on the new relationships between the characters, is made possible by their recollections of the destruction of Troy. The importance of the memories has been noted by others: Pyrrhus' sense of guilt,[18] the conflict between past (Hector) and present (Astyanax) in Andromaque,[19] the fatality of past inescapably weighing on present,[20] desire for freedom from the past (Pyrrhus) at odds with fidelity to it (Andromaque)[21] – these are some of the interpretations which offer insights into the workings of the play. What seems especially interesting, however, and is only touched upon here and there in these interpretations, is not simply Andromaque's clinging to the past as a bulwark against the advances of Pyrrhus, and his attempts to free himself (and her) from it and its present consequences, but the conflicting ways in which the two remember and imagine the past, and indeed imagine the future – for Pyrrhus attempts to detach Andromaque from the past and to attach her to an imagined future. Both past and future, each in its way, hold the power of myth over these two characters.

Let us consider first the case of Pyrrhus. The prolongation of the life of Astyanax is of course crucial to the situation: without it,

Oreste would have no pretext for his visit to Epirus, and Pyrrhus would have no means of blackmailing Andromaque, while she would not be placed in her impossible dilemma. For Oreste, Pyrrhus and Hermione, Astyanax is a pawn in the game of love and politics, and, naturally enough, they all speak of him with detachment. When Oreste approaches Pyrrhus with the demand of the Greek allies, he enters into an account of the present situation through the past, alluding to Pyrrhus' and Hector's part in the Trojan war. This is characteristically indirect diplomatic tactics, but the reference to Pyrrhus, not by name, but in the forms 'le fils d'Achille' and 'le vainqueur de Troie' (146, 150) is not simply flattering: it attaches present to mythical past, establishing the same kind of continuity as the one the Greeks fear from Hector to his son, who likewise is not actually named (159). This is, however, not merely a matter of temporal continuity: it also concerns a possible break, in the case of Pyrrhus, with the supposedly admirable patriotism and loyalty of his father (157ff.) and, in the case of Astyanax, the fear of a renewal of Hector's might in the person of his son (155ff.). Astyanax is imagined repeating the father's exploit in setting the Greek ships on fire (162–3), a clear echo of the *Iliad* (xv, 696ff.). And the other characters of the play are introduced through their relationships to some of the principal figures of the war itself – a kind of parallel of the Homeric 'naming them with all their names' – Hermione as the daughter of Menelaus (179) and Helen (245, 342), Oreste as the son of Agamemnon (178), Andromaque as the widow of Hector (108, 109). Like Oreste, Andromaque sees in Pyrrhus the son of Achilles (310, 359–60). But the overwhelming unseen presence is of course that of Hector. Oreste alleges that it is fear of the greatest of the Trojan heroes that haunts the Greeks (224; cf. 155ff.):

Ce n'est pas les Troyens, c'est Hector qu'on poursuit

For Pyrrhus, Hector and Astyanax are not the objects of fear, but obstacles in the way of his marriage to Andromaque. All these means of attaching the characters to their mythical past – the allusiveness contributing much to Racine's poetry – provide causes of dramatic conflict through their irreconcilable perceptions of that past.

In reply to Oreste's expression of Greek fears of a Trojan revival, Pyrrhus recalls the immediate aftermath of defeat, the distribution of the captives among the victors and his own independence, which he now seeks to safeguard in his treatment of Astyanax. Here, he conceals his true motive for refusing the Greeks' demand: in doing so, he recalls and uses aspects of the myth different from those of which Oreste reminds him. The sack of Troy is evoked from the standpoint of the present:

> Je songe quelle était autrefois cette ville . . .
> Je ne vois que des tours, que la cendre a couvertes . . .
>
> (197, 201)

Pyrrhus is arguing that the city's revival is unthinkable. Evocative through these lines are, he views the past unemotionally, dispassionately, endeavouring to put it behind him:

> Tout était juste alors . . .
> Mais que ma cruauté survive à ma colère?   (209, 214)

But that the past is not dead is Oreste's final argument (225): so long as the mythical Hector lives in his son, the Greeks will fear a new Troy, a myth of the future arising out of that of the past, the same past to which Phœnix appeals when encouraging Pyrrhus to abandon Andromaque. At the volte-face of Act II, scene v, he exclaims:

> C'est Pyrrhus. C'est le fils et le rival d'Achille.   (630)

Try as he may, Pyrrhus is simply not allowed to detach himself from the past. The figure of Hector, conjured up for him by the imagination of Andromaque, besets him still (649ff.), as it haunts his very desire of present love, in spite of the vain attempt at separation:

> Elle est veuve d'Hector. Et je suis fils d'Achille.
> Trop de haine sépare Andromaque et Pyrrhus.   (662–3)

But he is soon saying:

> Je croyais apporter plus de haine en ces lieux,   (951)

a hatred between his father and her husband and which is not stilled for her –

> Enfin voilà l'époux que tu me veux donner –   (1008)

as he recognizes:

> Andromaque m'arrache un cœur qu'elle déteste.   (1298)

62

Significantly, in his final appeals and threats, the past has disappeared, his attention now being concentrated on the present, on the construction of a new myth — unrealizable — of Pyrrhus the protector of the widow and orphan (cf. 282ff.), offering queenship to the mother (959) as he had offered future kingship to the child 331–2). Not that the cruelty is gone: it remains in the peremptory threats with which Pyrrhus takes his leave (967ff.). In his first preface, Racine claims to go no further than 'adoucir un peu la férocité de Pyrrhus'. At his next and final appearance, his only encounter on the stage with Hermione (IV, v), Pyrrhus is taunted with an evocation of the horrors perpetrated at Troy:

> Que peut-on refuser à ces généreux coups? (1340)

The myth of the hero is demolished. The cruelties of the past portend that of the present, of love disdained (1323–4). While coolly acknowledging his bad faith, Pyrrhus, in the face of Hermione's accusations, turns his back on the mythical past to which betrothal to her belongs. He imagines instead a future (1281, 1299–1300) which is doomed.

In their references to the Trojan war, Oreste, Pyrrhus and Hermione all use the myth as evidence in an argument. For Oreste and Hermione, it is myth in the sense of story already embedded in the annals of Greece: they did not experience the events directly. Pyrrhus did experience them, but, while he cannot deny them, he does try to repudiate them:

> Mais enfin je consens d'oublier le passé. (1344)

In the same way Oreste, in order to win Hermione, sets aside what he calls her 'devoir austère' (881), obedience to Menelaus, who belongs to the story of Troy but not to the play itself. Oreste thus abets Pyrrhus' breaking his solemn promise to her, in the same way repudiating the past — an irony in view of Oreste's recalling Pyrrhus to his duty to his allies. Meanwhile, until the point of no return is reached, Hermione deludes herself with the vision of another Pyrrhus, part real, part her personal myth:

> Sais-tu quel est Pyrrhus? . . .
> Charmant, fidèle enfin, rien ne manque à sa gloire.
> (851, 854)

Finally, that illusion is destroyed:

> Je t'aimais inconstant, qu'aurais je fait fidèle?
> Le perfide triomphe, et se rit de ma rage.　　　(1365, 1409)

Gone is the hero whose story belonged to myth:

> Ce prince, dont mon cœur se faisait autrefois
> Avec tant de plaisir redire les exploits . . .,　　　(1423–4)

only to re-emerge, remythified, after his death, as having lived 'une si belle vie' (1538).

If Pyrrhus offers a future myth to Andromaque, she resolutely refuses it.[22] He misjudges her, falling into an idle boast and bad faith, saying the reverse of what he has just said to Oreste:

> Votre Ilion encor peut sortir de sa cendre.
> Je puis, en moins de temps que les Grecs ne l'ont pris,
> Dans ses murs relevés couronner votre fils.　　　(330–2)

Pyrrhus is constructing in his mind an untold story which continues and reverses the myth he has lived.

Throughout this first encounter, Andromaque argues only from the present situation, pleading simply to be spared the embraces of her captor and for the safety of her son: she appeals to Pyrrhus' generosity (310), to his sense of duty to Hermione (342) and to his compassion (373–4). True, the memories of Troy and Hector live in her mind, and she does respond to Pyrrhus' mention of the walls of the fallen city by an apostrophe addressed to them and linked with her husband's name (355–6). True, she contrasts her plight as one of the defeated and bereaved with Hermione's good fortune (357–8). But these are here part of her 'souvenir cruel' (359), which she uses, as do the other characters, and as she will again face to face with Hermione, as part of an argument.

Andromaque's next encounter with Pyrrhus (III, vi and vii) begins, like the first, with threats, but this time Pyrrhus speaks of having already condemned Astyanax. Reduced to despair and inactivity, Andromaque makes her final plea thanks only to the persuasions of Céphise (927ff.). This is her first evocation of the myth of Troy: memories and recital lead to an apostrophe to Hector, the irony of which is calculated to shame Pyrrhus into being merciful. Its function is rhetorical, and it succeeds in bringing him to his final offer − and to his final threat, though with a short stay of execution.

Up to here, Andromaque's memories of the sack of Troy are, like those of the other characters, recounted at a distance: they form part of what Vinaver has called the comico-heroic aspect of the play. He argues that at this point Andromaque realizes that Pyrrhus is now in deadly earnest and that he has given her her last chance. The game of argument and manœuvre is over: 'Tout se passe comme s'il fallait que ce mécanisme s'arretât avant que ne s'epanouît sur la scène le poème tragique proprement dit.'[23] Vinaver's contention is that two different kinds of play succeed each other, one belonging to the dramatic traditions of the seventeenth century, the other to the world of authentic tragedy, a world upon which Racine, as it were fortuitously, stumbles when he has Andromaque accept that only her own total self-sacrifice can preserve both her fidelity to Hector and the life of his son. This view seems to me to take insufficient account of two important factors: first, that the creation of the dramatic situation by Oreste's embassy has given to Pyrrhus, in the first half of the play, the opportunity to intensify his blackmail; second, what flows from that, that these central scenes represent only the culmination of menaces to which Andromaque has been subject for a year. Act III, scene viii is the logical and necessary consequence of what precedes it. Andromaque must now face the myth of Troy within herself, to find her own way forward, no longer to persuade others. The use of the myth will not be rhetorical. Admittedly, and for this precise reason, it is here that the play becomes authentically tragic. The turning-point, whether Pyrrhus intends literally what he says or is threatening obliquely, seems to be '. . . Allons aux Grecs livrer le fils d'Hector' (900). Andromaque certainly takes him seriously, hence her cry of alarm.

The formula 'le fils d'Hector' is crucial. It confronts Andromaque with the impossible nature of her dilemma: Astyanax is not simply her son ('mon fils', 260), but Hector's ('son fils', 931). The distinction, however, is not made in terms of past and present:[24] Astyanax represents for his mother the living continuation of his father. Hector still lives in his son (1016). The apparent choice is not a choice. She refuses the new Pyrrhus evoked by Céphise (985–91), and he has already perceived that for Andromaque her husband still lives in his son:

> C'est Hector, disait-elle en l'embrassant toujours;
> Voilà ses yeux, sa bouche, et déjà son audace;
> C'est lui-même, c'est toi, cher époux, que j'embrasse. (652–4)

But when Céphise encourages Andromaque to accept the final offer of Pyrrhus,

Qui ne se souvient plus qu'Achille était son père,
Qui dément ses exploits, et les rend superflus,   (990–1)

the heroine remembers not him, but Hector:

Dois-je les oublier, s'il ne s'en souvient plus?
Dois-je oublier Hector privé de funérailles . . .?   (992–3)

It is over against Hector that Pyrrhus stands, and, following from

Quoi! je lui donnerais Pyrrhus pour successeur?   (984)

Andromaque enters again into the experience of Troy destroyed.[25] This is no longer the *récit* and argument of earlier evocations, but the living experience of a past recent, but already a myth; no longer a 'souvenir cruel', but a present vision into which she endeavours to draw Céphise: 'Songe, songe, Céphise . . . / Figure-toi Pyrrhus . . . / Songe . . . / Peins-toi dans ces horreurs Andromaque éperdue . . . / Voilà . . . Voilà . . . / Enfin, voilà l'époux que tu me veux donner . . .' Although this scene contains clear echoes of the Virgilian and Homeric narratives,[26] they are notable for their brevity, for the absence of picturesque details and of references to Hector's military prowess, for the increased emphasis on his devotion to wife and son — a shift of balance which remythifies the Trojan hero — and for the direct speech which he utters through Andromaque. Little is directly imitated from the source passages. Visualizing again the farewell and the defeat, she is given the poetic power to bring them visually before Céphise and the spectator, an example of the φαντασία discussed in the treatise *On the Sublime*.[27]

Similarly, when Céphise recalls her to the other reality, that of the present,

Hé bien, allons donc voir expirer votre fils,   (1012)

it is

Ce fils, ma seule joie, et l'image d'Hector   (1014)

that Andromaque sees. The vision is completed by her first remembering ('je m'en souviens') and then hearing and transmitting Hector's imperishable farewell words. He lives in her, not in a dead past: he is a present mythical figure. In order finally to arrive at her 'innocent stratagème', Andromaque must still consult Hector at the 'tumulum inanem' of Virgil's account quoted at the head of the prefaces. Those last words,

> Allons sur son tombeau consulter mon époux, (1048)

are inseparable from her first:

> Je passais jusqu'aux lieux où l'on garde mon fils, (260)

echoed again (1064, 1072) after the consultation. Hector, still present at his cenotaph, gives his command:

> Voilà ce qu'un époux m'a commandé lui-même, (1098)

the command of total self-sacrifice (1123–4). Those words represent Andromaque's realization of her tragedy. At the same time, her final instructions to Céphise reiterate her refusal of the imaginary future offered by Pyrrhus (1119–22). The conflict between them has been expressed as much by their manner of seeing and recounting the Trojan myth as by the dramatic situation itself. For Pyrrhus, it is something external, to be used or forgotten in the pursuit of his passion; for Andromaque, it has become an inescapable, demanding, overwhelming presence. While her encounter with that presence results from the drama leading up to it, it also results in the dramatic developments which follow, first the 'innocent stratagème', then all its consequences.

At this point, in the revised version of the play (1673), Andromaque, in 'calm of mind, all passion spent', comes to the end of her drama. Her reappearance in Act V of the original 1668 text strikes us now as odd and inappropriate, proclaiming as it does the fidelity of his widow to the dead Pyrrhus ('Pyrrhus de mon Hector semble avoir pris la place', 1494*t*) and an end to 'le souvenir de Troie' (1494*p*). While several reasons may be advanced for the excision of the passage in question,[28] one in particular seems important in our reading of the play. By the time he came to revise it for a new edition, Racine had written three further tragedies, beginning with *Britannicus*: no concessions were made in them to what has been seen as the 'baroque' ethic associated with Pyrrhus' offer of his new myth or of Andromaque's apparent acceptance of it at the end of the original text.[29] Had Racine realized that his Andromaque was the heroine of Acts III and IV, and that his concession — he was still a relative novice — to current moral and theatrical conventions was aesthetically and ethically discordant in her? The success of the tragedy had surely given him confidence enough to go his own authentic way. The modern myth of Andromaque, dependent as it is on her living and poetically speaking the

67

ancient myth of Troy, deformed, yet in its essentials remarkably respected and recreated, is that of the central scenes of the play as we now know it. The new myth, already established perhaps between 1667 and 1673, certainly existed before 1676, when the second preface was written, for there the dramatist congratulates himself on having expressed 'l'idée que nous avons maintenant de cette princesse'. Of whose making was that 'idea', the myth of the new Andromaque, if not of Racine's, thanks to 'la manière ingénieuse dont [il a] su accommoder la fable à [son] sujet'?

In her remarkable study of the theatre of Greece and Rome, Professor Erika Simon has suggested that the painters of Attic vases of the Archaic period, when depicting Dionysiac rites, did so theatrically, translating 'the action on the stage directly into myth. They portrayed what contemporary spectators saw in the tragedies: the myth itself.'[30] Would it be too much to claim, conversely, that in Racine's portrayal of Andromaque it is her living, in present words and action, the myth of Troy that brings her and the audience to awareness of her tragedy, and to the realization that that tragedy is inseparable from μύθος, both myth and dramatic action?

NOTES

1 For the detailed facts, see R. C. Knight, *Racine et la Grèce* (Paris, [1950]), pp. 266ff., and *Andromaque*, ed. R. C. Knight and H. T. Barnwell (Geneva, 1977). See also H. G. Hall, 'Pastoral, epic and dynastic denouement in Racine's *Andromaque*', *MLR*, LXIX (1974), 64–78.

2 '. . . Plato suggests that *muthoi* are inherently false but that there is often some truth in them . . .' Such stories were by then probably treated in a rationalizing way: see J. Creed, 'Uses of classical mythology', in *The Theory of Myth. Six Studies*, ed. A. Cunningham (London, 1973), pp. 13ff. In Racine's play no counterpart exists of the intervention of Zeus and Athene in the fight between Hector and Achilles in the *Iliad* (XXII, 168ff., 208ff., 213ff.).

3 G. S. Kirk, *Myth: Its Meaning and Functions in Ancient and Other Cultures* (Cambridge and Los Angeles, 1970), pp. 28, 31, 32–4, 250. Neither the euhemerist nor the allegorical approach to myth is, in this account, exclusive. See K. Apsley, in *Myth and Legend in French Literature: Essays in Honour of A. J. Steele*, ed. K. Apsley, D. Bellos and P. Sharratt (London, 1982), pp. 15ff. Cf. J.-P. Vernant, *Myth and Society in Ancient Greece*, trans. Janet Lloyd (Brighton, 1979), pp. 195–6.

4 *Principes de la tragédie*, ed. E. Vinaver (Manchester, 1944), ll. 39–41. Cf. ll. 58–62.

5 *Ibid.*, ll. 151–2. This terminological confusion is compounded by Vettori's phrase, 'extra fabulam', used to indicate those improbable events which the dramatist must situate outside the play itself. Racine translates as 'hors de la tragédie', going back to Aristotle's use of the word δράματος (*ibid.*). I will not raise the issue, unimportant here, of the derisory use of 'fable' as in *Andromaque*, 769–70, and *Iphigénie*, 754. Cf. Pascal, *Pensées*, La. 978.

6 See *Andromaque*, ed. Knight and Barnwell, pp. 205–6 and n. 9.

7 See Racine, *Oeuvres complètes*, ed. R. Picard, 2 vols. (Paris, 1964, 1966), II, 871.

8 See Corneille: for example, second *Discours*, in *Pierre Corneille: Writings on the Theatre*, ed. H. T. Barnwell (Oxford, 1965), pp. 43–7.

9 Like all his contemporaries, Corneille regarded the gods of antiquity as purely imaginary: see first *Discours*, ed. Barnwell, p. 25.

10 Corneille, second *Discours*, p. 44. See also Abbé d'Aubignac, *La Pratique du théâtre*, ed. P. Martino (Algiers, 1927), p. 65.

11 *Défense des fables dans la poésie*, in *Œuvres complètes*, ed. A. Stegmann (Paris, 1963), pp. 891–2.

12 *Art poétique*, III, ll. 163ff.; *Réflexions sur Longin*, IV.

13 *Observations sur Homère et Virgile* (1669), quoted by Ch.-H. Boudhors, in *Oeuvres complètes de Boileau. Epîtres, Art poétique, Lutrin* (Paris, 1952), p. 190; *Réflexions sur la poétique*, ed. E. T. Dubois (Geneva, 1970), p. 83.

14 Quoted in *Réflexions*, ed. Dubois, p. 168 (n. 137).

15 The formula, 'décor verbal', is that of R. Elliott, *Mythe et légende dans le théâtre de Racine* (Paris, 1969), pp. 186ff. Like the arguments of other critics whose objective is an understanding of the plays in themselves – R. C. Knight, 'Les dieux païens dans la tragédie française', *Revue d'histoire littéraire de la France*, LXIV (1964), 414–26, and 'Myth in Racine: a myth?', *L'Esprit créateur*, XVI (1976), 95–104; O. de Mourgues, *Racine or, The Triumph of Relevance* (Cambridge, 1967); M. Delcroix, *Le Sacré dans les tragédies profanes de Racine* (Paris, 1970) – Elliott's analyses are opposed by those who – like J. C. Lapp, *The Brazen Tower* (Saratoga, 1977), C. Delmas, *Mythologie et mythe dans le théâtre français, 1650–1676* (Geneva, (1985), and R. Barthes, *Sur Racine* (Paris, 1963) – argue, from largely anachronistic and external evidence, in favour of modern mythical interpretations.

16 See *Andromaque*, ed. Knight and Barnwell.

17 Cf. Knight, *Racine et la Grèce*, p. 396.

18 G.Defaux, 'Culpabilité et expiation dans l'*Andromaque* de Racine', *Romanic Review*, LXVIII (1977), 22–31.

19 P. Allen, 'The role of myth in Racine: *Andromaque, Iphigénie*,

Phèdre', in *Essays in Honour of A. J. Steele*, ed. Apsley, Bellos and Sharratt, pp. 93–116.

20 O. de Mourgues, *Racine*, pp. 78–9, 95–6; R. Elliott, *Mythe et légende*, p. 50; G. Poulet, *Etudes sur le temps humain* (Edinburgh, 1949), p. 139; J.-L. Backès, *Racine* (Paris, 1981), p. 87.

21 Barthes, *Sur Racine*, pp. 72–80. But Barthes's conclusions are dubious and partly based on misreadings of the text thanks to extra-literary preconceptions.

22 Cf. P. F. Butler, *Classicisme et baroque dans l'œuvre de Racine* (Paris, 1959), pp. 144ff.

23 E. Vinaver, *Entretiens sur Racine* (Paris, 1984), pp. 17ff., 27, and *Racine et la poésie tragique*, 2nd edn (Paris, 1963), pp. 115ff.

24 Allen, 'Role of myth', p. 104; E. Vinaver, *Entretiens*, pp. 32, 35.

25 See Vinaver's fine analysis: *Entretiens*, pp. 33ff.

26 Racine recreates the myth in many ways which I cannot explore here, for example by transporting details from one part of it to another.

27 See 'Longinus', *On the Sublime*, trans. D. A. Russell (Oxford, 1965), pp. 20ff. 'Longinus' gives examples, among others, from the three great tragic poets of Greece.

28 See *Andromaque*, ed. Knight and Barnwell, pp. 29ff.

29 Butler, *Classicisme et baroque*, pp. 144ff.

30 *The Ancient Theatre*, trans. C. E. Vafopoulou-Richardson (London, 1982), p. 8.

6
Ritual murder at Versailles: Racine's *Iphigénie*[1]

R. C. KNIGHT

Eager as I was to join in the tribute to the doyen of our dramatic studies, the title chosen for the volume gave me pause. I thought I had locked myself into a *prise de position* which Professor Ronald Tobin was magnanimous enough to let me publish in a special number which he collected and edited on myth-criticism.[2] I have realized since that I succeeded at most in proving that the concept of myth was absent from the conscious thought and theory of the seventeenth century, and not that it could not have existed then. Since that time myth-criticism has been quietly disengaging itself from the tentacles of Lévi-Strauss and Mircea Eliade and has shown itself decidedly helpful in the study of 'mythological' literature.[3]

But then a subject seemed to offer itself. I remembered a Nigerian postgraduate who was writing an Ibadan Ph.D. thesis with me on war and violence as seen by Racine and his sources. He came to me one day after he had reached the tragedy *Iphigénie* and said:

I wanted to tell you this. In my people, Oh, not now of course, but within living memory, we had human sacrifices − except that it was not always a man or woman then, but an animal, perhaps a dog, that they killed. But always, if there was a plague or a drought, the elders would come to the chief and they would say: 'Look − for three months now we have this plague (or, it has not rained). We must have a sacrifice; the people expect it.' And the chief − he might be a young man, he might be educated, a Christian even − he would give in and do it. Shall I put this in my thesis?

I told him how lucky he was to have a livelier sense of the reality of such things than we could have, or the French seventeenth century or even Racine himself. I have wondered since if he was so lucky, and even if *Iphigénie* was such a promising subject.

Sacrifice, such as Iphigenia underwent − or escaped − must surely belong to myth, being a mytheme, a bit of myth, a legend told to account for some local rite, what mythologists call an

71

aetion. To slaughter animals and burn their bodies on altars was a universal practice in worship at least up to the time of the first Apostles and until the destruction of the Jewish Temple in A.D 70, and must have had a place in the consciousness of every religious-minded European. And the conception of offering or penalty paid to the gods tinged all religious thought and found its sublime culmination in the Passion of Christ, as C. Delmas has reminded us.[4] But a human sacrifice is a higher penalty than usual, therefore for a heavier fault (like the vanity of Andromeda's mother). It can be represented as the result of a curse; it can therefore be made voluntarily, as an act of devotion, like that of the famous Decius Mus, who charged alone into the thick of the enemy to secure the victory foretold to his army, or an act of piety and patriotism, like that of Ménécée, in Racine's *Thébaïde* (621ff.). It had happened among the Jews, as Racine's Joas remembered (*Athalie*, 1259–62).

The story of Iphigenia is not so much complex, as all commentators remark,[5] as complicated, thanks to the meddling of many authors. Or, in another view, we must say that the story is a blank. In the vast plain of primitive myth there are outcrops, hardly visible, testifying that an Iphigenia was once sacrificed to Artemis (whom Racine calls 'Diane'), or on the contrary sacrificed victims to Artemis, or was identified with Artemis. Some early testimonies to this are found among lyric poets, as Racine found out.[6] He also found, when he came to the threshold of extant literature, that 'le père des poètes', Homer himself, had done what he had sometimes done before (as when he would not mention the monstrous sins marking the story of the House of Atreus) and blandly expunged the death of Iphigenia from the slate, showing Agamemnon[7] in the middle of the Trojan war as the father of three daughters whom he can offer in marriage, one of whom is called Iphianassa. So there is no death of Iphigenia here.

Did she die? Racine has taken a poll among his authors. The most impressive voice among the 'ayes' is Aeschylus. His strong tragic sense found high tragic possibilities in the conception of sin to be expiated: and the grim architecture (is it his invention?) of the *Oresteia* trilogy is built on an unending sequence of black crimes attracting retribution which takes the form of a vengeance itself to be avenged. Agamemnon, already under a family curse, kills Clytemnestra's daughter, Clytemnestra kills her husband and Orestes his mother. In the first of these tragedies, *Agamemnon* (when the victorious King returns to be murdered), a chorus of aged mariners who had been assembled with the host against Troy is made to tell how Artemis had sent a gruesome omen (two eagles which devoured a pregnant hare and her unborn litter), which Calchas interpreted as meaning that she detested the bloodshed planned by Zeus (205–16): Agamemnon, she foresaw, would commit sacrilege by burning Trojan temples over the heads of suppliants, and this he would have to expiate by sacrificing his own daughter to get a fair wind for the fleet; not that he could not refuse, losing thereby his rank and glory, but he would not, and would incur divine wrath. A tortuous form of retribution, we may think; but I follow Kitto[8] and Mazon.[9] This Iphigenia does suffer death, a death described with great pathos later in the same *Agamemnon* chorus. The death of a sacrificial victim could not seem a suitable tragic action to a Greek playwright – the victim has no fault, and the injustice of her fate could seem only revolting, μιαρον (*Poetics* 52ᵇ 36, ch. 13), as Racine saw, if dwelt upon (the exception is Polyxena). But the passage is acceptable here: it is lyrical rather than tragic, and it sets the mood admirably for what will follow. Reflected in the memories of horror-stricken witnesses, are evoked at a distance the girl's beauty and grace, her terror, and the humiliation and brutality she endures:

> Heedless of her tears,
> Her cries of 'Father!' and her maiden years,
> Her judges valued more
> Their glory and their war.
> A prayer was said. Her father gave the word.
> Limp in her flowing dress,
> The priest's attendants held her high
> Above the altar, as men hold a kid.
> Her father spoke again, to bid
> One bring a gag, and press
> Her sweet mouth tightly with a cord,
> Lest Atreus' house be cursed by some ill-omened cry.
>
> Rough hands tear at her girdle, cast
> Her saffron silks to earth. Her eyes
> Search for her slaughterers; and each,
> Seeing her beauty, that surpassed
> A painter's vision, yet denies
> The pity her dumb looks beseech,
> Struggling for voice; for often in old days,

When brave men feasted in her father's hall,
With simple skill and pious praise
Linked to the flute's pure tone
Her virgin voice would melt the hearts of all,
Honouring the third libation near her father's throne.

The rest I did not see,
Nor do I speak of it . . .[10]

There is no other tragedy in which Iphigenia dies. It is well, however, to remember how blank is our knowledge of tragedy in the Greek fourth century; it was wiped out with unimaginable remorselessness. Aeschylus and Sophocles both wrote plays entitled *Iphigenia*, and we have no idea what they, or the other works listed for us by scholars, contained.[11]

So the *Iphigenia in Aulis* is left to become the sole source and model of all the later plays about Iphigenia. It is a curious work to modern critical eyes: the long perspective of the sins and woes of the Atreidae has been (almost) cut away, and all that remains is the crisis of Agamemnon and his daughter. There are features which look like our poet's own invention: Agamemnon brings his daughter to the camp by a lie; he countermands his order (in a striking night-scene); his letter goes astray; wrangles are violent and innumerable; and the happy ending is due to a theophany (not, however, enacted). The poet seems to delight in deflating characters and motives. Kitto judges it a 'thoroughly second-rate play' − a melodrama, not a tragedy, by which he means, as he tells us, a play that aims 'first and foremost at being theatrically effective': 'there is no illumination, no catharsis, to relieve and justify its cruelty'.[12] But this is an old man's play, latest but one of the ninety-odd attributed to Euripides (Aeschylus and Sophocles, no less prolific in their time, are now represented by only seven tragedies apiece: what might we not be obliged to say if we could see their *fonds de tiroirs*?). The hasty denouement that draws attention to its own inadequacy is now generally attributed to the son who presented his father's play after his death.

Myth-criticism fails us here: we have just too little myth to go on. It is perhaps not impossible to prolong the story, if we descend to the archaic methods of *Quellen- und Einflussforschung*.[13]

Racine is in a position which has long been a subject of discussion. After a career as writer of historical tragedy, he feels himself drawn to the Greeks[14] − whether simply because of his own

74

reading, whether by reaction to the mythological subjects of Quinault–Lully opera,[15] or whether, as C. Delmas more plausibly suggests, by the contemporary tide of *pièces à machines*[16] (whether it affected him by attraction or repulsion). Primitivism seems to fascinate him; he worked for some time on the other Euripidean subject, which shows Iphigenia as sacrificing priestess.[17] It is only just to point out that he emphasizes the repellent nature, to him, of human sacrifice: Iphigénie abhors it, so does her suitor the Prince; Oreste is dear to her because, alone of all his house, he was not 'coupable' of the attempt to kill her which had been frustrated by an implausible cause.[18] Racine had researched the subject widely, and convinced himself that he was free to give Iphigenia whatever fate he wished: he knew that Sophocles speaks of her death;[19] there is nothing to prove that he ever discovered the full and moving story in Aeschylus.

He seems to have seen no faults in Euripides, to judge by the ardour with which he defends him (*Preface*). (It is odd to recall that the title τραγικωχιατοϛ, awarded as he says by Aristotle, was given because of the latter's propensity for unhappy endings,[20] a propensity Racine has resisted here.) Racine seems to have valued Euripides' tragedy for the pathos and violence of the human conflicts: he must have accepted the sacrifice theme; it may have seemed a good way of involving mortal characters in conflict with the will of an immortal (bringing them all, as he must, into the same tragic action). Later at least he must have discovered how dangerous, and how upsetting to moral standards, it was to introduce a divinity making cruel, immoral and arbitrary demands:[21]

> Les Dieux ordonneraient un meurtre abominable? (921)

The pathos and horror of the prospect are skilfully worked, following Euripides, with emphasis always on the moral and not the physical horror of the killing. They speak as if the father was himself to plunge in the knife, instead of presiding at the ceremony. If there is a tendency to speak as if the victim was to be stabbed in the heart (cf. 1275) – or even to have her heart extracted, as if to take omens (1304) – rather than have her throat slit, is must be because the heart lends itself to metonymy. If Agamemnon is made to say:

> . . . J'ignore pour quel crime
> La colère des Dieux demande une victime, (1221–2)

75

it was perhaps only because he must pay a high price for a high favour; that would surely be in the logic of pre-rationalistic myth. From the situation Racine wrings the mental torment of Iphigénie so well analysed by R. Pfohl:[22] he makes a biting study of the superstition and political ambition unleashed by the oracle, with tragic movements of *égarement* and *reconnaissance* in the perturbed Agamemnon,[23] more deeply perturbed than in any earlier treatment. Racine is obliged to adopt the clumsy denouement, for he will not let his heroine die (a very seventeenth-century attitude): 'Quelle apparence que j'eusse souillé la scène par le meurtre horrible d'une personne aussi vertueuse et aussi aimable qu'il fallait représenter Iphigénie? (*Preface*). Nor can he bring himself to adopt the 'machine' and the 'métamorphose' of girl into hind which contented Euripides (*ibid.*). Instead he finds that desperate expedient, 'cet heureux personnage d'Eriphile', for whom he provides a forged passport[24] and an enigmatic paternity – hidden under an ambiguous oracle in the worst manner of Corneille's *Oedipe* – creating thereby an identity tangle and a love-triangle between the two 'sisters', as modern commentators are only too eager to point out,[25] a tangle which almost takes our minds off the sacrifice. Not quite, however: for the suicide of the damned soul is necessary to the plot (but why did Diana want her death?). The denouement has to be amazingly brisk, to avoid loose ends and awkward questions, but it deprives us even of that reconciliation scene which had become a convention at the finale whenever there was a happy ending,[26] but of whose unreality several bitter ironies in Iphigénie's words of farewell make us only too aware (1653–4, 1661–2).

Racine's first encounter with the supernatural has been bought at almost too high a price; nevertheless, his imagination has been stirred, and he has conceived the mortal terrors of Agamemnon's religious conscience:

> . . . les Dieux toutes les nuits,
> Dès qu'un léger sommeil suspendait mes ennuis,
> Vengeant de leurs autels le sanglant privilège,
> Me venaient reprocher ma pitié sacrilège;
> Et présentant la foudre à mon esprit confus,
> Le bras déjà levé, menaçaient mes refus. (83–8)

But the goddess descends, and the winds at last blow, in an atmosphere of awe:[27]

> A peine son sang coule et fait rougir la terre,
> Les Dieux font sur l'autel entendre le tonnerre;

Les vents agitent l'air d'heureux frémissements,
Et la mer leur répond par ses mugissements;
La rive au loin gémit, blanchissante d'écume;
La flamme du bûcher d'elle-même s'allume;
Le ciel brille d'éclairs, s'entr'ouvre, et parmi nous
Jette une sainte horreur qui nous rassure tous.
Le soldat étonné dit que dans une nue
Jusque sur le bûcher Diane est descendue . . .   (1777–86)

The lesson appears to have stood the playwright in good stead
for *Phèdre*. There the morally repugnant and incredible conception
of 'Vénus' filling a reluctant mortal with sinful desire is avoided
not merely, as we used to say, by the fact that Racine has achieved
complete 'intériorisation' of the action in the soul and conscience
of the heroine, but also because the persecution is a figment of her
imagination, a product of ancient, amoral, anti-rational myth, a
conviction of which Phèdre never speaks to others and which no
other person suspects (save Oenone).[28]

This, then, was the ritual murder enacted during the festivities of
1674 in the park of Versailles, behind a 'théâtre de verdure' in an
avenue leading to the Orangery, intersected with some architectural
motifs and liberally sprinkled with gilt tritons, marble basins and
candelabra,[29] but not, probably, *pace* C. Delmas, any additional
'superbe palais': properly interpreted, Clytemnestre only says
(807–8) she feels no need of any. But where is Agamemnon's tent,
which should have blocked the whole vista? The over-florid taste
of Versailles was not noticeably propitious to 'spectacle' if that
meant dramatic requirements. (No doubt the Théâtre du Marais
made up for deficiencies.) It is no easier to know how spectators
of *Alceste* imagined Pluto in Hell in the Cour de Marbre or Apollo
descending (from nowhere) with his train to congratulate Admète
at the finale, than to imagine Argan comfortable in his bedroom
in the 'grotte de Thétis' (as in July 1674). The décor of *Iphigénie*
may well have been reminiscent of spectacular *pièces à machines*;
Racine may not have been best pleased. This, I am afraid, has been
a digression.

My paper has not been a study of the workings of myth.
Whatever we have seen of the myth of Iphigenia has been obscured
from us by the busy devices and calculations of men of letters,
assiduously consulting the heavily annotated and cross-referenced
pages of learned poets like Ovid, learned geographers like
Pausanias, learned mythographers like Pomey and Conti: myth has

created mythography, a bazaar of assorted legends among which playwrights, including Racine, can pick and choose. Racine's researches had made him aware of this; we note his strong approval of the opinion of the scholiast he found in Sophocles:

qu'il ne faut point s'amuser à chicaner les poètes sur quelques changements qu'ils ont pu faire dans la fable, mais qu'il faut s'attacher à considérer l'excellent usage qu'ils ont fait de ces changements, et la manière ingénieuse dont ils ont su *accommoder la fable à leur sujet.*[30]

Had the old Stagirite ever had a sense of humour, it might seem to have been an outrageous pun when he told his disciples to make the μυθos their chief concern – meaning, as we have no need to remind ourselves, not primitive man's explanation of the universe, but the story-line.[31]

So I offer this over-short study with diffidence as probably unworthy of the description myth-criticism, but only perhaps of another, once reputable, form of words, 'the classical tradition in literature'.

NOTES

1 I have received so much encouragement and help during a recent spell of ill-health from my friend Professor Harry Barnwell, that it would have been only just to ask him to add his signature to mine; but this would have been to embroil him in a controversy not of his seeking. I can only record my deep gratitude. At the same time I can and must take full responsibility for errors that may remain, and apologize to the reader for the short measure I have given him. I would also thank Dr June Salmons for the word-processing and George F. Evans and the readers of tapes whom he organized.

2 'Myth in Racine: a myth?', *L'Esprit créateur*, XVI: 2 (Summer, 1976), 45ff.

3 See, for instance, in *Myth and Legend in French Literature: Essays in Honour of A. J. Steele*, ed. K. Aspley *et al.* (London, 1982), Peter Allen, 'The role of myth in Racine: *Andromaque, Iphigénie, Phèdre*' (pp. 93ff.), and the admirably circumspect 'introduction' of K. Aspley, 'Myth as Proteus, or Myth, legend and literature' (pp. 1ff.); and C. Delmas, *Mythologie et mythe dans le théâtre français* (Geneva, 1985) (henceforth *Mythe*), a collection of earlier articles, to which I refer for convenience. C. Delmas has studied the connection between the *pièces à machines* and the revival from *Andromède* onwards of spectacular and mythological drama (*Mythe*, pp. 55, 67, 77ff., 223). He chides me for my 'tranquille incompréhension' of this tendency. What I should

apologize for is having ignored his edition of *Andromède* (Paris, 1974), which had appeared rather recently, only two years before. He must forgive me if I am unfavourably struck by the contrast between Claude's pastoral vision of antiquity and Torelli's sets as recorded by Chauveau, and cannot forget La Fontaine's cruel picture of a stage theophany ruined by a technical hitch: 'Un dieu pend à la corde et crie au machiniste . . .' (*Epître à M. de Niert, sur l'opéra* (Paris, 1677), v. 20; in *Oeuvres complètes*, ed. H. De Regnier, 11 vols. (Paris, 1883–92), IX, 156. For C. Delmas on *Phèdre*, see pp. 241–75.

4 *Mythe*, p. 171.
5 For example, J. Dubu (ed.), *Iphigénie*, Livre de Poche (Paris, 1986), p. 97. J.-M. Gliksohn, *Iphigénie: de la Grèce antique à l'Europe des Lumières* (Paris, 1985), p. 13.
6 See his preface to the play.
7 *Iliad*, IX.141ff.
8 *Greek Tragedy: A Literary Study*, 3rd edn (London, 1961), ch. 12, and especially p. 363.
9 *Eschyle: Agamemnon*, éd. P. Mazon (Paris, 1925), p. 3.
10 *Agamemnon*, 228–47 (Aeschylus, *The Oresteian Trilogy*, trans. P. Vellacott (Harmondsworth, 1956), pp. 50–1).
11 See Gliksohn, *Iphigénie*, p. 17.
12 Greek Tragedy, ch. 12, p. 362.
13 I do not find attractive the (Marxist? Frazerian?) explanation lately offered by J. M. Apostolidès, *Le Prince Sacrifié: Théâtre et politique au temps de Louis XIV* (Paris, 1985). According to him, the subject is 'le passage du féodal en monarchique', and the play is 'd'abord la tragédie d'Agamemnon, appelé à devenir le monarque absolu' (pp. 116–17). This does not happen, and Racine knew it; Greece never became a nation–state; Agamemnon never consolidated his power (against Achilles, for instance, as the *Iliad* makes clear). The only link attempted with myth-criticism is the figure of the 'feudal' King.
14 Cf. my *Racine et la Grèce* (Paris, 1950), ch. 26, especially p. 325.
15 Cf. E. Gros, *Philippe Quinault, sa vie et son œuvre* (Paris, 1926), pp. 730ff., 734–6, and my *Racine et la Grèce*, pp. 328ff.
16 *Mythe*, pp. 233ff.
17 *Iphigenia in Tauris*. See Racine's project in *Oeuvres complètes* (Paris, 1950), I, 965–9.
18 *Ibid.*, pp. 966–7.
19 See, in the Preface, the reference to the *Electra*.
20 *Poetics*, ch. 13, 53ᵃ 36.
21 R. C. Knight, 'Les Dieux païens dans la tragédie francaise', *RHLF*, LXXI (1964), 416–24.
22 *Racine's 'Iphigénie': Literary Rehearsal and Tragic Recognition* (London, 1974), pp. 142–3, 225.

23 Well analysed by E. Vinaver, in *Entretiens sur Racine* (Paris, 1984), pp. 147ff.

24 Cf. my *Racine et la Grèce*, pp. 316ff.

25 For example, Anne Delbée's Preface to *Iphigénie* (see n. 5 above). The girls are actually cousins.

26 See Corneille's remarks at the end of his Examen of *Nicomède* (*Pierre Corneille: Writings on the Theatre*, ed. H. T. Barnwell (Oxford, 1965), p. 153).

27 E. Vinaver has interpreted this 'horreur' admirably: *Entretiens*, pp. 143ff.

28 C. Delmas, 'La Mythologie dans *Phèdre*', *Mythe*, pp. 24ff. He speaks of Phèdre's 'mythomanie' (*ibid.*, p. 255). Professor E. M. Zimmerman has noticed that Phèdre never talks of Venus except to Œnone (*La liberté et le destin dans le théâtre de Racine* (Saratoga, Calif., 1982), p. 86).

29 According to Félibien; quoted in Delmas, *Mythe*, p. 224.

30 *Andromaque*, seconde Préface (my italics). The question at issue had been, oddly enough, how many sons had Clytemnestra? It was a real Greek scholiast, and not the German Camerarius, as all editors have told us since Mesnard: see *Andromaque*, ed. R. C. Knight and H. T. Barnwell (Geneva, 1977), p. 205 and n.

31 *Poetics*, ch. 6, 50ᵃ 39.

7
The myth of place in seventeenth- and eighteenth-century French theatre

MICHAEL O'REGAN

'Quant à l'unité de lieu je n'en trouve aucun précepte ni dans Aristote ni dans Horace', writes Corneille.[1] The supremacy of this rule in the French theatre of the seventeenth and eighteenth centuries was in fact far from unchallenged. It is true that in the few years when the purest classical tragedy flourished, Racine could obey the law faultlessly. Even he, however, was compelled, or tempted, to vary the setting for each act of *Esther* (though without straying, as he points out in his Preface, beyond the bounds of the palace). Successors like Campistron and Crébillon were equally capable in this respect, but the single locales in which their plays are set were contemporary with the multiplicity of scenes which other tragic dramatists, such as Quinault, Thomas Corneille and Houdard de la Motte, used for their opera librettos. Among Molière's plays, the one set of *Tartuffe* or *L'Avare* co-exists with the multiple scenery of *Dom Juan* or *Psyché*. The long careers of Pierre Corneille and Voltaire could likewise furnish many varieties of single and multiple place.

Diverging attitudes were displayed by theorists too, not least during the Enlightenment, as different articles in the *Encyclopédie* can show. In De Jaucourt's article on UNITÉ, the spectator's imagination of theatrical place is considered to be restricted by good sense:

Que le *lieu de la scène soit fixe et marqué*, dit M. Despréaux; voilà la loi. En effet, si les scènes ne sont préparées, amenées, et enchaînées les unes aux autres, de manière que tous les personnages puissent se rencontrer successivement et avec bienséance dans un endroit commun; si les divers incidents d'une pièce exigent nécessairement une trop grande étendue de terrain; si enfin le théâtre représente plusieurs lieux différents les uns des autres, le spectateur trouve toujours ces changements incroyables, et ne se prête point à l'imagination du poète qui choque à cet égard les idées ordinaires, et pour parler plus nettement, le bon sens.[2]

In the *Supplément*, however, Marmontel refuses to accept this law:

Non seulement je regarde le changement de lieu comme une licence permise, mais je fais plus, je nie que ce soit une licence.[3]

He credits the spectator with greater imaginative powers:

Il s'y transporte donc [à l'endroit de la scène] en esprit dès le premier acte. Or ce premier pas fait, pourquoi le second, le troisième lui coûteraient-ils davantage? Et si dans les actes suivants il est besoin qu'il se transporte dans un autre lieu, pourquoi s'y refuserait-il? La même vivacité d'imagination qui le rend présent à ce qui se passe dans la ville, lui manquera-t-elle pour voir ce qui se passe dans le camp, et pour y être présent de même?[4]

The unsigned article on SCENE finds scene changes unnatural:

En effet, il n'est pas naturel que la *scène* change de place, et qu'un spectacle qui commence dans un endroit finisse dans un autre tout différent et souvent très éloigné.[5]

Marmontel on the other hand sees no contradiction between imitation of nature and stimulation of the imagination. In his article on DECORATION, he divides 'les décorations théâtrales' into those which are 'de décence' and those which are 'de pur ornement':

Les décorations de décence sont une imitation de la belle nature, comme doit l'être l'action dont elles retracent le lieu. Un homme célèbre en ce genre en a donné au théâtre lyrique, qui seront longtemps gravées dans le souvenir des connaisseurs. De ce nombre était le péristyle du palais de Ninus, dans lequel aux plus belles proportions et à la perspective la plus savante, le peintre avait ajouté un coup de génie bien digne d'être rappelé.

Après avoir employé presque toute la hauteur du théâtre à élever son premier ordre d'architecture, il avait laissé voir aux yeux la naissance d'un second ordre qui semblait se perdre dans le cintre, et que l'imagination achevait; ce qui prêtait à ce péristyle une élévation fictive, double de l'espace donné. C'est dans tous les arts un grand principe, que de laisser l'imagination en liberté: on perd toujours à lui circonscrire un espace; de là vient que les idées générales n'ayant point de limites déterminées, sont les sources les plus fécondes du sublime.

It is true that Marmontel's example is one of Servandoni's sets for the Opéra, but even for tragedy, he continues,

Le manque de *décorations* entraîne l'impossibilité des changements, et celle-ci borne les auteurs à la plus rigoureuse unité de lieu; règle gênante qui leur interdit un grand nombre de beaux sujets, ou les oblige à les mutiler.[6]

There is, then, a lasting disagreement between those who hold to an aesthetic of fixity and those whose ideal is change. The aesthetic of change cannot be discounted even from tragedy and 'serious' comedy, though its predominance is in court spectacle and opera. It is paradoxical that Versailles, the symbol of monarchical permanence, was itself an ever-changing decor. One of the most striking instances of such metamorphoses was produced in February 1745 for the marriage of the Dauphin to the Infanta Maria-Teresa of Spain. The *Manège* was transformed by the Slodtz brothers first into a theatre with cloud-painted ceiling and curving, garlanded balconies for the performance of Voltaire's *La Princesse de Navarre*, and then into a ballroom whose walls were decorated with statues in niches, palm-trees, and rococo mirrors.[7] Earlier the cathedral of Notre-Dame had become a baroque mausoleum designed by Bérain as a setting for Bossuet's funeral oration for the Grand Condé in 1687.[8] The theatrical nature of funeral ceremonies, particularly royal ones, is especially well illustrated by those of Ch.-N. Cochin's engravings which give a side view of the proceedings. For the funeral, in 1746, of the Dauphine Marie-Thérèse, the gothic church of Saint Denis was converted by the Slodtz brothers into a vast and brilliantly lit auditorium, with spectators ranged all round in raked boxes.[9]

If buildings with such specific original purposes could radically change their appearance, how much more appropriately could such illusions transform an opera stage! There, change is part of the poet's inventive task, according to Cahusac:

Ce n'est pas assez d'imaginer des lieux convenables à la scène, il faut encore varier le coup d'œil que présentent les lieux, par les *décorations* qu'on y amène. Un poète qui a une heureuse invention jointe à une connaissance profonde de cette partie, trouvera mille moyens fréquents d'embellir son spectacle, d'occuper les yeux du spectateur, de préparer l'illusion. Ainsi à la belle architecture d'un palais magnifique ou d'une place superbe, il fera succéder des déserts arides, des rochers escarpés, des antres redoutables. Le spectateur effrayé sera alors agréablement surpris de voir une perspective riante coupée par des paysages agréables, prendre la place de ces objets terribles. De là, en observant les gradations il lui présentera une mer agitée, un horizon enflammé d'éclairs, un ciel chargé de nuages, des arbres arrachés par la fureur des vents. Il le distraira de ce spectacle par celui d'un temple auguste: toutes les parties de la belle architecture des anciens rassemblées dans cet édifice formeront un ensemble majestueux; et des jardins embellis par la nature, l'art et le goût, termineront d'une manière satisfaisante une représentation dans laquelle on n'aura rien négligé pour faire naître et pour entretenir l'illusion.[10]

The customary words which begin the stage-directions for each act of a *tragédie-lyrique* emphasize change. For instance, for Act II of Quinault's *Phaéton* (1683), 'Le théâtre change et représente le Temple d'Isis.' In addition, those who delight in change are not satisfied by a mere succession of different illusions, such as Cahusac describes. Change also becomes part of the action itself. Thus in the fourth scene of this act of *Phaéton*, 'On entend du bruit dans le Temple et l'on voit les portes se fermer d'elles-mêmes', and in scene v, 'Les portes de Temple s'ouvrent, et ce lieu qui avait paru si magnifique, n'est plus qu'un gouffre effroyable qui vomit des flammes, et d'où sortent des Furies, et des Fantômes terribles, qui renversent et brisent les offrandes, et qui menacent et écartent l'assemblée.' Similarly in Act IV, scene i, of the same author's *Armide* (1686), 'Une vapeur s'élève et se répand dans le désert qui a paru au troisième acte. Des antres et des abîmes s'ouvrent, et il en sort de bêtes farouches et des monstres épouvantables.'

Cahusac himself, who, as well as a librettist, was an amateur *machiniste*,[11] provides an example of a contrary transformation, from *désert* to lush countryside, in his book for the 'ballet héroïque', *Les Fêtes de l'Hymen et de l'Amour* of 1747. In the second *entrée*, 'Le théâtre représente d'un côté des rochers, de l'autre des arbres mal arrangés: les uns sont sans tige, les branches de quelques autres tombent jusqu'à terre. Dans la perspective, des rochers et l'entrée de plusieurs cavernes.' Then, in scene v, 'de riches berceaux de fleurs' are erected. 'Ces berceaux aboutissent dans le fond à un salon de fleurs et de verdure; il est percé à jour, et les rameaux qui le forment sont chargés de toutes sortes de fruits.' Finally, 'Le fond du théâtre change et représente une campagne fertile, chargée de moissons, de fleurs et de fruits.'[12]

In machine plays, operas and ballets, such miracles and enchantments abound, and the spectator's *bon sens* is not shocked by them (as De Jaucourt suggests it is). Even when the locations are not such common mythological sites as *la Vallée de Tempé*,[13] *l'antre des Parques*,[14] *le Mont Parnasse*,[15] *les jardins de Circé*,[16] or *le palais du Soleil*,[17] the conventionalized places, raised to the level of the mythological events so often depicted, have attained a mythic status. The audiences or readers who rejoice in change accept them as myth.

At the other extreme, De Jaucourt, theorist of fixity, demands not only unity of place but particularity:

Or non seulement le lieu général, mais encore le lieu particulier doit être déterminé; comme un palais, un vestibule, un temple.[18]

What is really required is the sort of precision that Racine provides in *Bérénice*: 'La scène est à Rome, dans le cabinet qui est entre l'appartement de Titus et celui de Bérénice.' Such exactitude is less common than the type of general statement that Campistron gives for his *Tiridate* (1691), 'La scène est à Dara, capitale de l'Empire des Parthes, dans le palais d'Arsace', or Crébillon for his *Pyrrhus* (1726): 'La scène est à Byzance dans le palais de Lysimachus.' Most often the actual place within the palace is not defined, but the palace is situated by stating who it belongs to, or where it is, or both.

Frequently the place of the action is no more precisely located than by the name of a town — Rome,[19] Memphis,[20] London,[21] — or of a region or country — 'en Hongrie',[22] 'en Brie',[23] 'dans Argos',[24] 'en Elide',[25] 'à Sparte',[26] 'en Picardie'.[27] Sometimes a spurious precision is given by situating the town geographically or historically. It is rarely as learnedly defined as by Pierre Corneille for *Sertorius* (1662), 'La scène est à Nertobrige, ville d'Aragon, conquise par Sertorius, à présent Catalayud', or by Racine for *Mithridate* (1673): 'La scène est à Nymphée, port de mer sur la Bosphore Cimmérien dans le Chersonèse Taurique.' More often the information given is minimal: 'La scène se passe à Séleucie, sur l'Euphrate' (P. Corneille, *Suréna*, 1674); 'La scène est dans Apamée, capitale de la Phrygie' (Th. Corneille, *Bérénice*, 1659); 'La scène est à Patare, capitale de Lycie' (Quinault, *Bellérophon*, 1665); '. . . à Sardis, capitale de la Lydie' (Campistron, *Alcibiade*, 1685); 'dans le ville de Los-Reyes, autrement Lima' (Voltaire, *Alzire*, 1736). Such places, already distant in time and place, further distanced by convention, become blurred instead of precise.[28]

In Gilbert's machine play, *Les Amours de Diane et d'Endimion* (1657), Endimion says to his divine rival, Apollon:

Je connais bien les Dieux, Je sais leur origine;
C'était des Conquérants, des Héros et des Rois,
Qu'on a déifiés pour leurs fameux exploits:
L'éclat de leurs hauts faits par le cours des années,
A fait jusques au Ciel monter leurs destinées.[29]

Similarly the sites of heroic actions have, by this blurring, and by the mechanics of the theatre, become magnified and mythologized. Just as the gods are debunked by Endimion, so this myth of place can be debunked, as when Piron ridicules the formula in *L'Endriague*:[30] 'La scène est à Cocqusigrüopolis, capitale de Vazviéder.'

In another kind of attempt at precise unity of place, it is the precision itself, rather than any blurring, that takes the setting of the scene into the realm of myth. The dramatic poet combines several of the favourite sites for tragic action into a single convenient locale, more ideal than truly *vraisemblable*. The proximity of a temple, a palace and a public square, for example, seems too good to be true. Voltaire makes use of just this juxtaposition for *Eriphyle* (1732), where 'La scène est à Argos, dans le parvis qui sépare le temple de Jupiter et le palais de la reine.' The setting for his *Rome sauvée, ou Catilina* (1752) is similar: 'd'un côté, le palais d'Aurélie; de l'autre, le temple de Tellus, où s'assemble le Sénat . . .'. He brings the same elements together again much later for *Agathocle* (1779): 'La scène est dans une place, entre le palais du roi et les ruines d'un temple.' Here, however, the scene does change, or rather opens up (*s'ouvre*) in Act II, scene iv. This hypothetical locality is indeed also to be found among the multiple sets of operas. The French version, with words by Du Rollet, of Gluck's *Alceste* (1776) situates the first act in 'une place publique; sur un des côtés on voit en avancement le palais d'Admète, dont la porte est surmontée d'un balcon en saillie; le fond du théâtre représente le portique du Temple d'Apollon'. Likewise in Act II of Beaumarchais's opera *Tarare* (1787) 'Le théâtre représente la place publique. Le palais d'Ataar est sur le côté; le Temple de Brama, dans le fond.' Here again the scene opens up (scene vii): 'Le fond du théâtre, qui représentait le portail du Temple de Brama, se retire et laisse voir l'intérieur du temple, qui se forme jusqu'au devant du théâtre.' The theatre of change, as well as the theatre of unity, employs this particular mythical place.

In all types of theatrical production the palaces are *palais à volonté*, the towns are fabulous. The reader or spectator is rarely confronted with a place he would recognize. This does happen occasionally in comedy, when it is intended to be close to reality, as in P. Corneille's *La Place Royale* (1634) and in *Le Menteur* (1644), the *Examen* of which states that 'le premier acte est dans les Tuileries, et le reste à la Place Royale'. Similarly in Dancourt's *La Foire Saint Germain* (1696) 'Le théâtre représente un des carrefours de la Foire.' In the play of the same name by Régnard and Dufresny (1695) 'La scène est à Paris dans l'enclos de la foire Saint Germain', and in their comedy *Les Momies d'Egypte* (1696) 'La scène est dans une boutique de la foire Saint Germain.' Even in more spectacular presentations real and recognizable places, such as Venice, are sometimes shown. In Régnard's ballet *Le Carnaval de Venise* (1699), for Act I 'Le théâtre représente la Place Saint-Marc à Venise', and for Act II 'la salle des Réduits à Venise'. In Act I of Houdard de la Motte's 'comédie-ballet' *La Vénitienne* (1705) 'Le théâtre représente des jardins; et dans l'éloignement, la Place Saint-Marc'.

The sets for such productions could certainly become realistic, in the period of the Englightenment and under the influence of neo-classicism, as can be seen in the design by Michel-Ange Slodtz for the ballet *L'Anglais à Bordeaux* (1763), which represents accurately the Place Royale at Bordeaux with the equestrian statue of Louis XV, since destroyed. 'Le dessin présente en vérité plus d'intérêt en tant que document qu'en tant qu'évocation de décor, car il ne rend pas du tout la fantasmagorie qui donnait son accent au ballet, d'une allégorie au demeurant fort banale.'[31]

A looser adherence to reality was the rule earlier – for instance on the rare occasions when Torelli imitated reality. Normally, for him, 'what was produced on stage had no connection with any real place or time'.[32] But his designs for Act I, scenes i and ii, of *La Finta Pazza* in Paris (1645) included in the background a view of the Pont Neuf, where, in fact, his almost identical set for the Prologue of *Bellerofonte* in Venice (1642) had shown instead the Piazzetta. 'Apart from the familiar background in each, there is no other attempt at realism.'[33] The bridge is shown merely as a flattering topical reference, quite out of context.[34]

Opera prologues under Louis XIV, usually pretexts for royal praise or propaganda, therefore sometimes showed real, royal places – the Tuileries, Versailles, Fontainebleau. Just as the King is virtually deified, so are his residences divinified. In the Prologue to Quinault's *Alceste* (1674) 'Le théâtre représente le palais et les jardins des Tuileries; la Nymphe de la Seine paraît, appuyée sur une urne, au milieu d'une allée dont les arbres sont séparés par des fontaines', and eventually 'les arbres s'ouvrent, et font voir les Divinités champêtres qui jouent de différents instruments, et les fontaines se changent en Naïades qui chantent.' Likewise the Prologue to his *Thésée* (1675) 'représente les Jardins et la façade du Palais de Versailles', where 'Mars paraît sur son char avec Bellone.'[35] In Houdard de la Motte's *Canente* (1700), the Prologue 'représente Fontainebleau, de côté du Parterre du Tibre et les bocages, où les Silvains sont endormis'. Thus even imitations of reality are mythologized.

As we have seen, the places represented in the theatre of unity and the theatre of change are not truly distinct, though to contemporaries the principles involved seemed almost irreconcilable. There were, however, attempts to find an ideal compromise – by recourse to simultaneity instead of succession. It is not surprising that Pierre Corneille, whose early plays were played in settings which must have been similar to Mahelot's *décors simultanés*, should have hankered after some such solution to the *duplicité de lieu*. The phrase, used in the *Examen* of Cinna, is appropriate to the kind of chicanery he first suggests:

Je voudrais . . . que ces deux lieux n'eussent point besoin de diverses décorations, et qu'aucun des deux ne fût jamais nommé, mais seulement le lieu général où tous les deux sont compris, comme Paris, Rome, Lyon, Constantinople, etc. Cela aiderait à tromper l'auditeur . . .[36]

This is, of course, the kind of blurring already mentioned, but Corneille's invention takes him a stage further, to envisage a kind of mythical no man's land:

Les jurisconsultes admettent des fictions de droit; et je voudrais, à leur exemple, introduire des fictions de théâtre, pour établir un lieu théâtral qui ne serait ni l'appartement de Cléopâtre, ni celui de Rodogune dans la pièce qui porte ce titre, ni celui de Phocas, de Léontine, ou de Pulchérie, dans *Héraclius*, mais une salle sur laquelle ouvrent ces divers appartements, à qui j'attribuerais deux privilèges: l'un, que chacun de ceux qui y parleraient fût présumé y parler avec le même secret que s'il était dans sa chambre; l'autre, qu'au lieu que dans l'ordre commun il est quelquefois de la bienséance que ceux qui occupent le théâtre aillent trouver ceux qui sont dans leur cabinet pour parler à eux, ceux-ci pussent les venir trouver sur le théâtre, sans choquer cette bienséance, afin de conserver l'unité des scènes.[37]

This conception appears to resemble the 'cabinet' of *Bérénice*, but Racine does draw attention to the room with its decor of linked initials,[38] which is an exact and specific place rather than the 'lieu composite',[39] the fictitious or mythical place that Corneille proposes.

Voltaire also suggests some compromises which recall the early days of the Hôtel de Bourgogne. In *Oreste* (1750), for instance, 'Le théâtre doit représenter le rivage de la mer; un bois, un temple, un palais, et un tombeau, d'un côté; et de l'autre, Argos dans le lointain.' The components, apart from the perspective of Argos in the distance, are those of Mahelot's lists of requirements. Troubled partly by the lack of action on the French stage (a consequence of the unity of place) and partly by the physical inadequacies of French theatres, Voltaire returns again, in his notes on *Olympie* (1764), 'esquisse légère et imparfaite d'un genre absolument nécessaire',[40] to the conventions of the early seventeenth-century stage. In this play, 'La scène est dans le temple d'Ephèse, où l'on célèbre les grands mystères. Le théâtre représente le temple, le péristyle, et la place qui conduit au temple.' And the set is described: 'Le fond du théâtre représente un temple dont les trois portes fermées sont ornées de larges pilastres: les deux ailes forment un vaste péristyle.' At the beginning of Act II, scene i, he writes:

Quoique cette scène et beaucoup d'autres se passent dans l'intérieur du temple, cependant, comme les théâtres sont rarement construits d'une manière favorable à la voix, les acteurs sont obligés d'avancer dans le péristyle; mais les trois portes du temple, ouvertes, désignent qu'on est dans le temple.[41]

He repeats his complaint at Act III, scene iii:

Il serait à souhaiter que cette scène pût être représentée dans la place qui conduit au péristyle du temple; mais alors cette place occupant un grand espace, le vestibule un autre, et l'intérieur du temple ayant une assez grande profondeur, les personnages qui paraissent dans ce temple ne pourraient être entendus: il faut donc que le spectateur supplée à la décoration qui manque.[42]

The actors remain downstage, and their acting space represents simulaneously the public square, the outside and the inside of the temple.

There is visual proof of the compromise by which in 1748 the Comédie-Française, with its spectators on each side of the stage, had changed the successive scenes required by Voltaire for his *Sémiramis* into a simultaneous set.[43] For the first and second acts the author demands 'un vaste péristyle' at the back, the palace with the hanging gardens above, on the right the temple and on the left the mausoleum. In Act III, scene vi, 'un cabinet du palais' is replaced by 'un grand salon magnifiquement orné'. Act IV takes place in 'le vestibule du temple', and Act V, where Azéma goes into the temple and Sémiramis into the tomb, presumably returns to the setting of Act I. The sketch by Gabriel de Saint-Aubin shows the set which was used throughout the play. At each side, steps lead up, on the left to the tomb, surmounted by an obelisk, from which Sémiramis emerges, and on the right to the doorway of the temple, while behind, three vistas are seen beyond the twin columns supporting the terrace. This set, designed by the Slodtz brothers, thanks to the King's generosity, is shown in more detail in their drawings of each of the six wing flats.[44] On the left, the first and third flats, though differing in detail, both show a pedestal, decorated with bas-reliefs, supporting a massive sculpture of flags, armour and fasces. Between them, the second flat shows, over the entrance to the tomb with its bas-relief, a sarcophagus surmounted by an obelisk. Another drawing shows the cave-like interior of the open tomb. On the right, the first and third flats each represent a pair of corinthian columns with cornice and balustrade decorated with urns above. The middle flat has an arched doorway of the same order under a cornice and a triangular pediment. Whether or not the Slodtz drawings refer to exactly the same production as the Saint-Aubin sketch, the set is basically the same, and it is clear that the King's money and artists were used to provide an elaborate set which could nevertheless serve for the whole of the play only by the benevolent exercise of the audience's imagination.

It is evident that, whatever the type of play, the number of different kinds of location that the playwright or designer created, and the audience accepted, was severely limited. Cahusac, in a passage previously quoted, talks of *mille moyens*, but describes only six or seven, and these could be compared with the sets provided for a model opera house belonging to Joseph Bonnier, Baron de la Mosson, and sold in 1745, after his death, to the Swedish ambassador, to be sent to Drottningholm: for Act I a forest and the sea; for Act II the Palace of the Sun; for Act III a *grotte affreuse*; for Act IV a landscape with the Temple of the Sun; for Act V a garden and then a public square.[45]

All types of set current in this period derive ultimately from Vitruvius' descriptions of the tragic, comic and satyric scenes[46] and from Serlio's illustrations of them.[47] D'Aubignac reduces all possible settings to three categories: miraculous, natural and artificial.[48] By 1681 the learned Claude-François Ménestrier could enumerate, he says, fifteen or sixteen species of *décoration*. *Les Célestes* include the rainbow, clouds, sunrise and sunset, and assemblies of divinities, *les Sacrées* temples and altars, *les Militaires* camps and towns under siege, *les Rustiques ou Champêtres* landscapes, with mountains, caves, valleys, and so forth, *les Maritimes* the sea, ports, storms, shipwrecks, *les Royales* palaces and gardens, *les Civiles* streets and private houses, *les Historiques* particular towns such as Rome, or other places such as the cave of the Sibyl, *les Poétiques* enchanted or supernatural places, *les Académiques* libraries and studies.[49]

In practice these categories overlap, and theatres could make do with a quite small stock of sets. Mahelot's drawings make it obvious that the Hôtel de Bourgogne used its prison, palace and cavern, for instance, over and over again for different plays.[50] Twice in the seventeenth century, stage designers working in Paris were recruited to provide an all-purpose collection of decors for the Swedish court in Stockholm. In 1647 Antonio Brunati arrived there to build, among other sets, one consisting of rocks, one of a mountainous landscape, two of gardens, one of a temple, one of a town, as well as both a small and a large sea.[51] In 1699 D'Olivet, perhaps with the collaboration of Bérain, built and painted in Paris another consignment which was shipped to Stockholm, after being tried out at the Hôtel de Bourgogne. The drawings, with extra folddown sections stuck on, to demonstrate how they could be varied, show very clearly that the gallery (an interior) had the same backdrop as the public square, which in turn could be modified for comedies by the addition of a flat with a usable door and window. By a further substitution of a backdrop of trees and landscape, and of trees for some of the buildings on the wing flats, the town became a village. This could be modified yet again to become a camp, if the remaining buildings were replaced by tents. Another set presented a palace courtyard for tragedies. If the central archway at the back was replaced by the trees, this set was suitable for 'les pastorales sérieuses'. The tragedy palace, as Agne Beijer says, resembles an opera decor, but '*visuellement* le domicile poétique des tragédies classiques n'était qu'une province du vaste pays féerique et intemporel de l'opéra de Quinault et de Lully'.[52] This is true not only of the palace, but also of the other places represented, which are equally *féeriques*.

The same elements were still in existence fifty years later. A *livre de service* used by the Comédie-Française in the 1750s still repeats the same items (the palace, the temple, the camp, the town, the village, woods, countryside, bedroom, *salon*, and so on), which could be re-combined: 'Les bois pour décoration avec la ferme de ville.'[53] Similar re-combinations of elements of decor also took place at the Opéra. An inventory of 1767 describes one of the sets for Rameau's *Castor et Pollux* (words by P.-J. Bernard, first performed in 1737):

Les Champs Elysées faits à neuf pour *Castor et Pollux* composés de seize châssis dont deux doubles à brisures, trois têtes d'arbres, quatre groupes d'arbres isolés; un Rideau de fond et deux terrains, toute cette décoration est chargée de fleurs et de fruit, plus un autre rideau ajusté pour sortir avec dix des susdits chassis dans *Erosine*. Le tout estimé la somme de deux mille cinq cents livres.[54]

Another inventory dating from 1767–71 repeats this description with a marginal note which reads:

Pour *les Fêtes Grecques et Romaines*, ballet remis le 28 juillet 1770. Cinq brisures ajoutées aux châssis. Le rideau d'*Erosine* repeint, servi pour l'acte d'*Hylas et Zélis*, le 6 juillet 1770. La dite peinture a été faite préparée [*sic*] pour la solitude d'*Issé* en 1769.[55]

These are composite sets in a sense different from Scherer's.

Some unified sets were designed for repeated use in classical plays, such as the *chambre de Molière* at the Comédie-Française. A new one was created by Brunetti after the removal of spectators' benches from the stage in 1759: a design 'traité à l'ancienne mode pour y représenter les comédies de Molière'.[56] Brunetti also constructed a Roman palace, or *palais rouge*, for tragedy; this was first used for Lemierre's *Hypermnestre*.[57] Even for court performances *passe-partout* sets, 'c'est-à-dire assez neutres pour servir à plusieurs pièces',[58] were provided by the Slodtz brothers: *palais vert, palais rouge, chambre verte*.[59]

Agne Beijer goes so far as to assert that 'nous pouvons parler de mêmes décors non seulement pour chaque pièce mais aussi *pour chaque genre dramatique*', but asks whether this 'déconcertante imprécision' does not make the *palais à volonté* the equivalent of Shakespeare's *wooden O* 'transporté dans le pays imaginaire des chandelles et des toiles peintes', whether there is not a link with the 'intemporalité' of the plays themselves. Did this convention, 'qui renvoyait la tragédie à son monde imaginaire et le comédie au sien', really lack any 'pouvoir de stimuler l'imagination'?[60]

That 'the collusion of the audience' was necessary is clear from the evidence of that 'bewildered spectator' (at Oxford in 1636) who could not understand the perspective and 'described the side wings as being like bookcases jutting out in a library'.[61] Examination of a series of *palais à volonté* will show that, given the audience's acceptance of perspective and their belief in the intemporal, imaginary world on the stage, the designer's imagination could be stimulated to create palaces in a variety of styles, yet all constructed according to the architecture of myth.

Torelli's design for the palace in Act IV of Corneille's *Andromède* (1650) established the pattern. Details of this design come from three sources: the description of the set, at the beginning of the act, in the text of the play published in 1650; the almost identical description in the programme, *Dessein de la tragédie d'Andromède*, also published in 1650; and Chauveau's engraving, published both separately and in the 1651 edition of the play.[62] We read that this structure is the *Vestibule* or *la grande salle* of the royal palace, but we see clearly that it is open to the sky, which is why Junon can fly in, in her chariot drawn by two peacocks. It is thus at the same time an interior and an exterior. On each side of the stage there is an arcade composed of nine round columns placed against square ones. Above each column, a flaming urn stands on the cornice. The stepped base of each column carries a life-sized statue of white marble. Each statue is different, but otherwise the arcades are identical and symmetrical. The courtyard, for that is what it really is, is closed at the back by a two-storey construction, each storey composed of three archways. This building is topped by a convexly curved pediment in the middle, linked by concave curves to a pedestal at each end. The pedestals and pediment each carry a sculpted fleur-de-lis — inappropriate to Ethiopia but flattering to France — the central one surmounted by a crown. The upper parts of further buildings are seen behind at either side. We are told that through the three ground-floor archways of the façade, three cypress avenues are visible, but these are beyond the three tunnel-like series of archways, converging to a central vanishing-point, seen in the engraving. An element of fantasy is introduced by the fact that the view through the three upper archways does not correspond at all with the ground-floor vistas. Indeed it is difficult to interpret this upper perspective, which appears to represent a courtyard closed at the back by a mansarded roof decorated with a sculpted coat-of-arms, though the outside of a low, curved roof above suggests rather a vast domed hall.

A touch of realism has been added to the side arcades by the engraver, who shows shadows of the left-hand arches cast on the ground to their right. This must be merely artistic licence, rather than an accurate representation of the stage lighting. At the same time it entirely does away with the pretence that the scene presented is an interior. The viewer has no notion of what, if anything, stands

Plate 1 Palace decor by Torelli for Corneille, *Andromède*, Act IV.

behind these arcades. They are perhaps merely free-standing arches, like those of the *Bosquet des Colonnades* in the gardens at Versailles.[63] Their resemblance to the three doorways at the back suggests, however, that they too may lead to further perspectives of arches. They are in fact quite without architectural reality, as is the whole scheme of this baroque Ethiopian palace.

The palaces created by Carlo Vigarani, Torelli's successor as court designer for fêtes and spectacles, generally follow a similar plan. We may take as an example a drawing for an unidentified opera,[64] where, as in the engraving for Torelli's design, colonnades on either side are blocked off at the back of the stage by a two-storey domed building. Here, however, the scene is more clearly meant to be an exterior. Vigarani's symmetry is more complex and more elaborately ornamented. The columns are twisted barley-sugar columns with garlands twined around them. On each side of the stage there are three pairs of columns, each pair supporting a massive continuous pediment which juts out above them. Between each pair of columns is a curved console supporting a smallish statue. The first one on the right is of an eagle. Alternating with the pairs of columns are statues of immense human figures on rectangular plinths. The first one on the right is of a man carrying a block of stone or wood. Beyond the third of these large statues on each side are three additional similar plinths, carrying smaller statues, not clearly visible in the sketch. There is a very noticeable change of rhythm and scale from the immense columns at the front, whose pediment, unlike Torelli's, disappears up into the flies, to the smaller blocks at the back. This trick of perspective is allied to another on the backdrop, where, under an upper storey which somewhat resembles the Pavillon de l'Horloge of the Louvre, a tall archway flanked by two more pairs of garlanded pillars leads to a stairway that leads the eye upwards to an even more distant archway, thus giving the perspective a different focus from that of the wing flats. The building at the back of Vigarani's set is also, typically, lower than Torelli's, adding to the different appearance of the perspective, as well as leaving more room for flights of divinities or vistas of celestial palaces. The style of Vigarani's palace is distinctive, but the lay-out follows Torelli's pattern.

Jean I Bérain succeeded Vigarani in 1680. A typical example of his style is a drawing from his workshop for Act III, scene iv, of the Quinault/Lully opera *Atys* (1676).[65] This is possibly a design for one of the *reprises* which took place in 1689–90 and 1699. The

95

Plate 2   Palace decor by Vigarani for an unidentified opera. (Reproduced, by permission, from Agne Beijer,

Plate 3 Palace decor by Bérain for Quinault/Lully, *Atys*, Act III, scene iv. (Reproduced, by permission, from François Lesure, *L'Opéra français XVIIᵉ et XVIIIᵉ siècles* (Geneva: Editions Minkoff, 1972).)

stage represents a room in the *palais du Grand Sacrificateur*, which in this scene is invaded by the God of Sleep and his suite of *Songes agréables et funestes*. This is again a symmetrical construction, though some of the symmetry is masked by the billowing clouds on the left on which the Dreams are borne. At first sight the design seems not to follow the established pattern, for this is an interior, with a ceiling, and the space is divided by a very open arcade into a downstage area, in which Atys is asleep on a couch, and an upstage area paved with square slabs, apparently a throne room — the throne not unlike Louis XIV's in Claude Guy Hallé's painting of the Doge of Genoa's audience in 1685.[66] This arcade consists of the usual three arches, supported by caryatids, two round ones and a wider central one flattened at the top. Above these are three slightly wider but very low arches of the same shape, which appear to open to the sky like windows. The upper openings are partially blocked by sculptures, the lower ones are draped with garlands hanging from masks at the keystones, and there are many other ornaments. However, but for the fact that this screen is much further forward, the principle is the same as in the palace backdrops of Torelli and Vigarani. The visible side wall of the nearer room has at the lower level two herms as caryatids, separating two decorated panels and with a rectangular doorway between them. Above the cornice that these support is an arcaded and balustraded gallery with round arches and flat pilasters adorned with carvings. The further room has at each side corinthian pilasters flanking a rectangular niche containing a seated statue, and above (apparently) a curved ceiling springing from a cornice higher than that in the first room. Yet again, the side flats consist basically of a sequence of columns and statues. The elements of the composition and their fundamental disposition are thus merely a modification of those of the early palaces, although the style of the decoration, particularly on the side panels, is characteristically Bérinesque. The details of this ornamentation are fanciful in the extreme, which adds to the impression that the architecture is that of a dream-world.

The design by Joachin Pizzoli for the Comédie-Française revival of the Molière/Corneille *Psyché* in 1684[67] is of the same period as Bérain's opera sets, but its style is much more sober, even though it must be intended to represent the enchanted palace created by Amour for Psyché. Once again the sides are constructed of columns and statues, and the backdrop has three archways. Again the

Plate 4   Palace decor by Pizzoli for the 1684 revival of Molière/Corneille/Quinault, *Psyché.*

columns are in pairs, and each pair encloses a curved console carrying the statue. The pairs of ionic columns, standing forward from flat pilasters but on the same rectangular bases, are separated from each other by tall archways. This pattern is repeated only once, so that the sequence on each side is column, statue, column, archway, column, statue, column, archway. The cornice above each pair of columns supports a flattened arch that spans the stage from side to side. The decor thus gives the appearance of consisting of two proscenium arches, one behind the other. The roofing that these arches provide extends forward only at the sides, leaving the main central areas uncovered, like two vast atria. The alternation of columns, statues and arches is continued at the back, but in a concave curve suggesting an oval. The two pairs of columns separating the three archways carry a triangular pediment, over the central arch, with two reclining figures on it. From the cornice a coffered ceiling curves inwards but stops just above the pediment, where there is a balustrade, apparently forming another, partly domed, atrium. Is this a courtyard or a vast hall? The ambiguity is complete. Even if a room is intended to be represented, it is open, through the three archways at the back, to a courtyard surrounded by colonnades. Here again, then, is the traditional layout, this time in classical style, of an architectural myth.

Jean-Nicholas Servandoni, painter and architect, designed sets for the Académie de Musique from 1726 to 1735 and provided *spectacles muets* at the Salle des Machines in the Tuileries from 1738 to 1742 and from 1753 to 1758.[68] A gothic palace attributed to him[69] shows radical departures in style and technique overlaying the traditional design. Pointed arches and crenellated round towers, not unlike some of Mahelot's prisons, define the style, and its medieval decrepitude is emphasized by weeds growing in the paved courtyard and bushes growing from between the stones of the towers. The scene is asymmetrical, a *scena per angolo* – the oblique perspective which Servandoni is generally supposed to have introduced to France. At the left the front of the stage is occupied by a stone wall, with a round-topped doorway or niche. Behind this is a round tower. Both wall and tower have battlements. From behind the tower a colonnade extends back towards the centre of the stage, where it turns at right angles downstage towards the right. The usual view has been swivelled round forty-five degrees, so that what would normally be the largest, central arch is the first arch visible on the left. This main arch is rounded and has a

Plate 5   Gothic palace decor attributed to Servandoni.

triangular pediment over it, but the other arches are gothic although supported by groups of four classical columns, whose cornices also carry large sculptures of flags and military trophies. Over the pointed arches, corbels that resemble machicolations bear a pierced balustrade. The result is an amalgam of classical and gothic, military and ecclesiastical architecture. Above the angle of this cloister-like construction, and behind it, rise two more round towers with battlements. Through the arches on the left, beyond a railing or fence, appear the buildings of a town, including a classical temple. Through the arches on the right, beyond the railings, further gothic vaults are seen. At the front of the stage, to the right, the scene is completed by two more round towers flanking a gothic doorway, all with battlements. One tower has a tiny pointed turret on its roof. These fortifications have no real relationship with the colonnade, which itself has no real architectural function. The palace simply evokes a mythical past. And, novel though its style and presentation are, it still presents the basic colonnaded court.

A drawing by the Slodtz brothers brings us back to classical times and style. This is a design for a revival of the Lully/Quinault opera *Thésée* at Fontainebleau in 1754.[70] The words 'rideau du palais d'Egée' are written at the top, so this is part of the set for Act II. Only the left-hand side of the backdrop is drawn; the other side would have been symmetrical. A round pavilion at the centre (on the right-hand side of the sketch) is topped by a dome supported by open arches. Through the huge arch below an avenue of trees is visible. On each side of the pavilion are three rectangular doorways with steps up to a hall or corridor, on the far wall of which columns alternate with statues in rounded niches. Above each doorway is a square, carved panel. Above these are a cornice and balustrade supported by corinthian columns on rectangular plinths between the doors. On the balustrade, above each column, is a statue. At each end, a slightly projecting wing has steps leading up to a round arch through which further columns and arches are shown. No doubt even more columns and arches graced each side of the stage. Only the dimensions (from the ground to the top of the balustrade, seven feet ten inches, for example) appear to distinguish this from an architect's drawing for a real building. But a real building constructed according to this design could have no purpose. The architectural perspective, painted to this design on the backdrop, transported the viewer's imagination to the mythical world of the play.

In 1778 the bust of Voltaire was crowned with laurels on the

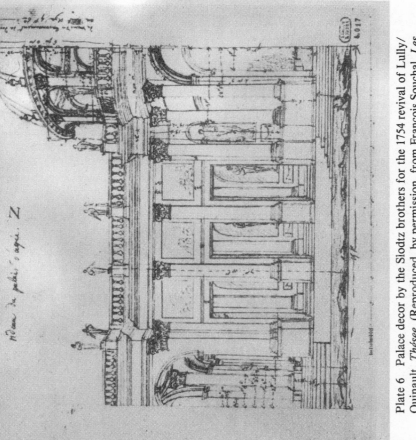

Plate 6 Palace decor by the Slodtz brothers for the 1754 revival of Lully/
Quinault, *Thésée*. (Reproduced, by permission, from François Souchal, *Les
Slodtz, sculpteurs et décorateurs du Roi (1685–1764)* (Paris: De Boccard
Edition-Diffusion, 1967).)

stage of the Comédie-Française, after a performance of his *Irène*, while the playwright looked on from his box. The engraving by Gaucher, after Moreau le Jeune, which commemorates this event shows Brunetti's set for the play, the palace of Constantine.[71] The architecture is of monumental proportions. At each side of the stage a vast square pillar rises. Beyond these, from a central position in the auditorium, two more huge square pillars would be seen to support a gigantic central arch, with two more arches going off into the wings. What is visible is merely a small section of an immense roofed arcade, the other three sides of which are seen behind, extending into the distance and forming a square courtyard. On the far side above the main arches a very much smaller arcade perhaps lights an upper walkway. Once more, in this set, we have a purposeless pillared courtyard, an architectural myth, this time in the neo-classical style.

Landscape is, if anything, more mythical than architecture in this land of the imagination. One of its traditional features is the cave, be it *grotte*, *antre* or *caverne*, which figures in stage designs at least from Mahelot to Christian Bérard's set for Cocteau's *Renaud et Armide* (1943).[72] Sometimes the cave is required by the dramatist rather than added by the designer, the best-known example perhaps being the magician's cave in P. Corneille's *Illusion comique*. A fantastic variant of the cave is the tunnel-like cavern which channels the view through the rock or mountain to a distant perspective of sea or landscape. This may be considered as the equivalent, in nature, of the arch or colonnade in architecture, through which a vista of courtyards or gardens is perceived.

Torelli's design for the Prologue of P. Corneille's *Andromède* is a prime example. The description tells us of a vast mountain − 'Le pied de cette montagne est percé à jour par une grotte profonde qui laisse voir la mer en éloignement' − and this is what Chaveau's engraving shows.[73] A drawing by Charles Errard (or Noël Coypel, or Gilbert de Sève) probably shows the similar set for the opening of Act III of Luigi Rossi's opera *Orfeo* performed at the Palais Royal in 1647,[74] to re-use the scenery of which Corneille was required to write *Andromède*. Torelli had used this device before, in Venice, for *Bellerofonte* (1642), where Act I, scene xi 'represented the grotto of the winds of Eolus as described by the ancient storytellers. In several places there were clefts, and, facing, the ruins of the cavern did not hide the view of the distant sea.'[75] A similar construction was ordered for Act II of Molière's *Dom Juan* (1665):

Plate 7 Palace decor by Brunetti for Voltaire, *Irène*, 1778.

'une grotte pour cacher la poutre au travers de laquelle l'on verra deux châssis de mer et le fond'.[76] It was produced yet again, by Buffequin, for the Prologue of Boyer's machine play, *Les Amours de Jupiter et de Sémélé* (1666), where 'A l'ouverture du théâtre, on voit de front un amas de rochers élevés les uns sur les autres, qui forment la Montagne de Parnasse, dont la cime est couverte de lauriers et d'autres arbres, et le pied étant percé à jour, laisse voir dans l'éloignement une agréable campagne.'[77] The Prologue of the Molière/Corneille *Psyché* (1671) also has 'dans l'enfoncement un rocher percé à jour à travers duquel on voit la mer en éloignement'. Another version appears in Act IV of Fontenelle's *Bellérophon*: 'Au fond du théâtre paraît un rocher . . .; il est percé par des grottes, au travers desquelles on découvre un paysage à perte de vue.'

These examples, from three different theatres, the Palais Royal (*Andromède, Dom Juan, Bellérophon*), the Marais (*Les Amours de Jupiter et de Sémélé*) and the Salle des Machines (*Psyché*), are sufficient to show how widely accepted was this form of landscape. Perhaps it had its origin in nature, as Corneille suggested: 'Le pied de cette montagne est percé à jour, à la façon de celle qu'on rencontre sur le chemin de Rome à Naples.'[78] Perhaps scene-designers borrowed from other artists. Mantegna painted a similar cavern pierced through a mountain, with a view beyond, in a fresco of huntsmen with hounds and horses in the Palazzo Ducale in Mantua.[79] This fresco is dated 1474. Rocky arches are still included in paintings by Claude. The *Pastoral Landscape* which dates from about 1630[80] has, centre right, a rocky arch, with a house and trees on top, through which part of the landscape is seen. In his *Coast Scene with Perseus (The Origin of Coral)* (1673), there is a rocky arch on the right, and the scene is closed on the left, like a stage set, by a tree.[81] The position of this arch and the subject of the composition recall the frontispiece of the Quinault/Lully *Persée* (1682), designed by Bérain.

Whatever its origins, this peculiar feature of stage landscapes demonstrates, as concretely as does the fantasy palace, the mythical quality of theatrical place in this period.

The artist who perhaps more than any other illustrates this quality is Lajoue. Very often it is simply not known whether his drawings and paintings are designs for the stage, for perspective frescoes to add space and openness to a room, or simply gratuitous fantasies. Even when it is evident that a drawing is for the stage, it is not known for what purpose it was produced, or whether the

Plate 8 Design by Torelli for Corneille, *Andromède*, Prologue.

set was ever realized. In his architectural fantasies of colonnades and fountains and curving, rococo stairways, often partly in ruins, garden and palace merge into uncertainty. This is the case, for instance, in a drawing called *Architecture et Escalier*,[82] where stairs swirl upwards to empty space under partly ruined open arches, and are linked by a colonnade to a curving, balustraded balcony that juts out over a shell-like fountain, showing more steps and part of the interior of a dome beyond and above. The merging of countryside and architecture goes even further in a painting entitled *L'Escalier* or *Le Parc*.[83] On the right a dark, cavern-like tunnel of trees leads the eye to a fountain and a distant landscape. In front of this, a stream or pool fed by two fountains contains fallen blocks of stone. From the middle left foreground a staircase rises towards the centre, where the far-off landscape is again visible, turning then at right angles towards the left with balustrades curving apparently into space. An immense stone urn stands on the inner corner of this turn in the staircase. An almost bare tree frames the painting on the left. Two dogs are on the steps and a few Watteauesque figures sit, stand, or lie, looking indolently round them or into the distance. These visitors seem to have strayed into the landscape of a dying myth.

The theatrical fiction of mythical place faded or was eliminated as the would-be realism of the *drame* took over in the eighteenth century. Beaumarchais needed four precisely described and defined different areas of the same château and house for *Le Mariage de Figaro* (1784) and *La Mère coupable* (1792). When, for his unperformed play *L'Ami de la maison*, he suggested a simultaneous set, it made no demands on the audience's imagination. The stage was to be divided into three compartments, each with its own curtain: 'un salon, un cabinet de toilette, et un cabinet de travail', three contiguous rooms of the same house, in which the action was to take place either simultaneously or successively.[84]

Diderot wished to sweep away the falsity and ignorance of myth, and replace them by nature and truth:

Mais ce qui montre surtout combien nous sommes encore loin du bon goût et de la vérité: c'est la pauvreté et la fausseté des décorations, et le luxe des habits.

Vous exigez de votre poète qu'il s'asujettisse à l'unité de lieu, et vous abandonnez la scène à l'ignorance d'un mauvais décorateur.

Voulez-vous rapprocher vos poètes du vrai, et dans la conduite de leurs pièces, et dans leur dialogue, vos acteurs du jeu naturel et de la déclamation réelle? élevez la voix, demandez seulement qu'on vous montre le lieu de la scène tel qu'il doit être.

Plate 9   Jacques de Lajoue, *Architecture et escalier.*

Si la nature et la vérité s'introduisent une fois sur vos théâtres dans la circonstance la plus légère, bientôt vous sentirez le ridicule et le dégoût se répandre sur tout ce qui fera contraste avec elles.[85]

The baroque and classical myth of place vanishes, but soon it will be the turn of the Romantics.

NOTES

1 *Discours des trois unités*, in *Pierre Corneille: Writings on the Theatre*, ed. H. T. Barnwell (Oxford, 1965), p. 63.

2 *Encyclopédie*, XVIII, 403. Spelling is modernized in this as in other quotations.

3 *Supplément*, s.v. UNITE (IV, 992).

4 *Ibid*.

5 *Encyclopédie*, XIV, 753.

6 *Ibid.*, IV, 701.

7 Cf. François Souchal, *Les Slodtz, sculpteurs et décorateurs du Roi (1685–1764)* (Paris, 1967), p. 436, and plates 63 and 64.

8 V.-L. Tapié, *The Age of Grandeur: Baroque and Classicism in Europe* (London, 1960), plate 105. Another view is reproduced in A. Tessier, 'Le genre décoratif funèbre', in *Revue de l'art ancien et moderne* XXVIII (1925), p. 181, and in R. A. Weigert, *Jean I Bérain, dessinateur de la chambre et du cabinet du Roi (1640–1711)*, 2 vols. (Paris, 1937), plate XII, fig. 26.

9 Cf. Souchal, *Les Slodtz*, plate 52(a).

10 *Encyclopédie*, s.v. *DECORATION (Opéra)* (IV, 702).

11 Jean-Philippe Rameau, *Oeuvres complètes*, XVIII (Paris, 1924), p. lvi.

12 *Ibid.*, XV (Paris, 1910), pp. 58, 93, 120.

13 Molière, *Mélicerte* (1666), *Les Amants magnifiques* (1670).

14 Quinault, *Isis* (1677), Act IV, scene V.

15 Fontenelle, *Bellérophon* (1679), Prologue; Régnard, *Les Chinois* (1692), Prologue; La Harpe, *Les Muses rivales, ou L'Apothéose de Voltaire* (1779).

16 Thomas Corneille, *Circé* (1675), Act II; Fontenelle, *Enée et Lavinie* (1690), Act III; Houdard de la Motte, *Canente* (1700), Act IV.

17 P. Corneille, *La Conquête de la toison d'or* (1661), Act V, scene VI; Quinault, *Phaéton* (1683), Act IV.

18 *Encyclopédie*, s.v. UNITE (XVII, 403).

19 Pierre Corneille, *Cinna* (1641); Thomas Corneille, *La Mort de l'empereur Commode* (1659); Quinault, *Amalasonte* (1658); Voltaire, *Brutus* (1730).

20 Quinault, *Le Mariage de Cambise* (1656); Boursault, *Phaéton* (1691).

21 Thomas Corneille, *Le Comte d'Essex* (1678); Boursault, *Marie Stuard, reine d'Ecosse* (1683); Voltaire, *L'Ecossaise* (1760).

22 Rotrou, *Laure persécutée* (1637).

23 Thomas Corneille, *Le Berger extravagant* (1651).
24 Thomas Corneille, *Timocrate* (1658).
25 Molière, *La Princesse d'Elide* (1664).
26 Quinault, *Le Feint Alcibiade* (1658).
27 Voltaire, *Le Droit du seigneur* (1762).
28 Cf. J. Scherer, *La Dramaturgie classique en France* (Paris, 1950), pp. 157–60.
29 Act III, scene vi. In *Recueil de tragédies à machines sous Louis XIV (1657–1672)*, ed. Ch. Delmas (Toulouse-le-Mirail, 1985).
30 'Opéra comique' (1723), in *Le Théâtre de la Foire*, ed. D. Lurcel (Paris, 1983).
31 Souchal, *Les Slodtz*, p. 479 and plate 71(b).
32 Per Bjurström, *Giacomo Torelli and Baroque Stage Design* (Stockholm, 1962), p. 73.
33 S. T. Worsthorne, *Venetian Opera in the Seventeenth Century* (Oxford, 1954), p. 154.
34 Bjurström, *Giacomo Torelli*, illustrations on pp. 61 and 137. The Pont Neuf set is also reproduced in Tapié, *Age of Grandeur*, plate 75.
35 Vigarani's design, with a rather insignificant Versailles in the distance leaving plenty of room for the machinery of Mars's chariot, is reproduced in Agne Beijer, 'Vigarani et Bérain au Palais Royal', in *Revue de la Société d'Histoire du Théâtre*, IX (1956), 184–96, fig. 1.
36 *Discours des trois unités*, ed. Barnwell, p. 78.
37 *Ibid.*, pp. 78–9.
38 *Bérénice*, 3–8 and 1321–5. Cf. *Le Mémoire de Mahelot, Laurent et d'autres décorateurs de l'Hôtel de Bourgogne et de la Comédie-Française*, ed. H. C. Lancaster (Paris, 1920), p. 113: 'un petit cabinet où il y a des chiffre [*sic*]'.
39 Scherer, *Dramaturgie classique*, p. 191.
40 Note to Act I, scene iv, *Oeuvres complètes*, vol. VI, *Théâtre*, tome V (Paris, 1877), p. 108.
41 *Ibid.*, p. 112.
42 *Ibid.*, p. 143.
43 Cf. P. Bjurström, 'Mises en scène de *Sémiramis* de Voltaire en 1748 et 1759', in *Revue de la Société d'Histoire du Théâtre*, IX (1956), 299–320; F. Souchal, *Les Slodtz* pp. 171, 476–7, 635–6 and plates 68(a) and (b).
44 There is some doubt about which brothers designed the set. Souchal, in the text of his book, says that it was Sébastien-Antoine aided by his painter brother Dominique-François who was responsible for it in 1748 (p. 471), and Paul-Ambroise with Dominique-François for the court performance in 1756 (Sébastien-Antoine died in 1754). The catalogue (p. 635) attributes the original design to Sébastien-Antoine and Paul-Amboise, and states that the drawings 'des Slodtz' date 'sans doute' from the 1756 revival at the Comédie-Française, quoting the specifications for six flats from the accounts of the Menus-Plaisirs for that year.

The description corresponds to what is shown in the drawings. According to Bjurström (p. 307), the drawings are by René-Michel (known as Michel-Ange) and were 'certainement' made for the performance at Fontainebleau on 24 October 1748. His figures 4 and 5, however, give their date as 1752.

45 Marianne Roland Michel, *Lajoüe et l'art rocaille* (Neuilly-sur-Seine, 1984), pp. 43, 108–9.

46 Vitruvius, *The Ten Books on Architecture*, trans. Morris Hickey Morgan (New York, 1960; reprint of 1914 translation), book v, chapter 6, p. 150.

47 Cf. *The Renaissance Stage: Documents of Serlio, Sabbattini and Furttenbach*, ed. B. Hewitt (Coral Gables, Fla, 1958), pp. 28, 30, 31; L. Dubech, *Histoire générale illustrée du théâtre* (Paris, 1934), ii, 263–5; N. Decugis and S. Reymond, *Le Décor de théâtre en France du moyen âge à 1925* (Paris, 1953), p. 40, plates 9, 10, 11.

48 Abbé D'Aubignac, *La Pratique du théâtre*, ed. P. Martino (Paris, 1927), p. 358.

49 C.-F. Ménestrier, *Des Représentations en musique anciennes et modernes* (Paris, 1681; repr. Geneva, 1972), pp. 171–4. These types are compared with Torelli's practice in P. Bjurström, *Giacomo Torelli*, pp. 198–211.

50 *Mémoire de Mahelot, passim.*

51 Agne Beijer, '*La Naissance de la Paix*, ballet de cour de René Descartes', in *Le Lieu théâtral à la renaissance*, ed. Jean Jacquot (Paris, 1964), pp. 409–22, especially pp. 413–14.

52 Agne Beijer, 'Le Théâtre de Charles XII et la mise en scène du théâtre parlé au XVIIe siècle', in *Revue de la Société d'Histoire du Théâtre*, ix (1956), 197–214.

53 Gösta M. Bergman, 'Le Décorateur Brunetti et les décors de la Comédie-Française au XVIIIe siècle', in *Theatre Research*, iv: 1 (1962), 6–28, especially p. 9.

54 Jean-Philippe Rameau, *Oeuvres Complétes*, viii (Paris, 1903), p. lxxiii.

55 *Ibid.*

56 Bergman, 'Le Décorateur Brunetti', p. 23.

57 *Ibid.*, pp. 14–15.

58 Souchal, *Les Slodtz*, p. 470.

59 *Ibid.*, p. 477 and plate 65(d).

60 Agne Beijer, 'Une maquette de décor récemment retrouvée pour le *Ballet de la Prospérité des Armes de France* dansé à Paris le 7 février 1641', in *Le Lieu théâtral à la renaissance*, ed. Jacquot, p. 402.

61 Roy Strong, *Art and Power: Renaissance Festivals 1450–1650* (Woodbridge, 1984), p. 156.

62 Cf. P. Corneille, *Andromède*, ed. Christian Delmas (Paris, 1974). The engraving is also reproduced in P. Bjurström, *Giacomo Torelli*, p. 153,

The myth of place

and in Decugis and Reymond, *Le Décor*, ch. 3, plate 26 (p. 68).
63 Cf. Gérald van der Kemp, *Versailles* (London, 1978), pp. 200, 201; Bernard Jeannel, *Le Nôtre* (Paris, 1985), p. 63.
64 Reproduced in Agne Beijer, 'Vigarani et Bérain au Palais Royal', fig. 10.
65 Reproduced in François Lesure, *L'Opéra classique français. XVIIe et XVIIIe siècles* (Geneva, 1972), plate 29; also in Decugis and Reymond, *Le Décor*, ch. 4, plate 29 (p. 88), and in *Lully et l'Opéra français*, special number of *La Revue musicale*, Jan. 1925, plate 15.
66 Cf. Luc Benoist, *Versailles* (Paris, 1947), plate 70.
67 Illustrated in Decugis and Reymond, *Le Décor*, ch. 5, plate 19 (p. 120) (here dated 1694). The left-hand side of this design is reproduced in *Album théâtre classique*, iconographie réunie et commentée par Sylvie Chevalley (Paris, 1970), p. 238, and in *Le Registre de la Grange 1659–1685*, ed. B. E. Young and G. P. Young, vol. II (Paris, 1947), frontispiece.
68 Cf. Per Bjurström, 'Servandoni décorateur de théâtre', *Revue de la Société d'Histoire du Théâtre*, VII (1954), 150–9, and the same author's 'Servandoni et la Salle des Machines', *ibid.*, XII (1959), 222–4.
69 Reproduced by Decugis and Reymond, *Le Décor*, ch. 4, plate 46 (p. 94), and by Eveline Schlumberger, 'Une Génie d'opéra. Servandoni', in *Connaissance des arts*, August 1965, p. 19.
70 Souchal, *Les Slodtz*, plate 66(b).
71 Bergman, 'Le Décorateur Brunetti', plate 7; Decugis and Reymond, *Le Décor*, ch. 5, plate 26 (p. 126).
72 Cf. Pierre Chanel, *Album Cocteau* (Paris, 1970), p. 153. On this subject, see also Naomi Miller, *Heavenly Caves: Reflections on the Garden Grotto* (London, 1982), especially ch. 5.
73 *Andromède*, ed. Delmas, p. 15.
74 Donald Oenslager, *Stage Design: Four Centuries of Scenic Invention* (London, 1975), pp. 44–5 illustration 15.
75 Worsthorne, *Venetian Opera*, p. 179.
76 'Marché de décors pour Dom Juan', in M. Jurgens and E. Maxfield-Muller, *Cent Ans de recherches sur Molière et sa famille et les comédiens de sa troupe* (Paris, 1963), p. 399.
77 *Dessein*, in *Recueil de tragédies à machines*, ed. Delmas.
78 *Andromède*, ed. Delmas, p. 170.
79 Cf. Mantegna, *La Camera degli sposi*, ed. G. Paccagnini (Milan, 1968), pp. 20, 22–3; Ronald Lightbown, *Mantegna* (Oxford, 1986), plates 86 and 89.
80 *L'opera completa di Claude Lorrain* (Milan, 1975), plate 1; H. Diane Russell, *Claude Lorrain 1600–1682* (New York, 1982), cat. no. 3 (p. 104).
81 Claude Lorrain, *Liber Veritatis*, ed. Michael Kitson (London, 1978), no. 184 and p. 167; also in Russell, *Claude Lorrain*, p. 32. Cf. also

Landscape with Hagar, Ishmael and the Angel (1668) and *Coast Scene with Aeneas Hunting* (1672) (*Liber Veritatis*, nos. 174 and 180).
82 Michel, *Lajoüe*, fig. 311 (cat. D. 222).
83 *ibid.*, plate 5 (cat. P. 93).
84 *Théâtre complet de Beaumarchais* (Paris, 1869), II, 229.
85 *De la Poésie dramatique*, in Diderot, *Œuvres complètes*, ed. J. and A. M. Chouillet (Paris, 1980), x, 404.

8
Marivaux mythologue

JACQUES SCHERER

Le 3 mars 1720, une très médiocre comédie en prose, dont Marivaux était peut-être l'auteur ou l'un des auteurs, est présentée anonymement par les comédiens italiens. Elle porte le titre, rendu mythologique par ses majuscules, de *L'Amour et la Vérité*. Une partie du dialogue de ces deux personnages nous a été conservée. On y apprend que l'Amour tendre s'est disputé avec l'Avarice et la Débauche parce que celles-ci ont poussé Plutus, dieu des richesses, à conquérir Vénus; de leur commerce est né l'Amour fripon. La Vérité se cache dans un puits, dont l'eau obligera ceux qui la boiront à dire le vrai; l'Amour se cache dans un arbre dont les fruits provoqueront l'amour. Parmi les autres personnages figuraient la Raison et Arlequin. Ces inventions sont d'une grande banalité. On y relève des emprunts à la mythologie gréco-romaine la plus classique, des personnages abstraits semblables à ceux de la 'moralité' médiévale, des valeurs magiques généreusement prêtées à un puits et à un arbre, et enfin Arlequin, qui est un mythe à lui seul. Mais tous les principaux ingrédients de la création mythologique sont déjà réunis dans ce premier essai.

La même année 1720, le 17 octobre, mais avec autrement de richesse et de solidité, Marivaux donne une de ses œuvres les plus parfaites, *Arlequin poli par l'amour*. D'une simplicité exemplaire, la fable est en apparence commandée par une Fée qui, appliquant le schéma racinien du pouvoir impuissant, règne sur tout, sauf sur l'amour. C'est en vain qu'elle aime Arlequin, puisque celui-ci et Silvia s'aiment, et triomphent grâce à un stratagème. L'amour et la vérité, mais ici sans majuscules, donnent leur vigueur à cette frêle intrigue. Dès la première scène est affirmé qu'Arlequin est l'Amour lui-même, ce qui peut avoir plusieurs sens: il est beau, il a inspiré l'amour de la Fée, il hérite des prestiges, et aussi des ridicules, de la tradition arlequinesque, qui est bien antérieure à Marivaux, et il est aussi, malgré sa balourdise initiale, un meneur de l'intrigue; ce Cupidon de campagne a du dieu le caractère direct, impitoyable et finalement triomphant.

L'autre composante de la mythologie d'*Arlequin poli par l'amour* est la vérité. Habituellement, les personnages de théâtre mentent, parce qu'ils combattent. Arlequin, cet asocial, ce rustre plus proche de l'animal que de l'homme et que seul l'amour pourra humaniser, dit toujours la vérité; c'est en quoi il dérange. Il en est de même pour Silvia, qui dit en propres termes: 'Je ne mens jamais.' Dans l'univers de mensonge que peint la comédie, Arlequin a pour rôle essentiel, suscitant l'étonnement des autres personnages, de proclamer une vérité provocante, dissonante et dénonciatrice. Cette vérité fait sa force parce qu'elle est également éclairante. Quand elle aura triomphé des motivations simplement réalistes des autres personnages, la pièce sera finie. Porteuse des conventions sociales, la cousine de Silvia lui conseille de dissimuler ses sentiments, c'est-à-dire de mentir. Mais ni Silvia ni Arlequin, amants de la vérité, ne peuvent jouer le jeu du mensonge et ils le transforment en respect maladroit d'une règle du jeu qu'ils ont eux-mêmes instituée. Dire le mensonge en prévenant qu'il est mensonge n'est pas efficace non plus. La liberté dangereuse de récuser les règles ('ne sommes-nous pas les maîtres?') détruit la faible objectivité que les règles pouvaient conserver. Le jeu est mort, tué par la vérité. Aussi bien est-ce par le geste et par le sentiment, non par une dialectique du jeu, que les deux personnages sont d'abord entrés en contact.

Dans certaines des œuvres suivantes de Marivaux, pendant une période qui va approximativement de 1725 à 1729, l'esprit de mythologie se met au service d'une critique sociale. Cette orientation n'était pas absente d'*Arlequin poli par l'amour*, où la Fée rassemblait les traits de la désinvolture amoureuse et de la dureté d'une grande dame se jouant impunément de la naïveté des paysans. Mais avec *L'Ile des Esclaves*, ce projet se place au centre. Le mythe est celui d'une inversion de la société: les maîtres deviennent esclaves et leurs anciens esclaves sont leurs maîtres. La règle du jeu est donc imposée de l'extérieur, ce qui n'empêche pas le couple des valets d'en chercher une autre, lorsqu'ils tentent de faire 'la belle conversation'. *L'Ile de la Raison ou les Petits Hommes* apporte un mythe plus étrange encore, et qui exige une mise en scène bien difficile à réaliser. Dans cette île de rêve, huit Européens captifs des insulaires ont rapetissé. Ils ne reprendront leur taille normale que dans la mesure où ils se guériront de leurs folies. Mythe didactique, comme celui de *L'Ile des Esclaves* et qui permet plus impitoyablement encore une mise en jugement des différents états sociaux. Le moins fou est le paysan, les plus durement traités, déclarés incurables, sont le poète et le philosophe.

Le Triomphe de Plutus, où ce dieu l'emporte sur Apollon dans une rivalité amoureuse, exprime schématiquement une idée banale, mais oblige à noter une fois de plus l'emploi, ici non nécessaire, de la défroque mythologique. Plus ambitieux est le mythe social exposé dans la troisième île de Marivaux. En 1729, les comédiens italiens présentent de leur auteur favori une comédie en trois actes intitulée *La Nouvelle Colonie, ou la Ligue des femmes*. Elle échoue et n'est pas publiée, mais Marivaux en donnera beaucoup plus tard une version réduite à un acte qui reprend l'essentiel. Les femmes ont pris le pouvoir. Mais leurs préoccupations superficielles, leur désordre et leur inexpérience provoquent l'écroulement de ce qui aurait pu être une révolution. En outre, le camp des femmes est divisé, car une opposition apparaît entre les bourgeoises et les aristocrates. Cette opposition est plus importante et plus réelle pour le public de Marivaux qu'une mythique révolte des femmes.

L'échec de *La Nouvelle Colonie* semble avoir dissuadé son auteur de faire du mythe un instrument de critique sociale. Il revient ensuite à un usage plus proprement esthétique de la mythologie. *La Réunion des amours*, jouée à la Comédie-Française en 1731, compare longuement les mérites de l'Amour (sentimental) et de Cupidon (sensuel) et conclut qu'il faut accepter les deux. Le thème et le traitement sont ceux d'une moralité du moyen âge. Le mythe est devenu un langage, et ne se lie pas nécessairement à un contenu émouvant.

Par contre, tout en poursuivant l'exploitation de l'abstraction médiévale, il se charge d'aspects moraux dans *Le Chemin de la Fortune, ou le Saut du Fossé*. Le décor y est aussi mythologique que les personnages. Pour parvenir au palais de la Fortune, le héros doit franchir un large fossé, devant lequel s'élèvent de petits mausolées élevés aux vertus perdues par ceux qui ont déjà sauté. Le héros hésite: le Scrupule tente de le dissuader, la Cupidité l'encourage. Il ne s'agit que d'une ébauche, jamais jouée, mais la pente de l'imagination y est significative. La mythologie de *La Dispute* est beaucoup plus élaborée et constitue le fondement nécessaire de l'intrigue. Cette dispute, ou discussion, s'élève à la cour d'un Prince sur la question de savoir si ce sont les hommes ou les femmes qui, les premiers, ont été infidèles. Pour y répondre, une expérience décisive est préparée depuis une vingtaine d'années: on a élevé des jeunes gens et des jeunes filles dans l'isolement le plus absolu depuis leur naissance, on les met en présence et ils jouent toutes les figures du sentiment marivaudien.

Ce postulat s'enracine dans la méditation, inlassablement reprise par les philosophes du dix-huitième siècle, sur l'instant premier, qui est aussi le lieu unique d'une vacance parfaite, grâce auquel on peut appréhender la situation de l'origine du monde, où des phénomènes vrais, non encore corrompus, peuvent apparaître dans la pureté; c'est un mythe de la primitivité.

Enfin, l'héroïne de *Félicie*, protégée par une Fée et accompagnée par La Modestie, est à son tour l'objet d'un conflit moral. Elle hésite entre le beau Lucidor et l'austère Diane, déesse de la vertu. Elle préfère Lucidor, mais la vertu l'emporte à la fin. On pourrait ajouter que pour les paysans naïfs des *Acteurs de bonne foi* le théâtre, dont ils ne comprennent pas toutes les implications, joue un rôle comparable à celui du mythe: s'imposant à eux par les prestiges de la cérémonie, il menace de prendre induement la place de la réalité.

Certes, dans cette dizaine de pièces qui doivent au mythe une partie essentielle de leur fond, sinon, pour les plus simples, la totalité de leur contenu, ne figurent pas les grandes œuvres de Marivaux. Leur nombre relativement important et la continuité du propos témoignent néanmoins de la profondeur de la préoccupation mythologique. Celle-ci s'exprime dès les modestes débuts et reste vivante jusqu'à la fin de la carrière dramatique.

Elle anime aussi plusieurs aspects d'œuvres de Marivaux plus réalistes que celles qui sont explicitement mythologiques en leur fournissant, surtout pendant les premières années, un personnage mythique, Arlequin, en qui convergent les deux objets principaux de la réflexion mythologique contemporaine, la recherche de la vérité et la recherche de la primitivité. Son originalité résulte de ce que sa fonction essentielle, dès l'*Arlequin poli* de 1720, est de dire la vérité et que, corrélativement, la vérité n'est bonne à dire que dans le mythe. Arlequin entraîne ainsi toute pièce où il figure efficacement dans un royaume de l'imaginaire. Son importance dans le théâtre de Marivaux ira en décroissant avec les années, mais il sera relayé par le mythe, plus didactique, de la primitivité.

Dans les grandes comédies dont le contenu réaliste est important, l'appel au mythe ne saurait être aussi direct que lorsqu'il suffit d'un événement imaginaire pour modifier du tout au tout la vie amoureuse, comme dans *La Dispute*, la vie sociale, comme dans *L'Ile des esclaves*, ou la vie politique, comme dans *La Colonie*. Il faudra alors disposer d'un instrument dramaturgique de relais, qui créera une situation mythique sans sortir, ou sans trop sortir, de la peinture juste du monde contemporain. Il s'agira de suspendre toute l'intrigue à la volonté d'un personnage puissant, mais bon, qui ne veut pas s'imposer et cherche à obtenir une solution acceptable pour tous. Alors que la méchante Fée d'*Arlequin poli par l'amour* est finalement vaincue, le Prince de *La Double Inconstance*, le père du *Jeu de l'amour et du hasard*, le Dorante des *Fausses Confidences*, le Lucidor de *L'Epreuve*, à la fois habiles et sincères, sont des créateurs de mythes privés. Sans bouleverser le monde par un coup de baguette magique, ils réalisent, par des moyens très simples qui prennent place aisément dans le cadre d'une maison seigneuriale ou même bourgeoise, ce miracle: diriger l'amour où il doit être dirigé.

Cette analyse, bien que nullement exhaustive, permet-elle de préciser, ce qui est le but de l'hommage rendu ici à William Howarth, le sens actuel de la notion de mythe? Il faut d'abord souligner que Marivaux est un mythologue singulièrement actif. Il déborde de beaucoup la définition, tournée vers le passé et non vers la création, du *Petit Larousse*: mythologue, savant qui étudie la mythologie. Cette définition implique que la mythologie est un corps de savoir déjà constitué, devant lequel on ne peut utiliser que l'observation, ou au mieux la réflexion, mais qui ne laisse aucune place à l'innovation. Pourtant, les mythes ont nécessairement eu des auteurs, même si la personnalité de ceux-ci se cache dans une époque très ancienne. Des commentateurs, des philosophes, des grammairiens, des écrivains variés ont, dans la Grèce antique, inventé ou modifié des mythes. Eschyle, Sophocle, étaient des mythologues. Marivaux aussi. Les définitions des grands dictionnaires courants ne sont pas non plus très éclairantes. Pour Littré, le mythe est un 'récit relatif à des temps ou à des faits que l'histoire n'éclaire pas et contenant, soit un fait réel transformé en notion religieuse, soit l'invention d'un fait à l'aide d'une idée'. Larousse dit du mythe: 'tradition qui, sous la figure de l'allégorie, laisse voir un grand fait naturel, historique ou philosophique'. Ces positions, lourdes de présupposés inexprimés, trahissent une certaine gêne vis-à-vis de l'histoire; or le mythe, et pas seulement celui de Marivaux, échappe au domaine historique. Et surtout, les hommes du dix-neuvième siècle ne comprenaient le mythe qu'au second degré. Il n'était que la traduction d'autre chose. Il fallait, derrière lui, retrouver le texte original, interpréter ou traduire, dégager un 'sens'. Plus opératoire, et plus proche de Marivaux, me semble la définition du mythe que donne Didier Anzieu dans son article

'Freud et la mythologie'.[1] Elle comprend quatre éléments. Le mythe est d'abord pour lui un récit composé d'un enchaînement de mythèmes, organisés dans une structure de discours. Si dans cette phrase nous remplacons *mythème* par *situation dramatique*, nous obtenons une excellente définition, non du théâtre, mais d'un ouvrage de littérature dramatique. On peut négliger le deuxième élément, qui constate que le mythe est indépendant des langues dans lesquelles il s'exprime. En troisième lieu, dit Anzieu, le mythe raconte des événements passés. Là est la différence la plus nette entre théâtre et mythe. Le théâtre est toujours au présent. Quatrièmement enfin, ce que raconte le mythe n'est ni histoire réelle ni pure fiction; c'est une histoire imaginaire, mais crédible et crue, et qui a une certaine part de vérité. J'ajouterais que cette *no man's land* entre vérité et imagination nous montre une fois de plus le chemin du théâtre. La notion de vrai–faux, que j'ai dégagée dans mon ouvrage *Dramaturgies d'Oedipe*, peut servir à désigner cette indécision. A partir de là, et en pensant à la variété des applications littéraires de la mythologie proposées par Marivaux, j'avancerais cette définition très générale du mythe, exempte du souci de traduire: récit, traditionnel ou inventé, dans lequel le personnage est plus qu'il ne semble être. Par cette puissance cachée, il peut décoller du réalisme et devenir exemplaire dans tous les domaines qu'on voudra. Il dispensera des leçons philosophiques, morales, sociales. Sa destinée semblera dotée d'un sens, bien que la critique échoue souvent à dire au juste quel est ce sens. Bref, il sera Arlequin, Plutus ou le Dorante des *Fausses confidences*.

NOTE

1 *Nouvelle Revue de psychanalyse*, I (1970), 124.

9

Fathers, good and bad, in Voltaire's *Mahomet*

HAYDN MASON

Of all Voltaire's tragedies, none ranked higher in the playwright's esteem, or in that of his contemporaries, than *Mahomet*. On few did he lavish so much care, making innumerable revisions between the original text, completed in March/April 1739, and the version put on at the Comédie-Française on 9 August 1742. Although it had to be withdrawn after only three performances because of its controversial nature, it briefly enjoyed greater success in its short run than had *Zaïre* or *Alzire*, and after its reinstatement at the Comédie-Française in 1751 it went on to establish itself as one of the most popular of all eighteenth-century tragedies.[1] A typically admiring reaction of the time was that of Diderot, who on several occasions refers to *Mahomet* as an incontrovertible model of literary excellence, describing it as 'un sublime ouvrage'[2] and 'un ouvrage de génie'.[3]

Voltaire's own deep attachment to the play is made manifest many times over in his correspondence. He considers it to be a bold new innovation, to the point of courting unpopularity. It is 'une pièce d'un genre si nouvau et si hazardé', and he wonders what success it will have 'chez nos galants Français'.[4] Two years later, the same point is being made: 'C'est un nouvau monde à défricher.'[5] Indeed, the assertion of its novelty is often reiterated during the years of composition and revision. The author is proud of his creation: 'Je commence à entrevoir que Mahomet sera sans aucune comparaison ce que j'auray fait de mieux . . .'[6] He is also deeply committed to it: 'Je travailleray dix ans à Mahomet s'il le faut. . .'[7] Though Voltaire was notoriously prejudiced in favour of his individual works at the time of composition, the repeatedly enthusiastic references and the very substantial amount of modification bear witness to an unusual degree of concern for the success of this tragedy.

The reasons for such commitment are not far to seek. For the playwright, the novelty of *Mahomet* lay in its subject: the destructive effect of religious zeal. One of his early letters about the play makes this clear: 'Je prends donc la liberté de lui [à Frédéric] envoyer ce premier acte d'une tragédie que me paraît, sinon dans un bon goût, au moins dans un goût nouveau. On n'avait jamais mis sur le théâtre la superstition et le fanatisme.'[8] The same claim to precedence in attacking superstition through tragedy is made to Frederick a few months later.[9] Long since appalled at the effects of unbridled fervour for a religious cause in instigating murders like those of Henri III and Henri IV by Jacques Clément and François Ravaillac respectively, Voltaire had finally decided to broach the topic openly on the stage. Some measure of religious intolerance had indeed been displayed already in *Zaïre*. But in that play the French nobles who represent such attitudes are shown to be also honourable, like Nérestan, or pathetic victims themselves of religious warfare, like Lusignan. Now, in *Mahomet*, all such reservations are removed: Voltaire wishes to convey the horror which he himself feels at such misdeeds. The 'Avis de l'éditeur' (composed by Voltaire) states the objective of the tragedy: 'C'est précisément contre les Ravaillac et les Jacques Clément que la pièce est composée . . .' and goes on to speak of 'l'horreur' which Voltaire inspires in all his writings 'contre les emportements de la rébellion, de la persécution, et du fanatisme'.[10] The same aim is announced in the *lettre ostensible* to Frederick of Prussia which Voltaire may at one point have intended as a dedicatory epistle at the head of the play: 'L'amour du genre humain, et l'horreur du fanatisme . . . ont conduit ma plume.'[11]

This preoccupation with the need to horrify his audience echoes throughout the dramatist's letters about *Mahomet*. Only by such shock tactics can people be made aware of the urgent need for free and critical enquiry and the avoidance of blind obedience. Voltaire's objective is to 'faire penser les hommes comm'ils pensent dans les circonstances où ils se trouvent, et représente[r] enfin ce que la fourberie peut inventer de plus atroce, et ce que le fanatisme peut exécuter de plus horrible . . .'. The author praises Molière's portrayal of hypocrisy in *Tartuffe* 'dans toute sa laideur', adding that 'Mahomet n'est icy autre chose que Tartuffe les armes à la main'. The playwright hopes that, dismayed at Séide's murderous act of submission to Mahomet's commands, the reader of his tragedy will be moved to ask himself 'pourquoy obéirais je en aveugle à des hommes aveugles qui me crient, haïssés, persécutés, perdés celui que est assés téméraire pour n'être pas de votre avis . . .'[12]

Since it was manifestly impossible to obtain official approval for putting on a play which would address itself directly to Catholic fanaticism, Voltaire was obliged to seek another creed for his purposes. Islam was to serve as a convenient substitute. The inspiration may have come from the coincidental fact that at the moment when Voltaire appears to have been thinking about his new play, he learned of the recent appearance of La Noue's *Mahomet second*, which immediately captured his interest.[13] But at the most the latter play could have provided only the idea of writing about Mohammed (*Mahomet second* did not reach Voltaire until he had virtually completed his own tragedy, and besides La Noue's play is of course about a much later and quite different historical figure). Voltaire could equally well have received the idea from the Marquis d'Argens's *Lettres juives*. For he had told d'Argens in 1737 that he had been reading the section of the *Lettres* relating to Clément and Ravaillac;[14] in that particular letter d'Argens makes an interesting conjunction (though in a quite different way from *Mahomet*) between religious fanatics like these, explicitly named, and the Moslem faith.[15] Or the notion may have occurred to Voltaire quite independently. He had already compared Christian and Moslem ways in *Zaïre* and drawn specific attention to it in one of the prefatory letters to that play.[16] As René Pomeau has pointed out, consciousness of Islam was in the forefront of European thinking in the early eighteenth century.[17] Voltaire himself, only some months before beginning work on *Mahomet*, had been reading with considerable admiration George Sale's edition and translation into English of the Koran.[18] The 'Preliminary Discourse' to that edition might well have supplied him with the source names for Séide, Phanor, Zopire and Omar[19] (even though he claims that Zopire is based on the historical Abusoftan, which is not incompatible).[20]

The fact that Voltaire for the most part in his works elsewhere refers to Mohammed favourably, in order to support his case for religious tolerance and deism,[21] is of no relevance here. Islam, on this occasion, serves the essential purpose of disguise, under which he can express himself freely about the dangers of the Catholic religion in which he was brought up. It is not the first such example in his writings. The Quakers had been employed, albeit more subtly, for similar ends in the third of his *Lettres philosophiques*. Indeed, George Fox and his followers are treated in not dissimilar language: 'Délivré de sa prison, il courut les champs avec une douzaine de

Prosélites, prêchant toujours contre le Clergé, & fouetté de tems en tems. Un jour étant mis au Pilori . . .'[22] As with Fox and his Quakers, Voltaire doubtless has Christ and his original disciples in mind in *Mahomet* also, which helps to account for the echoes of the *Lettres philosophiques*:

> Ses disciples errants de cités en deserts,
> Proscrits, persécutés, bannis, chargés de fers,
> Promènent leur 'fureur, qu'ils appellent divine. (I, iv)

Just as in the account of English Quakerism Voltaire asserts that 'l'Enthousiasme est une maladie qui se gagne',[23] so too the morbid image is repeated in the tragedy: 'De leurs venins bientôt ils infectent Médine' (I, iv).

But, whereas Fox was merely mad, Voltaire's Mahomet must be seen as truly menacing. So, to gain full effect, the author bases his plot on a theme which, as elsewhere in his writings (particularly in his poetry), touches a deep level of sensibility in him: the relationship between fathers and children, especially sons. This phenomenon, with its effects upon Voltaire's religious views (not wholly appreciated until the appearance of M. Pomeau's epochal work *La Religion de Voltaire* in 1956), has latterly received careful attention in two fertile and imaginative studies. A brilliant reading of Voltaire's first play *Oedipe* by J.-M. Moureaux has brought out the extent to which the character Philoctète, created by Voltaire as an extension of the Oedipus myth, demonstrates the playwright's concern with flight and freedom from the father-figure:[24] 'Reste probablement chevillée, au plus profond de l'inconscient de Voltaire, la hantise de ce jugement du père condamnant sans appel et qui, à un autre niveau de lecture, s'appellera l'angoisse du Dieu terrible et de la prédestination qu'il impose.'[25] Following an independent but similar line, M. Pomeau has examined the 'présence du thème père–fils' in other plays by Voltaire, most notably *Brutus* (1730) and *La Mort de César* (1731). Careful to avoid the charge of amateur psychoanalysis, the critic nonetheless demonstrates convincingly the importance of this theme in the plays considered. It is particularly striking in *La Mort de César*, where the playwright, taking his inspiration from Shakespeare's *Julius Caesar*, adds an entirely personal drama that is his own invention, including a case of double paternity in which 'le père putatif occulte le père réel'. Furthermore, the first Shakespeare play to have evoked a response from Voltaire, only a few months after his arrival in England, was *Hamlet* – where the filial relationship is of central concern.[26]

Fathers in Voltaire's *Mahomet*

It is now well known that Voltaire regarded himself as the natural son not of François Arouet but of a certain Rochebrune, with whom the young writer was closely acquainted up to the latter's death in 1719. As M. Pomeau has shown in his recent biography of Voltaire's early years, this hypothesis cannot be excluded, even though we have no conclusive evidence in its favour.[27] But whatever the truth may have been, it is at least clear that these views involved him in a complicated filial relationship, where dislike of his official father was paramount.

Following M. Pomeau's own prudence on the subject, it would be wise not to embark upon the risky business of attempting to define Voltaire's psychological outlook in these matters. Let us rather address ourselves to the greater assurance provided by the text of *Mahomet*. For even the most cursory reading of the play reveals that its author's concern with paternal identities, so strongly expressed already in earlier plays like *Oedipe* and *La Mort de César*, is equally evident here. The four central characters, comprising two 'fathers' and two sibling children, are viewed within a relationship of growing intensity.

Zopire, the true and natural father, is also for most of the play the clandestine father. Once again 'le père réel est occulté'. Zopire's children were taken from him while still young; he yearns for their return, if only to embrace them on his deathbed − a wish that is to be granted in savagely ironic fashion after his son has inflicted the murderous blow. When he meets Séide and Palmire, all his instincts incline Zopire to care for them. Before he knows the truth of their origins, he begins to suspect that his concern surpasses ordinary affection:

> Hélas! plus je lui [à Séide] parle, et plus il m'intéresse:
> Son âge, sa candeur, ont surpris ma tendresse.
> Se peut-il qu'un soldat de ce monstre imposteur
> Ait trouvé malgré lui le chemin de mon cœur?
> (*A Séide*)
> Quel es-tu? de quel sang les dieux t'ont-ils fait naître? (III, viii)

By the end of Act III he has decided that, whatever the relationship between them, he wishes to intervene:

> Dieux, rendez-moi mes fils! dieux, rendez aux vertus
> Deux cœurs nés généreux, qu'un traître a corrompus!
> S'ils ne sont point à moi, si telle est ma misère,
> Je les veux adopter, je veux être leur père. (III, xi)

As in *Brutus*, as in *La Mort de César*, as in *Zaïre*, the mother is absent. Her absence here serves only to heighten the pathos, as she has been killed in the fighting with Mahomet. The emphasis therefore falls unreservedly upon the father. Besides, Zopire is a father not only to his children but to the citizens of Mecca. Phanor makes this point explicitly to Zopire at the outset of the play:

> Nous chérissons en vous ce zèle paternel
> Du chef auguste et saint du sénat d'Ismaël.　　(I, i)

Indeed, as Phanor goes on to underline, now that Zopire has apparently lost all his family, he owes it to the State to channel his paternal feelings in that direction:

> Vous avez tout perdu, fils, frère, épouse, fille;
> Ne perdez point l'Etat: c'est là votre famille.　　*(ibid.)*

But Zopire will not be swayed from what he considers the path of duty by any such appeal, whether (as here) on behalf of his 'family' of Mecca or, as later, when his own children are involved. Mahomet goes on to reveal that they are still alive. But Zopire's joy is quickly dashed when Mahomet indicates the price to be paid for their return: 'il faut m'aider à tromper l'univers' (II, v). Zopire has already made clear that he would sacrifice his own life and liberty for them; but he will not acquiesce in Mahomet's demands:

> Mahomet, je suis père, et je porte un cœur tendre.
> Après quinze ans d'ennuis, retrouver mes enfants,
> Les revoir, et mourir dans leurs embrassements,
> C'est le premier des biens pour mon âme attendrie:
> Mais s'il faut à ton culte asservir ma patrie,
> Ou de ma propre main les immoler tous deux;
> Connais-moi, Mahomet, mon choix n'est pas douteux.
> Adieu.　　(II. v.)

The 'Adieu' is definitive, followed by Zopire's immediate exit, and any hope, however faint, of a compromise is at an end. Zopire and Mahomet have exchanged their last words with each other.

One curious aspect of Zopire's past needs, however, to be added to this otherwise saintly portrait. It emerges in the very first scene of the play that Mahomet too has lost a son. Worse, Zopire is his murderer. This seems a strange anomaly, on the part of one who still does not hesitate to tell Mahomet 'Ton nom seul parmi nous divise les familles' (II, v). Why this gratuitous detail? Not, certainly, to contrast Zopire's remorse with Mahomet's implacable hostility as one might have expected; for Zopire shows no regret at what he has done. Voltaire wishes rather to stress from the outset, it seems, that all possibility of reconciliation between them has disappeared:

> Le cruel fit périr ma femme et mes enfants:
> Et moi, jusqu'en son camp j'ai porté le carnage;
> La mort de son fils même honora mon courage.
> Les flambeaux de la haine entre nous allumés
> Jamais des mains du temps ne seront consumés. (I, i)

> Dans le cours de la guerre un funeste destin
> Le priva de son fils que fit périr ma main.
> Mon bras perça le fils, ma voix bannit le père;
> Ma haine est inflexible, ainsi que sa colère. (I, iv)

To Zopire's way of thinking, reciprocal hatred has been established definitively between the two fathers:

> Réponds, est-ce ton fils que mon bras te ravit?
> Est-ce le sang des miens que ta main répandit? (II, v)

Later, it becomes clear that Mahomet's desire for revenge is as strong as Zopire's:

> Je déteste Séide, et son nom seul m'offense;
> La cendre de mon fils me crie encor vengeance. (II, vi)

But in the interview with Zopire he seems ready to subordinate these feelings to collaboration with his enemy, if the latter is willing to serve his evil designs. Is this yet one more indication of how unnatural he is, compared with Zopire's straightforward expressions of hostility at filial loss? For Voltaire at no point permits any sympathy to be felt for this monster, even though as a father he has suffered as has Zopire.

The contrast between the two fathers is indeed total. Mahomet has brought up Séide and Palmire, but no bond of affection has resulted from it, only deep antipathy:

> De mes deux ennemis apprends tous les forfaits:
> Tous deux sont nés ici du tyran que je hais.
> . . .
> J'ai nourri dans mon sein ces serpents dangereux;
> Déjà sans se connaître ils m'outragent tous deux. (II, iv)

As we have seen, his detestation of Séide knows no limits: 'son nom seul m'offense' (II, vi). The relationship with Palmire is necessarily different since he lusts after her, preferring her to his wives and eventually offering her a place alongside him (V, ii: whether as wife or as concubine is unclear). But he feels no more tenderness for her than for Séide, and he deceives her as totally as he betrays her brother. Both have been reared by him, but as slaves, totally in his power:

> Elevés dans mon camp, tous deux sont dans ma chaîne.
> . . .
> Je tiens entre mes mains et leur vie et leur mort. (II, v)

As we have seen, Zopire accuses him of dividing families asunder:

> Ton nom seul parmi nous divise les familles,
> Les époux, les parents, les mères et les filles. (*ibid*.)

There seems to be some evidence for this: Séide and Zopire are but two of the captive children 'Qu'en tribut à mon maître on offre tous les ans' (III, viii). The others have been brought up in similar fashion, to give unquestioning obedience to Mahomet:

> Parmi tous ces enfants enlevés par Hercide,
> Qui, fermés sous ton joug, et nourris dans ta loi,
> N'ont de dieu que le tien, n'ont de père que toi. (II, iv)

Predictably, Mahomet rejects the natural law underlying familial relationships, adhering to a doctrine that appears ominously materialistic:

> Les cris du sang, sa force, et ses impressions,
> Des cœurs toujours trompés sont les illusions.
> La nature à mes yeux n'est rien que l'habitude. (IV, i)

In consequence, Zopire's children have lived in a state of psychological alienation, as they are well aware. Palmire expresses it openly to Zopire early on:

> Nous ne connaissons point l'orgueil de la naissance;
> Sans parents, sans patrie, esclaves dès l'enfance,
> Dans notre égalité nous chérissons nos fers;
> Tout nous est étranger, hors le dieu que je sers. (I, ii)

Séide echoes these sentiments later on, in characteristically more naive terms:

Fathers in Voltaire's *Mahomet*

Je n'ai point de parents, seigneur, je n'ai qu'un maître,
Que jusqu'à ce moment j'avais toujours servi
. . .
Son camp fut mon berceau; son temple est ma patrie:
Je n'en connais point d'autre . . .   (III, viii)

Despite the 'clémence' which he has enjoyed from Mahomet, the essentially abnormal nature of the situation emerges from his words as from Palmire's.

The predisposition to fanaticism is thus grounded in the isolated life which these virtual orphans have been leading for fifteen years and in the state of servitude which Mahomet and the couple are all agreed in recognizing to be their lot. Not surprisingly, therefore, when they are exposed to Zopire's humanitarian feelings for them, both children are touched deeply. Palmire has been moved by her father's kindness before the action of the play begins:

Mon penchant, je l'avoue, et ma reconnaissance,
Vous donnaient sur mon cœur une juste puissance.   (I, ii)

Similarly, when later Séide meets Zopire he is surprised and troubled by the new tone, to which he is a complete stranger: 'Que ce langage est cher à mon cœur combattu!' (III, viii). He has to confess that he cannot find it in himself to hate Zopire (or indeed anyone else) as he had been instructed to do by Mahomet, and Zopire recognizes the tumult going on within him:

D'où vient que tu frémis, et que ton cœur soupire?
Tu détournes de moi ton regard égaré;
De quelque grand remords tu sembles déchiré.   (III, viii)

But it is characteristic of Voltaire's pessimistic outlook in this tragedy about the power of fanaticism that for neither Palmire nor Séide will the claims of humanity triumph. Palmire's own hesitations come to a climax in a soliloquy where she speaks of the fear and mistrust that assail her:

Tout m'est suspect ici; Zopire m'intimide.
J'invoque Mahomet, et cependant mon cœur
Eprouve à son nom même une secrète horreur.
Dans les profonds respects que ce héros m'inspire,
Je sens que je le crains presque autant que Zopire. (III, ii)

Yet one interview with Mahomet is enough to resolve her doubts completely. By the end of the following scene, not only is she quite

won over by his blandishments; she is confidently promising him
to deliver Séide in a state of total obedience:

> N'en doutez point, mon père, il les [les serments] remplira tous:
> Je réponds de son cœur, ainsi que de moi-même. (III, iii)

What can explain such a radical change of outlook in such a
short time? In *Mahomet*, nothing less than the central protagonist's
unswerving claims to absolute authority over Palmire. He demands
that she put him unequivocally ahead of any feelings she has for
Séide. He warns her ominously of the dread she will feel on hearing
the secrets he must reveal to her. Finally, he reassures her am-
biguously that if she trusts in him she will be rewarded. It is the
language of obscurantist totalitarianism. Faced with it, Palmire,
already weakened through fifteen years of psychological
dependence upon Mahomet, makes an unconditional surrender.

The same brutal treatment is meted out to Séide. At the merest
hint of hesitation when he is told he must kill Zopire, Mahomet
turns upon him his most thunderous tones. Contempt and anger
are visited upon any attempt, however feeble, at independent exercise of thought and will:

> Téméraire,
> On devient sacrilège alors qu'on délibère.
> Loin de moi les mortels assez audacieux
> Pour juger par eux-mêmes, et pour voir par leurs yeux!
> Quiconque ose penser n'est pas né pour me croire.
> Obéir en silence est votre seule gloire. (III, vi)

Mahomet cites as an exemplary response to God's wishes that terrible instance of fatherly submission in the Old Testament where
Abraham, 'Etouffant pour son dieu les cris de la nature', stood
ready to obey God in sacrificing his only son, Isaac. The presence
of Abraham's tomb in Mecca is invoked to break Séide's will,
much as Lusignan used the setting of Jerusalem, the place of
Christ's death, to convert Zaïre. But, whereas in *Zaïre* Lusignan is
pathetic as well as cruel, old and dying as well as insensitive to
Zaïre's plight, here Mahomet is acting out of utter ruthlessness.
Séide's response is pathetically predictable: 'Je crois entendre Dieu;
tu parles: j'obéis' (*ibid.*).

It is this conjunction of paternal and divine authority that
Séide finds overbearing. Mahomet's charisma is not entirely to be
explained in psychological analysis. Mahomet overwhelms Séide

because he has yoked his power to divine omnipotence in claiming to speak as the prophet of the Almighty:

> Savez-vous qui je suis? Savez-vous en quels lieux
> Ma voix vous a chargé des volontés des cieux?   (*ibid.*)

Only adoration will suffice, and that is already present in Séide's attitude, as Palmire has told Mahomet:

> Séide vous adore encor plus qu'il ne m'aime;
> Il voit en vous son roi, son père, son appui.   (III, iv)

Palmire's words indicate that, while Séide feels filial respect for Mahomet, his attitude is also allied to a transcendental authority. Séide has already given evidence of it: 'O mon père! ô mon roi!' (II, iii). No others amongst the abducted children, Omar tells Mahomet, were as submissive as these two. So much docile credulousness, fostered and manipulated by Mahomet, will in the end be enough to lead to murder.

Thus the stage is set for the climactic scenes in Act IV, which Voltaire looked upon as 'le seul moyen de pousser . . . la terreur et la tendresse à son comble . . .'.[28] In a dialogue of collective bad faith, Séide and Palmire nudge each other towards the terrible deed that neither might have been able to achieve alone. Séide is inspired by the notion that Zopire, praying alone at the altar, is blaspheming, and begins to enter into a hypnotic trance of frenzied zeal:

> Ne vois-tu pas dans ces demeures sombres
> Ces traits de sang, ce spectre, et ces errantes ombres?   (IV, iv)

Palmire tries to stop him, but half-heartedly and too late. When Séide goes out to commit the act, she takes refuge in fatalism: 'Si le ciel veut un meurtre, est-ce à moi d'en juger?' (*ibid.*). Séide stabs Zopire and returns in an *état second* not unworthy of Diderot in *La Religieuse*. It is perhaps the most dramatically powerful scene in the whole of Voltaire's theatre.

But the dramatist reduces its force by the following scene, where Zopire survives anti-climactically rather too long for *vraisemblance*. This scene is, however, necessary if father and children are to appreciate the nature of their relationship and the full horror of Séide's action. Palmire, in acknowledging her responsibility, realizes a further terrible truth, that the reward she was awaiting in marriage to Séide would have been incest. Here

Voltaire exploits to the full his capacity for evoking horror, following to some extent the example of Crébillon in *Atrée et Thyeste*[29] and, like Crébillon, risking the danger of toppling over into melodrama. What, however, is significant for present purposes is that, though now made fully aware of Séide's murderous aims, Zopire dies reconciled with his children. As in *Brutus* and *La Mort de César*, where, respectively, father kills son and son kills father, reconciliation and resignation attenuate the cruelty.[30] In the end the good father drives out the bad, but at the cost of his own life and of yielding up all power to his enemy.

For in *Mahomet* the play does not end in reconciliation. The God of humanity and nature in whom Zopire believes does not triumph over the God of cruelty, deceit and blind submission. Both Séide and Palmire recognize their error too late. The poison already circulating in Séide's veins is symbolic as well as literal. He is destroyed by his act of destruction. His desire for vengeance over Mahomet, even had it been successful, could never have erased the atrocity of his fanatical deed. Voltaire is now more deeply aware of the negative spirit in human nature which can be placed, in suitable circumstances, at the disposal of tyrants hungry for power. So long as human beings subordinate secular to transcendental values, so long will credulousness hold out against rational persuasion. Mahomet, in the final scene, reminds his hearers that he will punish them 'd'avoir osé douter': the very phrase Voltaire had attributed to Locke in the *Lettres philosophiques*. In the world of *Mahomet*, there is no hope of an early change to the empirical spirit that had characterized the English thinker.

Mahomet himself is a commanding figure, but he lacks subtlety to the point of being virtually implausible. Did Voltaire come eventually to appreciate that the play he had written was not the one he might ideally have wished to write? It is certainly the case that, during the long period of revision, he recognized that 'Mahomet n'est pas le rôle intéressant'.[31] By now he wants to give the tragedy another title;[32] a few months later he goes further, telling Mlle Quinault that the new title should be *Séide*.[33] This is a striking change of heart. Evidently he had come to appreciate where for him the true dramatic centre lay: 'C'est un jeune homme né avec de la vertu, qui séduit par son fanatisme, assassine un vieillard qui l'aime, et qui dans l'idée de servir dieu se rend coupable sans le savoir d'un parricide; c'est un imposteur qui ordonne ce meurtre, et qui promet à l'assassin un inceste pour récompense.'[34] In this synopsis the role of Mahomet no longer holds first place. The accent is now firmly placed upon the son and his intolerable dilemma, in being driven to kill his true father. It was of course too late to turn *Mahomet* into *Séide*. Even by such simple criteria as the number of spoken lines and the amount of time on stage, the young fanatic lags well behind both Mahomet and Zopire. For most of the play he is amiable, but credulous, bewildered and passive. Only in Act IV does he come into his own. The only practical modification Voltaire could make was to amend the title to *Le Fanatisme, ou Mahomet le prophète*, which became the definitive one. In order to give Act IV its full value, the dramatist had to wrestle with the dangers of anti-climax in Act V. This final act was the cause of much trouble and dissatisfaction to him; as he put it, 'Le cinquième acte m'a fait suer sang et eau . . .'[35] In its final form it still remains somewhat slight, and it is by far the briefest in the play. Yet this was a necessary price to pay, because 'c'est le seul moyen de pousser dans cet acte [le 4ᵉ] la terreur et la tendresse à son comble . . .'.[36]

Had Voltaire set out from the start to compose *Séide*, the history of Voltairean tragedy could well read very differently. The potential alliance of a fervent attack on religious oppression with the mythical theme of fathers and sons leaves one regretful for what might have been. Behind Séide and his cruel master one can descry the lineaments of the terrible God-tyrant, in whose name Mahomet orders Séide to commit murder: the divine 'father' who had commanded Abraham's sacrifice, and for whom even Mahomet too feels only fear, as he admits in his final speech. On his side, the natural father Zopire prays to his own gods, the gods of mercy. They avail him nothing. As Séide confesses to Palmire, he does not understand

> Comment ce dieu si bon, ce père des humains,
> Pour un meurtre effroyable a réservé mes mains. (IV, iii)

It is the essential question of evil that Voltaire will never cease to pose of an incomprehensible universe. Here it is conceived within the dominant structure of paternity, true and false. *Mahomet* is not a masterpiece. Nonetheless, there are powerfully dramatic elements here which place it alongside *Zaïre* as his very best achievement on stage. Those elements derive their force from the father–son theme that could still, even in the early 1740s, serve as the essential channel through which to *écraser l'infâme*.

NOTES

1 Cf. C. Alasseur, *La Comédie Française au 18ᵉ siècle: Etude économique* (Paris, 1967), pp. 139–40; H. C. Lancaster, *French Tragedy in the time of Louis XV and Voltaire, 1715–1774*, 2 vols. (Baltimore, 1950), I, 209–10.

2 *Le Neveu de Rameau*, in *Oeuvres complètes*, ed. R. Lewinter, 15 vols. (Paris, 1969–73), x, 342.

3 *Essai sur les règnes de Claude et de Néron, ibid.*, XII, 683.

4 D 2040, to Helvétius, 6 July 1739: all references to Voltaire's correspondence will be to *The Complete Works of Voltaire*, ed. T. Besterman *et al.* (Geneva, Banbury and Oxford), LXXXV–CXXXV (1968–77), designating the letter by D and number.

5 D 2515, to Cideville, 19 July 1741.

6 D 2267, to d'Argental, 12 July 1740.

7 D 2259, to Mlle Quinault, 3 July 1740.

8 D 2048, to Frederick, Crown Prince of Prussia [*c*. 20 July 1739].

9 D 2106 [*c*. 1 Nov. 1739].

10 *Oeuvres complètes*, ed. L. Moland, 52 vols. (Paris, 1877–85), IV, 99. All references to *Mahomet* will be to this edition.

11 D 2386, 20 [Dec.] 1740.

12 *Ibid.*

13 Cf., e.g., D 1917, 1923, 1927, 1946, 1956, all written between 28 Feb. and 26 Mar. 1739.

14 D 1271, 28 Jan. [1737].

15 *Lettres juives*, 6 vols. (The Hague, 1737), I, 209 and n.

16 *Zaïre*, ed. E. Jacobs (London, 1975), p. 76.

17 *La Religion de Voltaire*, new edn (Paris, 1974), p. 146.

18 D 1588, to Thieriot, 14 Aug. [1738].

19 'He [Mohammed] soon made proselytes of those under his own roof, *viz.* . . . his servant Zeid Ebn Hâretha . . . [Mohammed] prevailed also on *Othmân Ebn Affân* . . . al *Zobeir Ebn al Awâm* . . . all principal men in *Mecca*, to follow his example': *The Koran* (London, 1734), p. 43. '*Mohammed* sent one of his disciples, named *Masáb Ebn Omair* home with them, to instruct them more fully in the grounds and ceremonies of his new religion' (*ibid.*, p. 47).

20 D 2392, to Frederick II, 31 Dec. 1740. Cf., however, other sources also used by Voltaire: Pomeau, *La Religion de Voltaire*, pp. 150–1.

21 Cf. Pomeau, *La Religion de Voltaire*, pp. 157–8.

22 *Lettres philosophiques*, ed. G. Lanson, rev. A. M. Rousseau, 2 vols. (Paris, 1964), I, 33.

23 *Ibid.*

24 'L'*Oedipe* de Voltaire: introduction à une psycholecture', *Archives des lettres modernes*, CXLVI (1973), 55–6.

25 *Ibid.*, pp. 87–8.

26 R. Pomeau, 'Voltaire et Shakespeare: du Père justicier au Père assassiné', in *Mélanges offerts au Professeur René Fromilhague, Littératures* (Toulouse, 1984), pp. 99–106.

27 R. Pomeau, *D'Arouet à Voltaire: 1694–1734* (Oxford, 1985), pp. 17–27.

28 D 2160, to Mlle Quinault, 4 Feb. [1740].

29 The similarity was noted by at least one contemporary: cf. D 2635, Le Blanc to Bouhier, 13 Aug. 1742. In both plays demands are made of a young person to murder someone known to him; in both the would-be killer changes from complete obedience to horror when the victim is named. But Voltaire adds to this situation the religious discussion of fanaticism, which does not appear in Crébillon's tragedy.

30 Cf. Pomeau, 'Voltaire et Shakespeare'.

31 D 2200, to Mlle Quinault, 19 Apr. [1740].

32 *Ibid.*

33 D 2259, 3 July 1740.

34 D 2386, 20 [Dec.] 1740.

35 D 2218, to Mlle Quinault, 3 June 1740; cf. also D 2149, 2154, 2158, 2160, 2266, 2267.

36 D 2160, to Mlle Quinault, 4 Feb. [1740].

10

From Raynal's 'new Spartacus' to Lamartine's *Toussaint Louverture*: a myth of the black soul in rebellion

E. FREEMAN

In any study of mythopoeia in French culture, the Romantic period, as in other countries, proves to be particularly fertile.[1] Love, Genius, Art, Nature, Paris, Revolution, the People, some of them inherited from ancient, medieval and Renaissance culture and refurbished, others a direct product of the events of 1789 to 1830, are among the many myths that find their expression in a number of major works of the period: *Les Méditations poétiques, Notre Dame de Paris, Episode de la vie d'un artiste, La Liberté guidant le peuple, La Confession d'un enfant du siècle, Le Rouge et le Noir, Chronique de 1830, Illusions perdues, On ne badine pas avec l'amour.* The title may, as in some of these cases, produce a thematic resonance of a fairly explicit sort. Or it may be enough to name the ego, often assuming mythic proportions in itself, that dominates the work; this is particularly the case in the theatre: *Hernani, Lorenzaccio, Antony, Chatterton, Caligula, Lucrèce Borgia.* And in at least one play of substance the techniques are combined: *Kean, ou Désordre et génie.*

Anyone examining the process whereby the raw material of personal experience (Lamartine's relationship with Mme Julie Charles), history (the brief life of Lorenzo de' Medici), or inherited literary theme (fated illicit love as in *Antony* or *Ruy Blas*) is transmuted into literary or dramatic myth can detect a number of common denominators in the more famous, or notorious, works of the period. Historical fact, where inconvenient, may be overlooked or flatly contradicted. Would England's Protector recognize himself in Hugo's Oliver Cromwell of 1827? Even more are the squalid last hours of the real Thomas Chatterton, dying of arsenic in his own vomit and almost certainly suffering from venereal disease, transformed into a metaphysical doom, a myth of martyrized genius to which a succession of artist–poets will subscribe during the rest of the century. And the example of Tebaldeo, the

136

naively idealistic artist in Musset's *Lorenzaccio*, will help us to realize that even that much-admired work, usually considered to be one of the most authentic evocations of a long past era, is more a skilful transposition of French Romantic complexes of the 1830s to a radically different Florentine world of three centuries earlier. Rhetorical enhancement of the moral and physical status of the hero – despite the fact that Lorenzo has a 'petit corps chétif' and Chatterton is also unimpressive – is an essential feature of this process. Hugo and Balzac are even more ostentatiously rhetorical in their exploitation of this paradox as a mythopoeic technique. As a common man on the lowest rung of the social ladder at a time when youth opportunities for Spanish lackeys are not highly developed, Ruy Blas possesses a greatness of soul – sufficient for the Queen of Spain, a married woman, to fall in love with him – in inverse proportion to the humbleness of his origins, as does Quasimodo in relation to his physical repulsiveness. Similarly the senile pauper Goriot, who exults in the adultery that he has beggared himself to finance for his own daughter, is deemed by Balzac, in an epithet as remarkable in its hyperbole as it is lacking in taste, to be a 'Christ de la paternité'. Elsewhere he employs this same rhetorical device, antonomasia, to dub Rubempré and Mme de Bargeton the Petrarch and Laura, Dante and Beatrice, and (separately) Byron and Corinne of Angoulême. At various times he presses into service Napoleon, Cromwell, Don Juan, Lady Macbeth and many others in case the reader is not sufficiently impressed by the actions alone of characters such as Gaudissart, Vautrin, Gobseck, Mme Cibot, etc.

Alphonse de Lamartine is the earliest French Romantic to use illustrious antecedents as an important part of the mythopoeic process. In 1817, simply by literary association rather than by the antonomasia wielded as a blunt instrument by Balzac, he calls forth Propertius' Cynthia, Petrarch's Laura and Tasso's Leonora to immortalize his composite 'Elvire'. She is mainly the provincial doctor's wife, Mme Julie Charles, as is well known, but other liaisons of the same period benefit from the same grandiose enhancement:

> Oui, l'Anio murmure encore
> Le doux nom de Cynthie aux roches de Tibur,
> Vaucluse a retenu le nom chéri de Laure,
> Et Ferrare au siècle futur
> Murmurera toujours celui d'Eléonore!
> Heureuse la beauté que le poète adore![2]

A name-change is part of the process: thus does the Neapolitan girl become 'Elvire' (she is also the later Graziella); for Lamartine it is both discreet enough and mythic to be 'le poète'. Though in this appropriation to himself of the privileged status, he eschews the capital letter sometimes affected by Vigny, the *sententia* of the last line is nevertheless testimony to the striving for lapidary permanence.

The play by Lamartine that I propose to examine within the terms of reference of this Festschrift, however, is not his *Saül*, dating from this period (1818) but admitted by him to be a 'froid pastiche de Racine et d'Alfieri'.[3] It is a work from a very different period of his life and in a very different vein: the heroic melodrama *Toussaint Louverture*, begun in 1839 and finished and performed in 1850 after the end of the Romantic era. Professor Howarth has argued in his necessarily brief examination of the play in *Sublime and Grotesque* (p. 348) that *Toussaint Louverture* in purely dramatic terms is a 'noble failure' (and Lamartine himself thought no more of it than he did of *Saül*). Undoubtedly the established names in French Romantic drama have left us with rather better plays by most norms of dramaturgy (but in some cases not much better). Yet perhaps it is Lamartine who reveals himself to have possessed a more original idea of what the theatre could be used for, and at the very least a less egocentric moral sensitivity, than Hugo, Musset, Dumas and Vigny, in elaborating a myth of rebellion in the black soul, rejection of the slave condition and mentality, and national regeneration through heroic action. As I hope to show, he anticipates by a hundred years – if in some cases only in fleeting perceptions – many of the views of Césaire, Senghor, Fanon and Sartre on precisely these subjects.

New World inhabitants of European descent lavish their attention on George Washington or Simon Bolivar as their heroes of continental independence. Yet the feat achieved by the black slave Toussaint Louverture was in many respects far more remarkable. As the leader of the only successful slave rebellion in history, he brought the rich French colony of Saint-Domingue, *la perle des Antilles*, to the brink of independence as the black republic of Haiti. He thus appeared to have answered the call for a 'Spartacus nouveau' made in 1770 by the Abbé Raynal in his highly influential anti-colonial and anti-slavery work of the Enlightenment, *Histoire philosophique et politique du commerce et des établissements des Européens dans les deux Indes*. John Morley in 1878, with what proof it is not too clear, believed that Toussaint in fact had read Raynal's immense work: 'Black Toussaint Louverture in his slave-cabin at Hayti laboriously spelled his way through its pages.'[4] The French source used by Lamartine for his play, General Ramel, who had been one of the participants in the conflict, stated that Toussaint Louverture 'croit fermement qu'il est l'homme annoncé par l'abbé Raynal, qui doit surgir un jour pour briser les fers des noirs'.[5]

Saint-Domingue was the western third of the large island 'discovered' for Europe by Columbus in December 1492. Hispaniola, as the island was at first called, was much disputed by the Spanish, French and British in the seventeenth century, before, as Saint-Domingue, it was won by the French from the Spanish in 1659 and developed as a classic negro slave colony thereafter. When Toussaint Bréda was born in the colony in 1746, it was in the process of becoming the most profitable European colony anywhere. Thanks to the prodigious fertility of its soil, Saint-Domingue produced sugar in quantities and at prices that British planters, notably in nearby Jamaica, despaired of trying to match. By 1789 it is estimated that the colony supplied half of Europe with sugar, cotton and indigo and accounted for something like half of all the foreign trade of France. The decade before the Revolution was particularly a boom time, with coffee production rising dramatically to come close to rivalling sugar in importance, although traditionally in the imagination of the general public – 'mythically', as one might say – the colony is associated almost exclusively with sugar. So too at this time did the annual number of imported slaves rise dramatically, to about forty thousand a year, as slave deaths far outnumbered births. On the eve of the Revolution the population consisted of some forty thousand whites, planters, *petits blancs* and (much resented) Paris-recruited officials, approximately half a million black slaves, and – constituting an increasingly sensitive and ambiguous class between them – some thirty thousand mulattoes. As R. and N. Heinl have observed, pointing out that in 1783 the Marquis du Rouvray compared the colony to a barrel of gunpowder primed to explode,

As the eighteenth century drew to a close, St-Domingue, for all its opulence, was a sick society at war with itself. The slaves mutely endured hideous grievances; the *affranchis* were systematically denied basic rights and freedoms theirs in law, and the white *colons* bickered selfishly, or blindly devoted themselves to the pursuit of wealth or pleasure.[6]

The French Revolution was the obvious spark that ignited the barrel, and it is perhaps not altogether surprising that it was the mulattoes who were the first to rebel, fruitlessly as it turned out. As a coachman on a plantation owned by the relatively enlightened Bréda family — established blacks usually graduated from the plantations to domestic work in their owners' households — Toussaint had far less to resent than most Saint-Domingue black slaves. Despite the claims by Morley and others that he was inspired by reading *L'Histoire des deux Indes*, Toussaint was not involved in the insurrection from the earliest moments and did more than a little to protect his master's family and property. The pattern of antagonisms and allegiances during the chaotic years 1791–1801 was in fact very complex. The French themselves were divided politically and socially. The plantation owners were for the most part counter-revolutionary, and detested the Republican commissioners after 1794 as much as they despised the mulattoes and feared the blacks. Nor were racial and ideological issues simple for the latter. Some mulattoes were richer and more educated than *petits blancs*, owned slaves and opposed emancipation, formed their own regiments and occasionally found themselves fighting whites and blacks at the same time. The conflict was thus anything but a straightforward one between white French planter and black slave. This consideration will be of some importance when we come to assess *Toussaint Louverture* as an example of French Romantic theatre, one of the most persistent criticisms of which is that moral issues are simplified in the extreme into a Manichaean division between villains and victims. In short, in the critical terminology which is sadly ironic in the present context, this theatre is often considered to be vitiated by its 'black and white' characterization.

The play that Lamartine has constructed against this ten-year-long backdrop of constantly shifting allegiances, chaos and suffering is a very substantial five-act work of approximately 2650 alexandrines (that is, considerably longer than a seventeenth-century tragedy by Corneille or Racine). The play begins in the last days of December 1801 at a time when, within the colony at least, Toussaint is the undisputed leader of Saint-Domingue, having fought successfully with the Republican and Directoire forces against the Royalist planters in alliance with the large British expeditionary force that occupied the territory from 1793 to 1798.[7] Lamartine has chosen a historical moment of maximum tension in which to situate the plot of the play. Bonaparte, now

140

First Consul, has despatched a large invasion force of twenty thousand men to re-establish French control over the colony and, it is feared, to restore slavery. Without consulting the French, Toussaint has virtually declared Saint-Domingue, rebaptized Haiti, independent with the proclamation of a constitution on 7 July 1801. The crisis is the centre of the plot of the play: will Toussaint accept the bland reassurances of Bonaparte and submit to the re-colonization of Haiti?

Lamartine states in his 1850 preface that it had been his intention to write not a literary work but a political one, 'ou plutôt, c'était un cri d'humanité en cinq actes et en vers'. Still adhering reasonably to the historical facts that could have been known to him in the 1840s, Lamartine has found the means of intensifying the Haitian leader's public crisis by weaving into the plot a private dilemma of the classic sort. The leader of the expeditionary force, General Leclerc, has brought with him not only his wife, who is Bonaparte's sister Pauline, but Toussaint's two adolescent sons. Toussaint had voluntarily sent them to France some five years earlier as hostages and pledges of his loyalty to the mother country that had abolished slavery. The changes of detail as regards the boys' names and ages are minor.[8] In the play the elder, Albert, on being united with his father turns out to have been impressed by his experiences in France, and declares that he will not take up arms against the Europeans who have treated him so well. Isaac, however, is faithful to his father's race and cause. Previously Toussaint has feared for their safety in the classic dramatic terms of the appalling choice:

> Liberté de ma race, es-tu donc à ce prix,
> Que pour sauver mon peuple, il faut perdre mes fils?
> Que pour sauver mes fils, il faut perdre ma race? . . .

Formulated in this way, via the binary alexandrine that serves so aptly as a vehicle for the extremes between public and private demands, the crux of the plot can be seen to be of a type that has antecedents in the French theatre. Two hundred years before Lamartine, Corneille trawled the murkier chronicles of obscure and provincial Roman history for awesome human conflicts. He would surely have detected here the beginnings of a plot in the dilemma of a provincial chieftain of a despised race whose sons are held hostage by the imperial authority and for whom nemesis is fast approaching. Indeed, a distinct Cornelian echo struck the ear of one of the most enthusiastic contemporary reviewers of the play, Théophile Gautier. He referred to the moment in the play when Père Antoine, a European monk who serves as both spiritual and political mentor to Toussaint, urges him to be resolute, despite his fears for his sons, and retorts to the latter's objection, 'Mais je suis père!', with the rhetorical 'Dieu ne l'était-il pas?' Gautier considered this to be a 'mot sublime à mettre à côté, sinon au-dessus du "Qu'il mourût!" de Corneille. Il y a dans cet hémistiche tout un monde d'idées et de sentiments.'[9]

In his enthusiasm Gautier seems to forget that the good monk, unlike *le vieil* Horace, is proposing to sacrifice another man's sons, not his own, and the analogy is not really exact. And when one looks hard at the dénouement of *Toussaint Louverture* the dilemma for the hero of a choice between his sons and his people is only apparent. Albert has to choose on his own account, and when he hesitates he is seized and carried off by French soldiers. This is most anguishing for Toussaint and for his niece Adrienne, who is in love with Albert, but responsibility for the latter's fate does not belong to his father. Lamartine has clearly tried to create for Toussaint a delicately balanced dilemma in having Albert urge him accede to Bonaparte's request, as set out in an ambiguous letter. But the equation is far too lop-sided. To retain the respect and allegiance of his first-born, he would have to forfeit the love of his other son, Isaac, and of his devoted niece, and risk being forced by Bonaparte to subjugate his own and other black populations in the Caribbean. There has never been any likelihood of his doing this; hence the dénouement of the play lacks the tension that one would expect in the purest classical tragedy. The scene of fatal hesitation was a *scène à faire*, just as 'Que pour sauver mon peuple, il faut perdre mes fils' was a *vers à faire*, but neither stretches the aesthetics of the play beyond the realm of melodrama as far as the mechanics of the plot are concerned. Lamartine would not have objected to this view, admitting that he wrote the play 'pour les yeux des masses, plutôt que pour l'oreille des classes d'élite au goût raffiné'.[10] And indeed the play ends minutes after the capture of Albert. The French troops attack; Adrienne dies heroically, shot as she waves the Haitian flag from the top of a rock to warn Toussaint's army. He takes the flag from the dying hands of the 'sublime enfant . . . ange de la victoire et de la liberté!', and the play ends thus:

TOUSSAINT (*revenant tout à fait à lui, s'élance à son tour sur le rocher, ressaisit le drapeau tombé des mains d'Adrienne et crie d'une voix terrible:*)
    Aux armes!!!

> *De toutes les cavités des rochers s'élancent des soldats blancs et noirs.*
> *– Le canon tonne dans le lointain.*
> *– Les fusillades s'engagent.*

    FIN

'Pour les yeux des masses' – Lamartine's confession is significant. In several places in the play he sets scenes, paints tableaux, groups his characters in attitudes. When Toussaint and Adrienne are reunited with Albert and Isaac, there is a succession of exclamations of joy, and then:

TOUSSAINT (*élevant les mains au ciel*).
                    Et toi, leur mère,
Femme qui de douleur t'enfuis au firmament,
Oh! mêle-toi d'en haut à cet embrassement!

> (*Ils se tiennent une seconde fois embrassés et groupés autour de Toussaint.*)

Act V opens with a very carefully composed grouping, consisting of Toussaint, le Père Antoine, Dessalines, Pétion, Adrienne and '*Généraux, Officiers, Soldats de l'armée de Toussaint, Peuple.*' They are clustered around Toussaint, who is

> ... *assis devant un tronc d'arbre renversé, recouvert d'une peau de panthère* ... *Adrienne est accroupie à terre, le bras appuyé sur l'épaule de Toussaint. – [Il] la regarde avec tendresse; il passe de temps en temps la main sur les cheveux de la jeune fille.*

And Lamartine's fondness for creating pathos out of an attitude is exemplified most succinctly of all in Act III when the disguised Toussaint suffers the anguish of being obliged by circumstances to remain silent and unidentified while his sons pine for home:

> *Toussaint soulève d'une main le lambeau de nattes de la cabane; il tend machinalement ses bras vers ses enfants et il écoute dans l'attitude de l'espion antique.*

Lamartine's scenic conception of his play, then, is characterized by a kind of visual sententiousness; literal *sententiae* – 'tout rôle est glorieux à qui sert la patrie' – may be found too, but the fact

143

remains that Lamartine evidently sought at many points to appeal emotionally to the 'eyes of the masses' by the most direct means: facial expression, physical gesture, spectacular effects. Thus Toussaint's heroic call to arms at the final curtain is a tropical *Liberté guidant le peuple* and Adrienne is a Gavroche before the letter ('C'est la faute à Raynal', perhaps?).

It is by means of scenic rhetoric such as this that Lamartine elaborates a myth of black emancipation. That he should have chosen to end the play with Toussaint storming into battle is not inappropriate, since that was the latter's most admired capacity; he was a military leader possessing both genius and immense personal courage (he was allegedly wounded seventeen times). But the problem facing Toussaint as Leclerc's invasion force landed and strengthened its grip on the island was to hold out long enough until yellow fever started to take its annual massive toll of unseasoned European troops. The decisions required of the hero were tactical and military. But this is scarcely promising material for the Romantic hagiographer. Showing Toussaint waiting for the enemy to die of yellow fever — and then making the mistake of not waiting long enough — would have been both aesthetically and ideologically appropriate, even highly appealing, to Brecht in 1939 but not to Lamartine or any other French Romantic in 1839.

The next phase of Toussaint's decline and fall also had its limitations by the standards of French dramaturgy in the nineteenth century. Instead of doing what he was best at, inspiring his ragged army to fight a guerilla war as successfully as it had done in the previous ten years, Toussaint started to negotiate with Leclerc. On 7 June 1802 he was lured to a meeting by a fulsome letter from a French general, unceremoniously arrested and trussed up, and bundled on to a ship bound for France. After seven and a half months of incarceration in the damp, chill Fort de Joux high up in the Jura, denied heating and a doctor, François Dominique Toussaint Bréda, called Toussaint Louverture,[11] died on 7 April 1803.

Now to die a champion of liberty in a tyrant's cell is a fate not without a certain mythic grandeur. A castle not very far from the Jura inspired some of English Romanticism's most famous lines celebrating the

> Eternal Spirit of the chainless Mind!
> Brightest in dungeons, Liberty! thou art.

Thus in 1816 did Byron remind his contemporaries of the existence

144

of François Bonnivard, an obscure Genevan patriot, dead some 250 years, but living on thereafter in the European imagination of the Romantic period as the Prisoner of Chillon. But just as Byron conferred a mythic status on Bonnivard, 'consigned to fetters and the damp vault's dayless gloom', so in the very month when Toussaint was being transported under heavy guard from Brest to the Fort de Joux did Wordsworth enquire whether the latter's 'head be now pillowed in some deep dungeon's earless den'. As treated by the two English Romantics, the subject is a trigger for philosophical reflections on the nobility of martyrdom. 'Freedom's fame finds wings on every wind', wrote Byron, echoing Wordsworth's moving farewell to Toussaint:

> Thou hast left behind
> Powers that will work for thee; air, earth and skies;
> There's not a breath of the common wind
> That will forget thee; thou hast great allies;
> Thy friends are exultations, agonies,
> And love, and man's unconquerable mind.
>
> ('To Toussaint Louverture', *Morning Post*, 2 Feb. 1803)

In the nineteenth century at least, the place for lines such as these, in England as with their equivalent in France, was the sonnet, not the stage. The sonnet, like the cell, is the place for reflection, not for action. The theatre required more rousing conclusions. So Lamartine does not wait for his black Prometheus to be caged. He has him immortalized in the final heroic pose, *essentializing* the life he has lived and for which he is best remembered. He is thus captured, not as he was historically and squalidly by the French, but, metaphorically, in *image d'Epinal* fashion on the retina of the admiring onlooker of 1850. Haitian flag in one hand, the other pointing towards the sound of gunfire, impersonated by the great Frédérick Lemaître (who liked nothing better), lit from below, Lamartine's final curtain image of Toussaint Louverture is as mythic as a Soviet poster celebrating the defence of Stalingrad.

It is not just in the shaping of the end of the play that Lamartine selects among historical alternatives to bring about a mythic enhancement of his subject appropriate to the artistic medium he is using at a given point in time. Toussaint, both literally and figuratively, has to be looked up to. Just as at the final curtain Toussaint leaps up high on to the rock to lead the counter-attack, so the first stage direction at the opening curtain directs our attention to the fact that, in a totally different setting, 'une petite lumière brille seule à travers la fenêtre haute d'une tour où travaille Toussaint Louverture'. There is no reason why this act should take place at a time when it is 'presque nuit'. It is simply a means of focusing, via a solitary lamp, on the looming background presence – high up, ever watchful, paternalistic – of the saviour of the nation. 'La lampe de Toussaint! C'est l'étoile de l'île; / Sa clarté nous conduit à la gloire!', explains one character. Another instructs artillerymen to open fire as soon as the signal is given from the tower. An atmosphere of suspense is immediately created, and then sustained throughout the whole of the act by the fact that Toussaint does not make an appearance. This initial, extended absence of the eponymous hero, who is constantly talked about, helps paradoxically to magnify his stature in advance; the same technique was used for comic effect by Molière in *Tartuffe*. Thus Frédérick Lemaître, as well as finishing gloriously, could not have wished for a better entry on stage than the one provided for him at the opening of the second act. It takes place in the tower, and not surprisingly Toussaint is alone, lit by just the one lamp referred to from outside in Act I. In fact he is frequently alone throughout the play, and much stress will be laid via hyperbole on the momentousness of the decisions he must take by himself: 'Je pèse avec la mienne un million de vies!' A number of themes that will recur – Toussaint's moral height above ordinary mortals, the awesome responsibility resting on his shoulders alone, his Christian and biblical frame of reference (he opposed voodoo vehemently), and his assimilation either by himself or by others to the ranks of epic leaders of the human race – all are densely packed into his first speech. Toussaint, like the audience, has had a long wait:

> (. . . *seul. Il se promène à pas interrompus et inégaux*).
> Cette heure du destin si longtemps attendue,
> La voilà donc! . . . En vain je l'avais suspendue,
> En vain je suppliais Dieu de la retenir;
> Pour décider de nous elle devait venir!
> Entre la race blanche et la famille noire,
> Il fallait le combat puisqu'il faut la victoire! . . .
> (*Il s'arrête un moment.*)
> A quelle épreuve, ô ciel! cette nuit me soumet!
> J'ai monté, j'ai monté . . . voilà donc le sommet
> Où mon ambition, de doutes assiégée,
> Par ma race et par Dieu va demeurer jugée:
> Moïse ainsi monta pour voir du Sinaï

Quelle route il ferait aux fils d'Adonaï.
Du haut de sa terreur et de sa solitude,
Il vit là le Jourdain et là la servitude.

The last line of the passage quoted (which is just a fragment of the whole speech) also exemplifies another technique, antithesis, which is used abundantly by Lamartine not just to dramatize the freedom/slavery theme, but to characterize Toussaint rhetorically. Thus, to stress his dramatic rise as a military leader —

> J'étais parti soldat, je revins général —

to compare him to Bonaparte —

> Lui, le premier des blancs, moi, le premier des noirs! —

to point to his role as the leader called for by Raynal (whose name however never appears) —

> Que les blancs ont un juge et les noirs un vengeur —

to warn of the consequences of succumbing to French blandishments —

> Rebelle aux yeux des blancs, aux yeux du peuple traître.

The chiasmus of the last example is used rhetorically elsewhere: 'Mille morts pour les blancs et pour vous mille vies!' retorts Toussaint to Pétion's protest 'Liberté pour nos fils et pour nous mille morts!' But normally the antithetical structures are neatly parallel. If he can, as in the examples of chiasmus just quoted, Lamartine finds an opportunity of avoiding the *noir/blanc* dualism, the dangers of abusing which must have been apparent to him:

> Gouverneur pour le blanc, Spartacus pour le libre.

The fact that he does it in these cases by differentiating the Haitians as 'le peuple' and 'le libre' — thus generalizing them as human beings — while leaving the French to continue being designated by nothing more than the colour of their skin, will be of significance later when we examine the ideological dimension of *Toussaint Louverture* beyond the solipsism of the Romantic hero. For the moment, still studying Lamartine's rhetorical technique of projecting Toussaint, we should notice that in the last example he also employs antonomasia: the black liberator is 'Spartacus'. Thus to the *quantitative* hyperbole — Toussaint *alone* (an exaggeration historically, since he could call on the services of a number of competent military and political advisers, including Europeans who threw in their lot with him) taking responsibility for a million lives in Haiti or, in another scene, a quarter of the human race all told − is added *qualitative* hyperbole. We have already seen that this is common in Balzac and that Lamartine, by a comparable although not identical technique, exalted Julie Charles to the ranks of Petrarch's Laura. Now, also employing antonomasia precisely, as well as simile and association by juxtaposition, Lamartine elevates Toussaint to stand alongside Moses, Romulus, Mahomet, Washington and, most obviously, Spartacus. Shortly before Lamartine, Comte had promoted Toussaint Louverture to a similar pantheon in the *Calendrier positiviste*,[12] and the process continues in modern times, with classical allusions predominating: Leonidas, Lycurgus,[13] Vercingetorix,[14] etc. Within the play, as we have already seen, Lamartine has Toussaint adopt '*l'attitude de l'espion antique*' − for once a titbit for the 'classes d'élite au goût raffiné' surely, since Toussaint is both spying on his children, as did Odysseus on his household,[15] and spying on the enemy, like Odysseus amid the Trojans on another occasion.[16] And, although he does not spell it out, the author was doubtless shaping this scene along the lines of another famous mythic parallel in having 'blind' Toussaint led by his devoted niece. Could Gautier be far wrong? 'Le faux Oedipe, guidé par son Antigone, le pas lourd, les mains étendues, la tête basse comme un homme qui ne peut plus chercher la lumière au ciel . . .'.[17]

But it is not just because of the grandiose heroic conception of the historical Toussaint Louverture and the character's domination of the play − Lemaître would have had 956 lines to deliver if the full text had been performed − that the work finds its place in this volume. The original conception appears to have been more thematic. The first working titles in 1839 and the early 1840s, long before the virtuoso actor was involved, were *Les Noirs, Haïti ou les Noirs* and *Les Esclaves*.[18] The texts of four of Lamartine's speeches, delivered between 1835 and 1842 either in the Chambre des Députés or at political banquets, and published in the 1850 edition of *Toussaint Louverture*, bear witness to the intensity of his opposition to slavery. It is often claimed that Lamartine lived in a fantasy world of his own, tastefully rearranged past. While this is undoubtedly true of his private life about the time he was proclaiming his undying devotion to Julie Charles (to take probably the most obvious example), there is no reason why we should doubt his

sincerity when he depreciates his play *qua* play and points to what
had mattered to him more in 1848: 'Si mon nom est associé dans
l'avenir de la race noire aux noms de Wilberforce et des abolition-
nistes français, ce ne sera pas pour ce poëme [term *sic*], ce sera
pour le 27 février 1848, où ma main signa l'émancipation de
l'esclavage au nom de la France.'[19] *Toussaint Louverture* is very
much about *la race noire*. As much as the play celebrates the life
of a remarkable individual, it is an imaginative affirmation of that
individual's blackness and of the blackness of the whole of his race.
We have already seen that Toussaint angrily rejects Bonaparte's
proposal that he should use his Haitian forces to subjugate other
colonial populations in the Caribbean. He asserts his solidarity
with the 'noirs de nos climats':

> Tout affront par un noir en mon nom supporté
> Me ferait détester ma propre liberté.

But it is to Lamartine's credit that he is alive to subtler racial
sentitivities than this. It is a historical fact that consciousness of
colour and of class, and the complicated relationship between them
– exemplified most obviously, but not exclusively, by the
ambivalent mentality and political allegiance of the mulattoes –
was a major factor in the upheavals of the 1790s. Adrienne is in
fact a mulatto, daughter of Toussaint's sister by a white man, and
initially at least she has an identity crisis:

> Enfant abandonné, fruit d'un perfide amour,
> A la sœur de Toussaint, hélas! je dois le jour;
> La sang libre des blancs, le sang de l'esclavage,
> Ainsi que dans mon cœur luttent sur mon visage;
> Et j'y trouve vivante en instincts différents
> La race de l'esclave et celle des tyrans.

She resolves her 'instincts différents' by throwing in her lot with
Toussaint and the Haitians. However, Albert does not wish to be
reminded by his brother of their blackness, and worships
Bonaparte and things French generally. With his aspiration to the
status of 'le noir civilisé, devenu citoyen', he is an early example
in literature of that *évolué* mentality satirized a century later by
Aimé Césaire in *Cahier du retour au pays natal* (1939) and by
Frantz Fanon in *Peau noire, masques blancs* (1952). In both of
these works, and also in Fanon's *Damnés de la terre* (1961), the
spiritual and psychological alienation of the colonial subject,

crippled by the complex of his personal and cultural 'inferiority',
is laid at the door of the European conscience. A corollary of the
colonial process is that it is not just the dominated subject that is
debased. The master too is at the very least coarsened by his
involvement:

> L'habitude de vivre au sein de l'esclavage
> Donne aigreur à la voix et rudesse au langage,

says Albert to Isaac, apologizing for the contempt of their European tutor, Salvador. (One of the crudest melodramatic features of
the play is that the latter turns out to be Adrienne's long-lost European father.) and Père Antoine understands the deadly dialectic of
the relationship between master and slave which, however violently
it began, needs a degree of complicity to be perpetuated:

> L'esclave au cœur du maître a trop appris à lire;
> Tu sais qu'on ne voit pas des bœufs baisser leurs cous
> Sans que l'on soit tenté de leur tendre les jougs!
> Que le maître et l'esclave auront dans l'attitude
> De leur ancien état l'invincible habitude . . .

In the course of welding the slaves into an effective, revolutionary
force, Toussaint has had to fight not only a military battle with the
French, but also, and more importantly, a psychological battle with
his fellow-blacks ('ces faibles esprits'): 'Les noirs pour leur couleur
n'avaient que du mépris.' It is evident in the opening scene of the play
that this battle has been largely won. A satirical chorus of articulate,
exuberant black and mulatto women, friends of Adrienne, clearly
possess a collective liberated mentality in rejoicing that they will no
longer be the victims of their white mistresses' jealousy because of
their beauty. 'Notre beauté' − the words are clearly used by
Lamartine's Haitian characters without irony or ambiguity. As
Léon-François Hoffmann has observed in *Le nègre romantique:
Personnage littéraire et obsession collective*, this was anything but a
standard French perception in the 1840s:

Les écrivains français ont rarement célébré la beauté noire. Pour certains,
la notion même de 'beauté noire' paraissait une contradiction dans les
termes . . . Ce n'est pas la peau noire qui gêne, l'écrivain pouvant choisir
tout un éventail de métaphores: 'peau d'ébène', 'couleur de la nuit', etc.
Le noir, couleur péjorative, a par contre l'avantage de faire ressortir la
blancheur des yeux et des dents . . . Mais comment célébrer les cheveux
crépus, le nez épaté ou les lèvres épaisses?[20]

In short, in Hoffmann's words, 'célébrer la beauté de la Négresse frisait le paradoxe, ou constituait une prise de position philan-thropique'.[21] Philanthropic Lamartine undoubtedly is, but he avoids in his physical portrayal of the black women both the coy, apologetic kind of European liberalism that could not (and still cannot) think in any other than Eurocentric terms of beauty and, at the same time, another kind of European response, the stress on exotic sensuality, much in fashion in his time, which is also a kind of racism. The women, like their menfolk, are liberated not just politically but spiritually:

> Les bras de nos amants ont affranchi notre âme.
> Gloire à Toussaint, Vive la liberté.

They simply take their beauty for granted; they do not need to assert it, expand upon it, justify it in European terms; nor does anyone else in the play. *Toussaint Louverture* is very much about the liberation of the soul. In that his black women no longer have to be the victims of the subordinating, subjugating gaze of the mistress —

> Son œil pour nous punir d'attirer un regard
> Contre notre beauté se tournait en poignard —

and, I think, by implication are free enough to resist it in future, Lamartine, exactly one hundred years before the publication of Senghor's *Anthologie de la nouvelle poésie nègre et malgache* in 1948, anticipates the psychological premise of its militant introductory essay, Sartre's 'Orphée noir':

Voici des hommes noirs debout qui nous regardent et je vous souhaite de ressentir comme moi le saisissement d'être vus. Car le blanc a joui trois mille ans du privilège de voir sans qu'on le voie . . . Aujourd'hui ces hommes noirs nous regardent et notre regard rentre dans nos yeux . . .[22]

Toussaint, Adrienne, le Père Antoine all understand the paralysing effect on the blacks, as on any subject people or class, of fear and an inferiority complex. As Sartre's Jupiter in *Les Mouches* confesses to Egisthe, the 'secret douloureux des Dieux et des rois' is that their power depends on the people — not just those of Argos — not knowing that they are free. Lamartine similarly generalizes from the narrow base of Haitian blacks when he has a French officer formulate the confidence trick at the crux of the master-slave dialectic:

> Commandons! noirs ou blancs, le peuple est ainsi fait;
> Celui qu'il croit son maître est son maître en effet.

Another white man in the play, le Père Antoine — a unique character creation at this time, as Hoffmann has shown — puts over a remarkable perception, one hundred years before Fanon's Algerians, of the blacks as the 'damned of the earth', in a lengthy harangue of which the following is a short extract:

> Vous, insectes humains, vermine au feu promise,
> Contre qui la colère aux plus doux est permise,
> Que le plus vil des blancs peut encor mépriser,
> Que le fou peut railler, que l'enfant peut briser,
> Qu'un revendeur de chair vend, colporte et transplante,
> Comme un fumier vivant qui féconde une plante;
> Sans pères, sans enfants, nomades en tout lieu,
> Hors la loi de tout peuple et hors la loi de Dieu;
> A qui, pour conserver plus de prééminence,
> Le blanc comme un forfait défend l'intelligence,
> De peur que vous lisiez au livre du Sauveur
> Que les blancs ont un juge et les noirs un vengeur!

Le Père Antoine is here the embodiment of the spirit of Abbé Raynal, or to be more precise of that Enlightenment conscience that Raynal compounded from the promptings of Diderot, Pechméja and Louis-Sébastien Mercier when writing the section of the *Histoire des deux Indes* dealing with slavery.[23] But appropriately it is Toussaint himself, in the most powerful scene in the play, who looks deepest into the metaphysical abyss of the race he leads. When interrogated by Leclerc and Rochambeau about his own attitude towards the French, the 'blind beggar' warms to the task. The following tirade is one of the most remarkable in Romantic drama. It lacks the poetic brilliance — and the rhetorical flashiness — of Victor Hugo at his most demonstrative; yet it goes far deeper than Victor Hugo was ever capable of going into one of the most tragic problems of his, and our, time: the psycho-spiritual alienation that leaves paroxysmic violence as the only means whereby oppressed peoples, like individuals, can liberate themselves, realize their potential, inherit their share of the planet. With its obvious antitheses, the first part of the speech has a certain Hugolian ring to it, true enough; but what of the rest? What is the substance of Hernani's complaint, once you scrutinize his wordy posturing, compared with the *real* and very modern syndrome described in the second half of the following speech? 'Oh! ma haine s'en va!', says Hernani when he is suddenly given the girl and the castle, and his life's pledge to avenge his father vanishes in as much breath as it

The black soul in rebellion

takes to declaim half an alexandrine. Thus Hugo's 'Castilian' conception of the character, and of the whole play, is revealed as the
shoddy tinsel it is. Whereas Hernani's 'trois mille braves' can conveniently be forgotten, things are not quite so easy for Toussaint
and his fellow-blacks. What does he, Toussaint, think of the
French?

> Peut-être, il l'ignore lui-même.
> De la haine à l'amour flottant irrésolu
> Son cœur est un abîme où son œil n'a pas lu,
> Où l'amer souvenir d'une vile naissance
> Lutte entre la colère et la reconnaissance.
> Le respect des Français du monde triomphants,
> L'orgueil pour sa couleur, l'amour de ses enfants
> L'attrait pour ce consul qui leur servit de père,
> Leur absence qu'il craint, leur retour qu'il espère,
> La vengeance d'un joug trop longtemps supporté,
> Ses terreurs pour sa race et pour sa liberté,
> Enfin, l'heureux vainqueur de ses maîtres qu'il brave,
> Le noir, le citoyen, le grand homme et l'esclave,
> Unis dans un même homme en font un tel chaos
> Que sa chair et son sang luttent avec ses os,
> Et qu'en s'interrogeant lui-même il ne peut dire
> Si le cri qu'il contient va bénir ou maudire.
>
> *(Les généraux se regardent avec*
> *étonnement et effroi)*
> Soudain sera l'éclair qui le décidera;
> Mais, quel que soit ce cri, le monde l'entendra.
>
> *(Les généraux paraissent de nouveau*
> *se troubler.)*
> Ne vous étonnez pas, Francais, de ces abîmes
> Où le noir sonde en vain ses sentiments intimes.
> Comme le cœur du blanc, notre cœur n'est point fait:
> La mémoire y grossit l'injure et le bienfait.
> En vous donnant le jour, le sort et la nature
> Ne vous donnèrent pas à venger une injure;
> Vos mères, maudissant de l'œil votre couleur,
> Ne vous allaitent pas d'un philtre de douleur.
> Dans ce monde, en entrant, vous trouvez votre place
> Large comme le vol de l'oiseau dans l'espace.
> En ordre, dans vos cœurs, vos instincts sont rangés;
> Le bien, vous le payez, le mal, vous le vengez.
> Vous savez, en venant dans la famille humaine,
> A qui porter l'amour, à qui garder la haine:
> Il fait jour dans votre âme ainsi que sur vos fronts.

La nôtre est une nuit où nous nous égarons,
Lie abjecte du sol, balayure du monde,
Où tout ce que la terre a de pur ou d'immonde,
Coulant avec la vie en confus éléments,
Fermente au feu caché de soudains sentiments,
Et, selon que la haine ou que l'amour l'allume,
Féconde, en éclatant, la terre, ou la consume.
Nuage en proie au vent, métal en fusion,
Qui ne dit ce qu'il est que par l'explosion! . . .

And in exhorting the Haitians elsewhere to realize that the only way to attain their freedom is to be prepared forthwith to be as ruthless as the enemy (and proving it in one of the most melodramatic pieces of action of all),[24] that they should feed on insults rather than be subjugated by them ('de ces affronts des blancs faisons notre gloire'), and that responsibility for their destiny lies in their own hands, Toussaint would seem an aberrant creation to those who know only the Lamartine of the *Méditations poétiques*. But the languid Mâconnais landowner-poet who gazes at us serenely from the famous Decaisne portrait is also the man whose *Histoire des Girondins* was believed to be one of the causes of the 1848 revolution, who put a case for Robespierre, and who brought about his own downfall later that year by trying to keep Ledru-Rollin in the provisional government.[25] In his literary treatment of the blacks of Saint-Domingue–Haiti Lamartine reveals himself to have possessed a power of empathy, and ability to leap the imagination gap of race and class, considerably in advance of his time. Begun in 1839 and completed in 1848/9, *Toussaint Louverture* anticipates some of the themes of Césaire's *Cahier du retour au pays natal* and of Senghor's *Anthologie* by exactly a century. Despite the manifest differences of form from these modern works, in that *Toussaint Louverture* was written for the theatre and even achieves some of its most striking mythopoeic effects in enhancing Tousaint himself precisely by action, the lyrical and elegiac force of the play should not be forgotten. The very long passages just quoted, as well as the chorus of Haitian women examined much earlier, make a vital contribution too to the myth of black humanity, solidarity and cultural values, in short *négritude*.

I have claimed much for Lamartine, but not at least that he invented that word. Nevertheless that is what *Toussaint Louverture* is about. And in decrying the work as theatre and preferring for it the designation 'poem' Lamartine points to a fundamental

The black soul in rebellion

aesthetic dilemma, which he never really resolved, between the conception and the execution of *Toussaint Louverture*. For, however much the dramatic form might have been an appropriate artistic medium in Lamartine's time for a myth of a modern Spartacus, a variant of the Promethean and Napoleonic myths which populate the era, it is possible that the *blackness* of the Spartacus in question and the existential trauma of the race he leads require for their most appropriate expression the intimacy of the lyric mode. Perhaps no one has appreciated better than Sartre the appropriateness of poetry to the deeper levels of the *négritude* myth. It is significant that, in seeking a title for his celebrated essay commemorating the spiritual renascence of the black race, he looks to the mythic archetype of Orpheus, not to the Prometheus of sundry Romantics or to the Spartacus that Lamartine inherited from Raynal. In concluding, fittingly I hope, with Sartre's homage to 'Orphée noir', we nevertheless do not diminish the value of Lamartine's mythopoeic treatment of the black man's first successful bid for his political and cultural emancipation in the modern era:

Mythe douloureux et plein d'espoir, la Négritude, née du Mal et grosse d'un Bien futur, et vivante comme une femme qui naît pour mourir et qui sent sa propre mort jusque dans les plus riches instants de sa vie; c'est un repos instable, une fixité explosive, un orgueil qui se renonce, un absolu qui se sait transitoire; car en même temps qu'elle est l'annonciatrice de sa naissance et de son agonie, elle demeure l'attitude existentielle choisie par des hommes libres et vécue *absolument*, jusqu'à la lie. Parce qu'elle est cette tension entre un Passé nostalgique où le noir n'entre plus tout à fait et un avenir où elle cédera la place à des valeurs nouvelles, la Négritude se pare d'une beauté tragique qui ne trouve d'expression que dans la poésie.[26]

NOTES

1 Cf. Jean-Yves Tadié: 'Dans son langage abondant, divers, souvent secret, le 19e siècle a sans doute été (avec le 16e siècle) dans notre littérature le siècle le plus créateur de mythes', in *Introduction à la vie littéraire du 19e siècle* (Paris, 1984), p. 121. Pierre Albouy goes so far as to base his *Mythes et mythologies dans la littérature française* (Paris, 1969) on the following rationale: 'Comme la création mythique proprement dite, qui consiste à donner des sens nouveaux à des mythes anciens, ne commence qu'avec le Romantisme, nous ne ferons que de brèves allusions aux siècles précédents et nous consacrerons notre étude au XIXe siècle, avec les mythes de la révolte et les figures de Satan,

155

Caïn, Prométhée, et au XXe siècle, avec les mythes de la connaissance et les figures de Narcisse et d'Orphée' (p. 14).

2 'A Elvire', *Oeuvres poétiques complètes*, ed. M.-F. Guyard (Paris, 1963), p. 1802n (third poem of *Méditations poétiques*, 1820).

3 Lamartine, *Saül*, ed. J. des Cognets (Paris, 1918), p. viii.

4 J. Morley, *Diderot and the Encyclopædists* (London, 1878), p. 210.

5 *Toussaint Louverture*, 1850, 'Notice', p. xviii.

6 R. and N. Heinl, *Written in Blood: The Story of the Haitian People 1492–1971* (Boston, 1978), p. 37; cf. also Robert Rotberg, *Haiti: The Politics of Squalor* (Boston, 1971); T. O. Ott, *The Haitian Revolution, 1789–1804* (Knoxville, 1973); R. L. Stein, *The French Slave Trade in the 18th century: An Old Regime Business* (Madison, 1979).

7 D. P. Geggus, *Slavery, War and Revolution: The British Occupation of Saint Domingue 1793–1798* (Oxford, 1982).

8 Historically, Toussaint's sons were Isaac (the elder) and Saint-Jean. The latter was not sent to France. Isaac was accompanied by Toussaint's step-son, Placide (five years older than Isaac). Cf. R. Korngold, *Citizen Toussaint* (London, 1945), p. 175.

9 Théophile Gautier, *La Presse*, 8 Apr. 1850; reprinted in *Les Maîtres du Théâtre Francais* (1929), p. 330.

10 *Toussaint Louverture* (1850), p. xiii.

11 How Toussaint came by the nickname 'Louverture' has never been satisfactorily explained. Suggestions range from the Hugolian grotesque, a gap in his front teeth, to the sublime, his military panache in forcing gaps in the enemy's ranks.

12 Cf. Maurice Bitter, *Haïti* (Paris, 1976), p. 48.

13 Cf. Charles-André Julien, Preface to Aimé Césaire, *Toussaint Louverture: La Révolution française et le problème colonial* (Paris, 1961), p. 7.

14 Bitter, *Haïti*, p. 49.

15 The second half of the *Odyssey*.

16 *Odyssey*, IV.240ff., and Euripides, *Hecuba*, 239ff. I am grateful to my colleague Dr Richard Buxton of the Department of Classics and Archaeology, University of Bristol, for help with this allusion.

17 Gautier (see n. 9 above), p. 330.

18 A. de Lamartine, *Oeuvres poétiques complètes*, ed. M.-F. Guyard (Paris, 1963), pp. 1926–7.

19 *Toussaint Louverture* (1850), p. xxx.

20 Hoffmann, *Le Nègre romantique* (Paris, 1973), p. 216.

21 *Ibid.*, p. 248.

22 L. S. Senghor (ed.), *Anthologie . . .* (Paris, 1948), p. ix.

23 On the whole of this complicated question, see H. Wolpe, *Raynal et sa Machine de Guerre: L'Histoire des Deux Indes et ses Perfectionnements* (Stanford, 1957); Virgil Topazio, 'Diderot's supposed contributions to Raynal's work', *Symposium*, XII (1958), 103–116; Yves

The black soul in rebellion

Benot, 'Diderot, Pechméja, Raynal et l'anti-colonialisme', *Europe*, XXIX (1963), 137–53; W. Womack, 'Eighteenth-century themes in the *Histoire philosophique et politique des deux Indes* of Guillaume Raynal', *Studies on Voltaire and the Eighteenth Century*, 96 (1972), 129–265; Michèle Duchet, (1) 'Diderot collaborateur de Raynal: à propos des fragments imprimés du fonds Vandeul', *Revue d'histoire littéraire de la France* LX (1960), 531–56, (2) 'Le *Supplément au voyage de Bougainville* et la collaboration de Diderot à l'*Histoire des deux Indes*', *Cahiers de l'AIEF*, XIII (1961), 173–87, and (3) 'Bougainville, Raynal, Diderot et les sauvages du Canada: Une source ignorée de l'*Histoire des deux Indes*', *Revue d'histoire littéraire de la France*, LXIII (1963), 228–36.

24 One of the many plots against him that Toussaint had to deal with was that mounted by his nephew, Moïse, who was summarily tried and shot. In the play Moïse is stabbed by the 'blind beggar' in the middle of Leclerc's HQ at the moment of betrayal. 'A la faveur de la confusion' thus created, Toussaint jumps off a cliff into the sea to escape – the kind of third-act curtain 'coup de théâtre' that could give the play a bad name.

25 Cf. W. Fortescue, *Alphonse de Lamartine: A Political Biography* (London, 1983).

26 Senghor (ed.), *Anthologie*, p. xliii. We have thus moved a long way from the apocalyptic vision of the Abbé Raynal, which can serve as an epilogue to this article: 'Il ne manque aux nègres qu'un chef assez courageux pour les conduire à la vengeance et au carnage. Où est-il ce grand homme que la nature doit peut-être à l'honneur de l'espèce humaine? Où est-il ce Spartacus nouveau, qui ne trouvera point de Crassus? Alors disparaîtra le code noir; et que le code blanc sera terrible, si le vainqueur ne consulte que le droit de représailles' . . . Il paroîtra, il lèvera l'étendard sacré de la liberté. Ce signal vénérable rassemblera autour de lui les compagnons de son infortune. Plus impetueux que les torrens, ils laisseront partout les traces de leur juste ressentiment . . . Tous les tyrans deviendront la proie du fer et de la flamme . . . partout on bénira le nom du héros qui aura rétabli les droits de l'espèce humaine, partout on érigera des trophées à sa gloire' (Abbé Raynal, *Histoire des Deux Indes*, 1770 (1774 & 1780 edns respectively quoted)). Toussaint Louverture was, in the words of C.-A. Julien, 'moins qu'un dieu mais plus qu'un homme'.

11
Alfred de Musset: Don Juan on the Boulevard de Gand

MERLIN THOMAS

'The necessity of tailoring the imaginary world to the scale of a three hour theatrical performance inevitably means that there is no room fully to establish a mythological world with its own coherent logic.'[1]

MYTH. A purely fictitious narrative (usually involving supernatural persons, actions, or events, and) embodying some popular idea concerning natural (or historical) phenomena. Often used vaguely to include any narrative having fictitious elements.

Of course my brackets around part of the above definition of *myth* from the *Shorter Oxford Dictionary* may be thought a cheat, but, if not, then I have every reason to believe that Professor Howarth would allow Musset to deal with 'some popular idea concerning natural phenomena' within three hours and get away with it quite successfully . . .

There is at least one 'popular idea' or theme which underlies most of Musset's theatre and gives to his mixture of emotion and flippancy some 'coherent' logic. This 'idea' can be variously described as that of the heartless seducer, of the disillusioned dandy, or of the Don Juan myth. There are of course other 'ideas' in Musset's writings — the 'Belle Dame sans merci', and what may be called the 'tart with a golden heart', for instance. But the Don Juan motif is of particular interest, since Musset uses it a great deal — in prose, in poetry and in drama — and gives it an original and personal touch.

There is no need here to list all the various Don Juans from Tirso onwards, but Musset in the second canto of *Namouna* makes it clear that he knew Molière (of course), Byron and Hoffmann, and he also adds for good measure Richardson's Lovelace and Laclos's Valmont.

Namouna (1833) is indeed a key text, perhaps not as well known as it should be. This may be because it comes to a somewhat abrupt conclusion – I wonder if during an evening on the Boulevard de Gand someone like Tattet came up with suggestions for a *partie fine* somewhere in the country outside Paris? Anyway, *Namouna* is a great deal more revealing about Musset the man and Musset the poet than most of the standard anthology pieces that have so greatly contributed to a false understanding and assessment of him. (I have always thought that the comment allegedly attributed by French *lycéens* to the little pelicans is quite appropriate – 'Quoi! Encore des tripes?'.) What a relief it is to find a French Romantic poet with an irreverent sense of humour such as is shown in *Ballade à la lune*, *Mardoche*, the *Dédicace* to *La Coupe et les lèvres* and, of course, *Namouna*. How lucky he was to have been born later than the grave, even self-important, Lamartine, Vigny and Hugo, and to be twenty in 1830, already in print, well-read, vivacious, with a genuine understanding of Shakespeare and Byron, attractive, sexually adventurous and capable of *both* laughter and tears!

The influence of the 'serious' Byron on the French Romantic movement has of course been endlessly discussed: that of the 'satirical' Byron is equally important in the case of Musset. *Childe Harold's Pilgrimage* may lie behind *Rolla*, but, thank God, Musset was open to other moods as well:

> And from the gate thrown open issued beaming
> A beautiful and mighty Thing of Light,
> Radiant with glory, like a banner streaming
> Victorious from some world-o'erthrowing fight:
> My poor comparisons must needs be teeming
> With earthly likenesses, for here the night
> Of clay obscures our best conception, saving
> Johanna Southcote, or Bob Southey raving.
>
> 'Twas the archangel Michael; all men know
> The make of angels and archangels, since
> There's scarce a scribbler has not one to show,
> From the fiends' leader to the angels' prince;
> There also are some altar-pieces, though
> I really can't say that they much evince
> One's inner notions of immortal spirits;
> But let the connoisseurs explain *their* merits.
>
> (The Vision of Judgment, XXVIII, XXIX)

Vous me demanderez si j'aime la nature.
Oui; – j'aime fort aussi les arts et la peinture.
Le corps de la Vénus me paraît merveilleux.

La plus superbe femme est-elle préférable?
Elle parle, il est vrai, mais l'autre est admirable,
Et je suis quelquefois pour les silencieux.
Mais je hais les pleurards, les rêveurs à nacelles,
Les amants de la nuit, des lacs, des cascatelles
Cette engeance sans nom, qui ne peut faire un pas
Sans s'inonder de vers, de pleurs et d'agendas.
La nature, sans doute, est comme on veut la prendre.
Il se peut, après tout, qu'ils sachent la comprendre;
Mais eux, certainement, je ne les comprends pas.

(From the *Dédicace* to *La Coupe et les lèvres*)

And, coming closer to my theme, what of this little confrontation?

And Julia's voice was lost, except in sighs,
Until too late for useful conversation;
The tears were gushing from her gentle eyes,
I wish, indeed, they had not had occasion;
But who, alas! can love, and then be wise?
Not that remorse did not oppose temptation:
A little still she strove, and much repented,
And whispering, 'I will n'er consent' — consented.

(*Don Juan*, I)

Et quel crime est-ce donc de se mettre à son aise,
Quand on est tendrement aimée, — et qu'il fait chaud?
On est si bien tout nu, dans une large chaise!
Croyez-m'en, belle dame, et, ne vous en déplaise,
Si vous m'apparteniez, vous y seriez bientôt.
Vous en crieriez sans doute un peu, — mais pas bien haut.

(From — yes of course — *Namouna*, Chant Premier)

Byron's Don Juan is a lighthearted and very efficient sex-machine, but Musset has different ideas, set out very clearly in *Namouna*, Chant Deuxième, XIV–LIV. In the course of these 250 lines or so, we see first the vicious roué typified by Richardson's Lovelace:

. . . beau comme Satan, froid comme la vipère . . . (II, 14)

Corrompant sans plaisir, amoureux de lui-même,

Et, pour s'aimer toujours, voulant toujours qu'on l'aime. (II, 15)

C'est le roué sans cœur, le spectre à double face,
A la patte de tigre, aux serres de vautour,
Le roué sérieux qui n'eut jamais d'amour. (II, 20)

Next, in a very brief transition, is a glimpse of Molière's Don Juan, a standard vulgar French roué:

Quant au roué Français, au don Juan ordinaire,
Ivre, riche, joyeux, raillant l'homme de pierre,
Ne demandant partout qu'à trouver le vin bon,
Bernant monsieur Dimanche, et disant à son père
Qu'il serait mieux assis pour lui faire un sermon . . .   (II, 23)

The last line of this stanza is fascinating:

C'est l'ombre d'un roué qui ne vaut pas Valmont

— there are few intelligent remarks about Laclos before
Baudelaire's notes on *Les Liaisons dangereuses*, written in the
1850s. We may wonder how Musset would have continued his fragment *La Matinée de Don Juan* (also 1833), which is very much in
the same tone.

This leads in to the key passage:

Il en est un plus grand, plus beau, plus poétique,
Que personne n'a fait, que Mozart a rêvé
Qu'Hoffmann a vu passer, au son de la musique,
Sous un éclair divin de sa nuit fantastique,
Admirable portrait qu'il n'a point achevé,
Et que de notre temps Shakspeare aurait trouvé.   (II, 24)

'Plus grand, plus beau, plus poétique' — such is the Don Juan
imagined by Musset: neither the heartless destroyer nor the vulgar
womanizer, but a guilty tragic figure always in vain pursuit of an
ideal not to be found on earth. What redeems this Don Juan is that
he *did* love his victims *à sa guise*. This is spelt out further in II,
42–4, in admittedly a rather more inflated tone:

Elles t'aimaient pourtant, ces filles insensées
Que sur ton cœur de fer tu pressas tour à tour;
Le vent qui t'emportait les avait traversées;
Elles t'aimaient, don Juan, ces pauvres délaissées
Qui couvraient de baisers l'ombre de ton amour,
Qui te donnaient leur vie, et qui n'avaient qu'un jour!

Mais toi, spectre énervé, toi, que faisais-tu d'elles?
Ah! massacre et malheur! tu les aimais aussi,
Toi! croyant toujours voir sur tes amours nouvelles
Se lever le soleil de tes nuits éternelles,
Te disant chaque soir: 'Peut-être le voici',
Et l'attendant toujours, et vieillissant ainsi!

Demandant aux forêts, à la mer, à la plaine,
Aux brises du matin, à toute heure, à tout lieu,

161

La femme de ton âme et de ton premier vœu!
Prenant pour fiancée un rêve, une ombre vaine,
Et fouillant dans le cœur d'une hécatombe humaine,
Prêtre désespéré, pour y chercher ton Dieu.

Love of course is a major theme in European Romantic literature, but *sex* is a good deal rarer, except hidden and/or agonizing (see Mario Praz's famous study, or the frankly dirty poems − some indeed by Musset and George Sand − which, if you have a reason and some patience, you can read in the Enfer of the Bibliothèque Nationale). What do you think *happened* on that boat on the Lac du Bourget, and was Wordsworth really at cross-purposes in the Lake District as Max Beerbohm's delightful cartoon suggests? We do not need to try and establish a list of Musset's lovers − 'toi qui la première' (*Nuit d'octobre*) to Louise Colet (Flaubert must have been glad of the rest) − in order to make the clear point that he had a great number and that none of his relationships lasted long. True, once sex had lowered its tantalizing head, lasting friendship occasionally ensued − notably in the case of Madame Jaubert. Is it then surprising that so much of his writing is concerned with sexual desire, pursuit and disillusionment?

But again from *Namouna* there is this:

Je confesse, pour moi, que je ne sais pas bien
Comment on peut donner le corps sans donner l'âme. (i, 62)

This is perhaps what distinguishes Musset from Baudelaire's 'latrine'.[2]

The brief here is of course to consider Musset's theatrical activities. This I propose to do by brief allusions in the light of what I have so far said. There are two starting-points to this: first, to suggest that, up to 1939 at any rate, with the possible exception of Claudel (and that depends on whether you can stomach his peculiarly disagreeable religiosity), Musset is the last dramatist who can rate more than − shall we say? − something like β? + ; secondly, to make the very obvious point that most of Musset's theatre is based upon his very personal view of love. Romantically amoral if you like: it certainly seems to have little or nothing to do with marriage, and even less with the procreation of the species. What indeed would happen if Jacqueline had a child by Fortunio? Musset's heroes are clearly aware of what Valmont had called 'les précautions'. Yet this view of love is susceptible to many variations, and Musset is able to use these variations to excellent effect — sometimes comic, sometimes ironical and even bitter, sometimes pathetic or even tragic.

It should also be remembered that — with two small one-act exceptions — *all* the best Musset plays were published by the time he was twenty-seven, and nearly all of his best poetry and prose as well. I do not wish to suggest that this is a merit, but it is surely worth remembering.

Indeed love is treated by Musset from the standpoint of youth, often lighthearted and predatory, but also subject to depression and disillusion. Some would say he never passed this tantalizingly fertile stage, typified by

> l'heure
> Où (quand par le brouillard la chatte rôde et pleure
> Monsieur Hugo va voir mourir Phoebus le blond.[3]

or

> Je suis venu trop tard dans un monde trop vieux.[4]

I confess that I find him *sympathique*, and I am sorry he burnt himself out so soon.

It is not difficult to apply some of the foregoing suggestions to his work for the theatre: here are a few rapid allusions.

Fertilized, if that is an appropriate term, by Shakespeare and Marivaux, he contrived to write virtually the only plays in nineteenth-century French literature which remain firmly in the repertoire, neither as occasional revivals out of curiosity nor as vehicles for actresses (camellias) or actors (large noses).

It can be reasonably suggested that in all Musset's plays — except *Lorenzaccio*, which is indeed a special case — the theme of love is dominant and that the outcome of the play depends on the honesty of the characters with regard to their feelings — *On ne badine pas avec l'amour*, in fact. If you do, then separation or even death ensue: if you take it seriously and do *not* cheat, then it *vincit omnia* — at least, one feels, for a time.

There would seem to be only one purely 'Lovelace' character of any importance in Musset's theatre — Alexandre de Médicis in *Lorenzaccio*. Julien Salviati in the same play is another, but only a minor character. One might feel, of course, that were he ever to lift his robes Cardinal Cibo might be a third, but in a full-scale tragedy there have to be villains, and villains these three certainly are, for differing reasons. A relatively recent production of the play (by the students of the Paris Conservatoire) shed an interesting, if controversial, light by playing Alexandre and Lorenzo virtually as lovers. It must be admitted that the text, spattered in places with 'mignons' in both directions (I, 4; IV, 1, 11) – and with, from Alexandre, 'Renzo', 'Renzino' – gives rather more authority to such an interpretation than did Molière's *Tartuffe* to Roger Planchon. There would seem to be something to it, and, if so, it is unique in Musset's theatre and it also gives an interesting twist to Lorenzo's remark to Philippe Strozzi in III, 3: 'le vice . . . est collé à ma peau'.

Once past 'Lovelace', the other two categories suggested – may they be called *Molière* and *Namouna* for convenience – overlap to a considerable extent. I would suggest that there are only two straight *Molière* characters – Clavaroche (*Le Chandelier*) and Steinberg (*Bettine*), both nasty, one vulgar, the other devious and corrupt.

Perhaps the reasons for the overlap are that none of the characters to be mentioned is deeply dislikable. This is no doubt because the *Namouna* kind are let off since they do have genuine feelings for the women with whom they are concerned, and in some cases, if they occasionally behave, or perhaps begin, in a *Molière* fashion, they are redeemed or converted and occasionally pay the price for 'falsity' in love. And, moreover, if they are very young – like Fantasio ('. . . moi qui suis plein de sève et de jeunesse', *Fantasio*, I, 2) or Fortunio ('Il est vrai que je suis un enfant', *Chandelier*, I, 6) – their sexual ambitions may qualify them as Don Juans *en herbe* (especially in the case of Fortunio with his 'Chantez donc, monsieur Clavaroche'); but they both possess such agreeable Musset-like charisma that any audience is bound to be on their side. There are then the penitents – Chavigny (*Un Caprice*) and Valentin (*Il ne faut jurer de rein*) who add to the growing impression that *Namounas* are like Musset himself and hence all right. Finally what of the two plays that end unhappily – *On ne badine pas avec l'amour* and *Les Caprices de Marianne*? Neither really fits the pattern so far outlined. Perdican *does* love his Camille: those nuns are deeply to blame for his naughty attempt to arouse her true feelings (which succeeds), and it is theatrically touching if implausible that Rosette should flake out as she does. (Was there an autopsy, and if so did they find a fractured heart?) As for *Les Caprices de Marianne*, its title tells us where to look – echoes perhaps of 'toi qui la première'. Célio, as we have all been told, is one part of Musset and Octave the other. Marianne is certainly not worth dying for, Octave behaves at the end with the utmost propriety, and Musset is already at twenty-three a good enough dramatist to invent a wonderful curtain line. No *Don Juannerie* here. I think that *Namounas* are indeed all right.

Sainte-Beuve was willing to be relatively generous to his contemporaries when they were dead, as is shown by the last two sentences but one of his *Causerie du lundi 11 mai 1857* (the very last sentence is too pompous to be quoted with decorum):

Poète qui n'a été qu'un type éclatant de bien des âmes plus obscures de son âge, qui en a exprimé les essors et les chutes, les grandeurs et les misères, son nom ne mourra pas. Gardons-le particulièrement gravé, nous à qui il a laissé le soin de vieillir, et qui pouvions dire l'autre jour avec vérité en revenant de ses funérailles: 'Notre jeunesse depuis des années était morte, mais nous venons de la mettre en terre avec lui.'

NOTES

1 W. D. Howarth, *Sublime and Grotesque* (London, 1975), p. 338.
2 *Mon cœur mis à nu*, XVI.
3 *Mardoche*, stanza I.
4 *Rolla*.

12
Avatars of Jupiter in Sartre's
Les Mouches and Giraudoux's
Amphitryon 38

ODETTE DE MOURGUES

[JUPITER] . . . henceforth I am omnipotent.
All else had been subdued to me; alone
The soul of man, like unextinguished fire,
Yet burns towards heaven with fierce reproach, and doubt,
And lamentation, and reluctant prayer,
Hurling up insurrection, which might make
Our antique empire insecure, though built
On eldest faith, and hell's coeval, fear . . .

(Shelley, *Prometheus Unbound*, III, i)

Culture, as the present volume will abundantly illustrate, is based
on myths which endlessly require to be rejuvenated according to the
aspirations or problems of each successive age. In our Western
civilization no mythical domain has proved so rich in tantalizing
possibilities of transformation and elaboration as the fabulous
universe of Greece and Rome. Such is its protean malleability and
compliance that it has, not long ago, obligingly provided the
psychologist with a slick label (the Oedipus complex) or the essayist
with a fitting ponderous symbol (Camus's myth of Sisyphus).

I am concerned here with some aspects of the survival and
metamorphoses of pagan deities.

There was a time, during the Renaissance and post-Renaissance
period, when the greatest glory for man was to be represented as
one of the Olympians. In innumerable poems, paintings, sculptures
and court pageants noble personages appeared under the guise of
Jupiter and Mars, Juno or Ceres. When we come to our modern
age the mythological fiction which expresses the relation between
man and the deity moves in a very different direction. Man is no
longer carried upwards to be triumphantly enthroned in the
empyreal sphere. On the contrary the gods are brought down to
earth, there to fight, if they can, for their now contested power,
and among them, first of all, the most powerful, Jupiter.

Avatars of Jupiter

Two French plays in the twentieth century, Giraudoux's *Amphitryon 38* (1929) and Sartre's *Les Mouches* (1943), offer interesting examples of the new role, or better roles, assumed by the king of gods.

Ignoring chronology I shall consider *Les Mouches* first. The subject of the play is one which, since Homer's mention of the story, has inspired Aeschylus, Sophocles, Euripides and a number of other tragedians: Orestes' return to his native city, Argos, where he avenges the death of his father Agamemnon by killing his mother, Clytemnestra, and her lover Aegisthus.

The most obvious modification brought by the twentieth-century playwright to this episode of the traditional saga of the Atreides is the absence of an element which had seemed essential in the unrelenting destruction of a doomed family: fate. The well-known statement of the Racinian Oreste, 'Je me livre en aveugle au destin qui m'entraîne', would not be uttered by Sartre's hero. The central point of the play is Orestes' discovery that he is free and can assume complete responsibility for his acts. Where fate should be and is not, Jupiter steps in. *Les Mouches* is a variation on the Promethean theme which already in the nineteenth century had attracted Romantic writers like Shelley, man's revolt against God – not an easy revolt in the case of the Sartrian Orestes.

Thus Jupiter becomes a central character in the play. He is present throughout, doubly present. His statue adorns the public square of Argos and the throne room in the palace – a statue hideously besmirched with blood and made more sinister by the vacant stare of its blank eyes. Jupiter himself appears early in the first act as an unknown traveller coming by chance – or so it seems – across Orestes and his tutor. The latter, however, has noticed that he seems to have dogged their steps during their journey to Argos. He has also been struck by a telling detail in the appearance of the stranger: the majestic beard which has reminded him (for he is a cultured man) of the statue of Jupiter Ahenobarbus in Parma. But his reliance on sceptic philosophy prevents him from seeing in the bearded man anything more than a shady-looking customer, perhaps a spy of Aegisthus. Yet some of Jupiter's ambiguous remarks are self-revealing and leave Orestes puzzled: 'Quel homme êtes-vous?' (I, i) and, later to the tutor, 'Est-ce un homme?' (I, ii). Still as a travelling companion, ready to oblige with good advice ('leave this city, young man') and even practical help ('I can provide good horses for your journey') Jupiter remains beside Orestes, sometimes openly, as during the ceremony for the dead, sometimes hidden, as when spying on the conversations between Orestes and Electra. Eventually he drops all pretence, first in front of Aegisthus at the end of Act II, and then in his supreme confrontation with Electra and Orestes (III, ii).

The part ascribed to him is that of an evil god whose sway is based on terror, who needs crime because crime brings punishment in the form of the most abject display of remorse. His minions, the classical Furies, here the Flies, take on the repellent aspect of monstrous insects harassing men with their bites, their buzz, their sickly taste for putrefying flesh. For Jupiter is also the god of death, enlisting the dead in his system of intimidation. During the *Fête des Morts* which takes place in the middle of the play, the deceased inhabitants of Argos, conjured up by the high priest, arise, invisible, from the mouth of a cave to avenge themselves on the living. Jupiter watches with satisfaction over the correct unfolding of the ritual. He interferes twice: once to stop Orestes, who draws his sword when Aegisthus gets ready to face the dead Agamemnon – 'Ruffian! je ne te permettrai pas de mêler le nom de mon père à tes singeries!' (II, i) – and a second time to nullify by a supernatural flash of light Electra's attempt at breaking the ghastly spell of collective hysteria.

The god is no less hateful in his moments of false bonhomie: offering to guide Orestes as in the past Minerva, disguised as Mentor, accompanied Ulysses' son, or, playing the benevolent father figure, reducing Electra to an infantile craving for his protection.

Perhaps his most pernicious and devastating power is to corrupt good itself through the enforcement of a fallacious moral order and to leave men without any means of judging of right and wrong. Even nature, hostile to man, is Jupiter's accomplice. Hence the shock, the feeling of an appalling dizziness experienced by Orestes when he discovers that everything around him is suddenly nothing more than an immense void. His next move, we know, is to acknowledge his freedom and find in himself and for himself a reason to live and a basis for a code of ethics. Nothing of course can suppress the basic horror attached to our existence. Jupiter, or whoever created the world, if anybody did, has placed humanity in a desperate situation in face of a meaningless reality. This men must realize, but as a starting-point only. And here Sartre has placed the most remarkable utterance in the play: '. . . la vie humaine' says Orestes, 'commence de l'autre côté du désespoir' (III, ii).

Jupiter is not completely defeated. Although he foresees the twilight of his reign, he is determined to carry on. But he reveals to Aegisthus his intolerable lassitude, far beyond the weariness expressed by the human tyrant himself: 'Depuis cent mille ans je danse devant les hommes. Une lente et sombre danse . . . Tu mourras. Moi, non. Tant qu'il y aura des hommes sur cette terre, je serai condamné à danser devant eux' (II, v). And indeed throughout the play Jupiter has been, in many ways, like a comedian and, what is worse, a second-rate performer in a second-rate music hall: a few tricks with lightning and thunder, the cabbalistic hocus-pocus of the superannuated conjurer to charm the flies, and, during his great show of power against the traditional backdrop of a sky studded with stars, the need of a resounding amplifier to give his purple patch of rhetoric an impressive number of decibels.

As Dorothy McCall has rightly said, 'Jupiter is both a terrible god and the parody of a terrible god.'[1]

When the play was first produced he may also have stood, according to the opinion of many, for Nazism, with Aegisthus and Clytemnestra as collaborators and Orestes as the hero of resistance. This interpretation is disputed.[2] Sartre's intentions on that point are not very clear, and the Germans did not object to the production of the play. *Les Mouches* appeared primarily as a dramatic presentation of Sartre's philosophy, and more particularly of his ethics of freedom. However, the reactions of the audience were bound to be coloured by the existing climate of occupied France. It was not so much that we saw Jupiter as Hitler, as that we could not fail to see in the evil moral order established by Jupiter, and delighting him, an image of the sickening moral order which Vichy preached and tried to enforce.[3] The degradation of the citizens of Argos seemed to reflect our own. This is perhaps why we could accept what in the play might well repel spectators today: Jupiter's recurrent lapses into crude, even vulgar expressions, the sordid details, and a too vivid and nauseating impression of a city rotting in filth and stench.

Critics have been hard when judging the dramatic value of the play, and some have suggested that it is better read than performed on the stage. I would not agree. It has, I think, great theatrical possibilities. The decor matters; many scenes need the visual and auditive effects. In any case the dramatic impact does not depend on careful reading. Sartre's use of language is in no way subtle. The play lends itself easily to translation, and one of the most successful productions I have seen was, some time ago, in Cambridge – an English adaptation superbly staged and acted.[4]

After the sombre atmosphere and the brutal starkness of the dialogue which we find in *Les Mouches*, it is undoubtedly a relief to turn to a witty play written some years earlier in the century in a lighter vein: Giraudoux's *Amphitryon 38*.

Here, again, the subject is traditional; it has inspired not only Plautus and Molière but also a number of other playwrights – thirty-seven exactly in all, according to the title of the play. Not that Giraudoux has counted them, leaving to painstaking scholars the dreary task of checking. He just *knew*, with the immediate precise knowledge of one who possesses a very special gift of clair-voyance.[5] The gods will not have any secrets from him, not even Jupiter's private life.

The play has the well-known ingredients of the bedroom comedy: disguise, mistaken identity, adultery (two for good measure, Amphitryon's as well as Alcmène's), happy ending – a pattern for the modern Boulevard vaudeville. But it is a deceptive pattern. The farcical element is entirely absent. The dramatic movement has been given a particular slant. The comic is related to different aspects of the protagonists' situation and has its own very sophisticated characteristics.

It has been said, more than once, that the title of the play should have been *Alcmène*, as she is given the central role. But it might be equally just to see her function as that of a catalyst and to suggest that the subject of *Amphitryon 38* is basically the humanization of Jupiter.

This transformation of Jupiter into a man is a gradual process, somewhat jerky at times, and only satisfactorily achieved at the end of the play.

From the beginning it is clear that he envies the subtle ritual of human love-making. This he will be able to experience in taking the form of Amphitryon. But even for an all-powerful god it is not so easy to become an exact replica of a man. In the first act it takes Mercure's critical advice and skill as a 'dresser' to suggest the necessary readjustments: some signs of wear and tear on clothes which should not look eternally new, the softening of the dazzling brightness of the eyes with the help of a gold-flecked transparent film, the acquired sensation of the rush of blood in the arteries, the imprints of age on the skin and even a completely different set of mental reactions.[6]

Avatars of Jupiter

Perhaps the most human sign of this new Jupiter is to want the impossible: to look like a man and to be loved as a god. In fact he finds himself in the comic situation of being a prisoner of his human form, unable to take advantage of, even less to reveal, his divine nature. He fails immediately in his attempt to be welcomed by Alcmène as a lover and not as a husband. He fails again later when he repeatedly tries to give an exceptional character to the night they have just had together. His first exclamation, which combines complacent self-satisfaction with a wish to flatter Alcmène, 'Quelle nuit divine!' (II, ii), meets with a derisive comment: 'Tu es faible, ce matin, dans tes épithètes.' Other adjectives are equally unsuccessful. Nor does the mention of his own name in the course of the conversation give him an opening for a semi-revelation or even help him to restore in the eyes of Alcmène Jupiter's overwhelming superiority as the creator of the world. She is totally unimpressed and unconvinced by his lecture on the subject. Yet the moment has come, according to the usual scenario of his past conquests, to reveal himself in all his glory to the mortal woman he has seduced. Giving up at last the indirect approach, he relies on a more straightforward technique. Unfortunately his final effort – the sudden majestic expression, the solemn tone and the dropping of the intimate *tu* – is tenderly but briskly dismissed by Alcmène as an ill-timed flight of lunacy.

Jupiter confesses his failure to the surprised Mercure and tells him the discovery he has made, that men are not what the gods think they are. Men rebel against divine ascendancy. In their insolent pride they claim as their own creation the most generous gifts bestowed on them by the gods. We find here again the Promethean theme, but given very different implications from those in Sartre's play.

Alcmène has proved indomitable: 'C'est elle le vrai Prométhée' (II, iii). Through her, as through a prism, he has perceived qualities which are purely human and beyond the reach of his power. But, far from experiencing a feeling of anger or bitterness at the baffling revelation brought about by the first really human being he has met, he takes pleasure in imagining how delightful it would be to share Alcmène's everyday life, down to the humdrum ritual of breakfast in her company.

At the end of the play he faces Alcmène without disguise, hoping this time that she will at last agree to yield to him. Alcmène remains unconquered, but as a consolation she offers him a precious

171

treasure which the gods do not know: friendship. His curiosity aroused, Jupiter accepts the gift after being initiated as a docile pupil — a little slow in the uptake — in the ways and means of this new relationship. One more touch remains to achieve in him the perfect fusion of the divine and the human. In order to remove any trace of uneasiness which still lingers in Alcmène's mind as to what has really happened between them, he tactfully denies having slept with her and, granting her wish, wipes out the whole day from her memory: a subtle way for a god of attaining the delicacy of the true gentleman. Jupiter and Alcmène are now on the same plane and can enjoy in their last exchange of words the very civilized flavour of tender badinage.

Throughout the play Giraudoux's Jupiter has appeared rather lovable and — or because — sweetly comic, with a spontaneity and at times a naivety only conceivable on a divine scale. Most of the comedy of the character springs, we know, from the recurrent interference of his fundamental nature with the role he has chosen to play. For instance, given his prescience — as a god he sees the unfolding of events at a glance — he brings out as an original lyrical outburst in front of Alcmène's house 'Salut demeure chaste et pure', and Mercure has to point out the utter banality of this borrowing from Gounod's *Faust*. And, again, when Jupiter welcomes Amphitryon as the victorious general of the battle of Corinth, Mercure reminds him that the battle will only take place in five years' time. It is also because he is a god, having the stereotyped reactions of a god, that with the best will in the world some of his responses to human situations are often slightly wrong, whether below or beyond expectation, or beside the point. We have a good illustration of this kind of slippage when Alcmène tests his newly acquired knowledge of friendship with hypothetical cases. What would he do as a friend about the absence of a husband? Jupiter suggests a comet to guide him but does not think of restoring his presence. What about a sick child? He automatically falls back on pathetic fallacy: the general sadness of the universe, the flowers losing their perfume, the animals looking dejected, but it does not come to his mind simply to cure him.

The comic is thus related to the two-world clash which is the central theme of the play. And this is where Giraudoux's deft handling of words at the service of a very personal imaginative vision shows its true value. His stylistic flexibility is no gratuitous virtuosity or recherché quaintness. He has been seen as a *maniériste*, as a *précieux*. The last label, used by Claude-Edmonde Magny in her excellent book,[7] has been taken up several times by later critics. It is not, however, the one I would choose; I should prefer to use the term 'wit', with all its serious implications. Wit seems to me the key to a poetic irony which suffuses the whole play and renders admirably the complex relations between the divine outlook on things and the human one, between the distant myth and the present reality. It is based on unexpected links, by means of juxtaposition, parallel, comparisons or fusion between elements which are very far apart and seemingly incompatible.[8]

For Jupiter the universe he has created is a vast frieze of concepts, of impressive generalities, which he unrolls with a large sweeping gesture for Alcmène to admire; the prodigious idea of water as an elastic and incompressible force, the continents, the earth with all its wonders.

'Et le pin?' asks Alcmène, puncturing with monosyllabic precision the flimsy web of abstractions. For her it is not the existence of the terrestrial globe and its undifferentiated beauty that matters, but the landscape, which requires the pine-tree and even all the different species of pine-tree. Alcmène's world is that of the concrete, the individual, the specific detail. In vain does Jupiter describe the rainbow, in terms of molecular collision, vibration and refraction, as a masterpiece of scientific technique. How colourless, retorts Alcmène, compared with the subtle nuances of her favourite tints: 'le mordoré, le pourpre, le vert lézard'.

This outlook presupposes an intimacy between man and nature which Jupiter had not realized; for nature here is not, as it is in *Les Mouches*, the god's accomplice but man's closest ally. When Jupiter mentions immortality to Alcmène she states firmly her solidarity with everything on earth which is destined to die: 'Ne me parle pas de ne pas mourir tant qu'il n'y aura pas un légume immortel' (II, ii). The alliance between the last two words is the most striking as it seems so comically preposterous. The French word *légume*, much more than its English equivalent, which derives a kind of protective ambiguity from its different denotations, relates to nothing more than its humble nutritive value. But in the context this essentially unpoetic word acquires an unexpected lustre and nobility.

So do, throughout the play, the familiar adjuncts of man's and woman's everyday life: the stripes on a tunic, the pumice-stone and nail-file, the carpet on the floor. It is, in fact, part of Jupiter's humanization to penetrate into this world of concrete details, of individualized forms of the living world. It is significant that after his night with Alcmène and their conversation afterwards he should move from lofty considerations on his discovery of an 'infini humain' to the honey and spices, and spoon and plate of a morning meal with her. Significant also that at the end of the play, when trying to grasp the meaning of the abstract word friendship, he should tentatively recall some particular scenes which have previously been for him totally inexplicable: the playful games between an ocelot and a young wild boar, regular conversations in the alley of a park between a high civil servant and a gardener.

The familiar, never trivialized, is given a pleasing naturalness by the use of anachronisms delicately tempered by the local colour of ancient Greece and oblique references to myths. These elements are wittily combined in different ways, all contributing to the poetic atmosphere of the play. The Trumpeter, part of the stylization of the Greek decor, acquires an individuality and a lifelike presence through his pride in having invented musical scores of silent variations as overtures to the only note his instrument can produce. Ecclissé, Alcmène's servant, for the benefit of the Theban women who have beset the house on hearing of Jupiter's imminent seduction, describes the attitude and appearance of the chosen woman like a modern reporter presenting a star or a royal bride: 'Son costume, vous voulez savoir son costume? Non, elle n'est pas nue. Elle a une tunique d'un linge inconnu qu'on appelle la soie, souligné d'un rouge nouveau appelé garance' (II, v). We are, however, in the wonderland of mythology, and the imaginary picture created by the servant includes a gigantic eagle – Jupiter's bird – which Alcmène is supposed to be nonchalantly feeding with diamonds.

The rich mythological lore of Jupiter's fantastic deeds is sparingly used and introduced only when in keeping with the main theme of the play. The most relevant feature of the god's personality is evidently his strong penchant for metamorphosis: metamorphosing either himself (temporarily) or human beings (definitively) to bestow on them honours, punishments or consolation. But, as we may expect from Giraudoux's wit, the well-known stories provoke unexpected comments or are given an original twist. When, in Act I, scene iii, Amphitryon imagines that their conjugal life will be blessed in their old age by their being transformed into trees like Philemon and Baucis, Alcmène objects to the tedious regularity of having to change one's foliage every year. Besides, how dangerous the power which can according to its whims arbitrarily upset the pattern of the natural world! Near the end of the play Alcmène expresses the fear that Jupiter, in revenge, might play a malicious variation on the fate of Procne and Philomela and change Amphitryon and herself into beings of a different species, forever incapable of communicating with each other: a nightingale and a toad, a willow and a fish, perhaps.

Leda's visit to Alcmène brings about a new development in the plot based on the traditional device of mistaken identity often found in comedy. But at the same time she calls up one of Jupiter's most graceful metamorphoses, and this fugitive grace is exquisitely preserved in the basically matter-of-fact conversation between her and Alcmène.

Turning away from the immaculate whiteness of a regal swan flying to the zenith and thinking back to the glib-tongued, bearded traveller in the streets of Argos, the terrifying Satanic buffoon, one might be tempted to wonder whether it is Jupiter's seemingly inexhaustible store of disguises that so conveniently entitles him to survival, for better or for worse.

We see how differently he has appeared when conjured up by a philosopher and by a poet.

Not his last avatars, I suspect.

NOTES

1 *The Theatre of Jean-Paul Sartre* (New York and London, 1969), p. 18.
2 See particularly Anthony Manser's *Sartre: A Philosophic Study*, 2nd edn (London, 1967), pp. 246–7.
3 To give one example, not among the most sinister: the institution in all the state schools of a compulsory weekly hour of 'action morale', with topics chosen by Vichy and going from the writing of a fulsome letter of thanksgiving addressed to the Maréchal to the edifying visit to a German armoured train.
4 Margaret Drabble acted the part of Electra in a very impressive way, and also, from what I gathered, had very much to do with the text and producing of the play.
5 See Claude-Edmonde Magny's excellent remarks on the arbitrary and god-like characteristics of Giraudoux's omniscience in *Précieux Giraudoux* (Paris, 1945), pp. 79–81.
6 Paul A. Mankin in his work *Precious Irony: The Theatre of Giraudoux* (The Hague, 1971) has devoted a number of very interesting remarks

to Mercure's function in the play, this function being primarily 'that of an interloper, essentially disinterested, yet all-knowing' (p. 67).

7 Magny, *Précieux Giraudoux*.

8 This presence of clashing elements in Giraudoux's plays has been commented on by Jacques Guicharnaud with slightly different implications, and he has expressed it in most felicitous terms: 'His plays are in the form of debates: but the debates are not really discussions: they are *an aesthetic equilibrium between contrary definitions*' (my italics) (*Modern French Theatre, from Giraudoux to Genet* (New Haven and London, 1962), p. 28).

13
Reality and myth in Montherlant's
Don Juan

RICHARD GRIFFITHS

Despite the failure of his *Don Juan* in the theatre in 1958, Montherlant remained convinced, to the end of his life, that it was one of the best of his plays:

Cette pièce qui passa pour grossière ne peut être comprise que par des esprits très déliés et très cultivés: c'est dire que son avenir est sombre. Mais, s'il existait une postérité tout idéale, où les œuvres d'art fussent jugés selon leur mérite, *Don Juan* occuperait la première place de mes œuvres de théâtre . . .'[1]

He eventually republished the play in 1972, under the title *La Mort qui fait le trottoir*.[2] In contrast to Montherlant's own view of it, however, this remarkable play has received critical neglect, and, in some cases, vilification.

It appears that one of the things that led Montherlant to single out *Don Juan* in this way was its concern with 'truth'. On another occasion, linking it with *Pasiphaé*, he said: 'Les deux pièces où j'ai été assez loin dans l'expression de la vérité, *Pasiphaé* et *Don Juan* . . .'[3]

The statement is striking, and at first sight paradoxical. For these are the only two plays in which Montherlant takes as his central character a figure of myth. Mythology, as Montherlant saw it, was at variance with the aims of his mature theatre, which was particularly concerned with the complexity of truth. He himself, after early experimentation with mythology in his abortive play *Les Crétois*, had bemoaned the undramatic nature of the symbolism that stems from myth:

Je voyais tant de sens divers à la fable de Minos, que si je voulais les indiquer tous dans ma pièce, celle-ci perdait son unité, devenait une manière de monstre encombré d'idéologie et d'ésotérisme, et l'intérêt dramatique sombrait.[4]

Pasiphaé (1936), though a fragment of *Les Crétois*, was produced years after the latter had been abandoned,[5] and had moved far from this symbolic plane. As Montherlant himself put it,

177

J'anéantissais tout l'appareil ésotérique de l'anecdote pour ne conserver que sa signification morale . . . Nul besoin pour y pénétrer de connaissances mythologiques, historiques, archéologiques . . . La nécessité de la pièce est ailleurs, elle est en ceci: un être humain se trouve placé devant un acte que l'opinion de son temps reprouve, et qu'il a envie de faire. Il se décide à le faire. Durant ces moments, que se passe-t-il en lui?[6]

This short scene, in which Pasiphaé discusses with the Chorus the act which she is about to commit (copulation with the bull), is thus stripped of all mythological overtones; and, though the format is reminiscent of poetic drama, the content is psychological, in the sense that Montherlant's mature drama was to be. In the case of *Pasiphaé*, the apparent paradox in relation to 'truth' appears to have been resolved.

When we come to *Don Juan*, however, the paradox redoubles. For there, in the very period when Montherlant was pre-eminently concerned with dramatic reality and truth, we find a play in which the dramatic techniques themselves, as well as the central subject, seem to be aimed at producing an impression of unreality. In this, *Don Juan* stands apart from all Montherlant's other dramatic output.

'Assez loin dans l'expression de la vérité'? We must obviously look more closely at the meaning of 'truth' in Montherlant's artistic vision, and at his attitudes to 'myth' and 'reality' in *Don Juan*.

In Montherlant's mature theatre, his view of 'reality' rested on a rejection of all that was artificial in the traditional artistic depiction of it, and on a positive desire to depict human nature in all its complexity and inconsistency. In this, his aims were closer to those of modern novelists than of modern playwrights. Human nature, he believed, is full of contradictions, as is human thought. He ridiculed all futile attempts at explaining such things by 'synthesizing' them. Stressing the artificiality of stage conventions, he wrote:

Le théâtre est fondé sur la cohérence des caractères, et la vie est fondée sur leur incohérence. L'inconstance de Ferrante est une des données de *La Reine morte*. La cohérence de ce caractère est d'être incohérent.[7]

One of the dangers of dramatic art was, in his view, 'la simplification à outrance des caractères'. So his plays are filled with inconsistencies; a character may justify a course of action to himself; and then do the opposite. 'Là est la vie',[8] says Montherlant. 'Une pièce, selon moi, vaut par ce qu'elle expose de vérité humaine, et, autant que possible, neuve.'[9]

In this search for 'vérité humaine' through the depiction of human psychology, Montherlant relied heavily on a tradition of 'realistic' staging (despite the occasional stylization of exchanges in his historical dramas). His plays, both historical and modern, lay right outside the main trends in the modern French theatre, and eschewed the striking innovations in theatrical techniques used by playwrights from Jarry to Ionesco. Everywhere, that is, except in *Don Juan*. The appearance of this play, in 1958, seemed a remarkable reversal of all that had gone before.

The return to a mythical subject was an unexpected one. The dramatic techniques used were, however, even more surprising. They appear to stem from a number of non-realistic sources, from the *commedia dell'arte* to the modern theatre. The audience is made perpetually aware that it is watching a performance, that the world that is depicted is artificial. La Comtesse, in the midst of her theatrical lamentations on the death of her husband Le Commandeur, translates for the benefit of the audience:

Angelillo del cielo, permite, que yo ponga mis labios de terciopelo carmesi (*au public*) 'que je pose mes lèvres de velours cramoisi' *en tu frente purisima. Unidos! siempre unidos!* (*au public*) Ça, naturellement, ça veut dire: 'Unis! unis à jamais!' (110)

Similarly, Don Juan includes the audience in his gesture, pointing out all the cuckolds around him:

(*Désignant l'un après l'autre les passants*) Un cocu! Encore un. Encore un. (*Son geste circulaire englobe maintenant la salle, et désigne les spectateurs*) Encore un. Là, encore un autre. (22)

The 'Carnavaliers', in Act II, act as a kind of stylized chorus. At one point, they repeat 'en sourdine' behind a speech of Don Juan's: 'Quel imbécile! Non, mais quel imbécile!' (78). At another, when the Commandeur has commented that he has the impression that someone is watching them, and Don Juan, after looking, replies, 'Mais non, voyons. La solitude est absolue', we have a stage direction which runs: *Les carnavaliers sont très apparents* (87).

Much of the play is filled with details which reinforce the audience's uncertainties about what is real and what is unreal. The three Penseurs-qui-ont-des-idées-sur-Don-Juan (III, ii) are clearly two-dimensional caricatures of the same type as Ionesco's Bartoloméus I, II and III in *L'Impromptu de l'Alma*, which had first been produced at the Studio des Champs-Elysées in February 1956, three months before the writing of *Don Juan*, and two years before its publication and performance.[10] The influence of Ionesco, indeed, appears to be present at various points, including the 'horloge dérangé' which strikes 'les onze coups de minuit' (II, ii) and the 'coq détraqué' which crows to announce 'L'aube quand la nuit tombe' (III, iv). In Act I, scene i, Don Juan gives directions to passers-by who ask the way, and they always go in the opposite direction. This culminates in the occasion when Don Juan himself makes a mistake in his instructions to an old lady, telling her to turn left; luckily he is then certain that she will conform to the pattern of the others:

DON JUAN Que le diable l'emporte! Je lui ai dit tout cela au hasard. Heureusement qu'elle va prendre le quai à droite. (*La vieille femme s'en va et tourne sur le quai à droite.*)   (36)

All these apparently incidental details, and many others, which are in no way central to the action, alert the audience to the debate about reality and unreality which is central to the play. At the heart of that debate is the whole question of the 'myth' of Don Juan. Of this, Montherlant has written:

La pièce fut écrite en mai 1956 . . . C'est seulement en la relisant, en novembre 1956, que je vis que je l'avais écrite en réaction contre l'abondante littérature qui a voulu faire de Don Juan un personnage chargé de sens profond: un être démoniaque, ou un Faust, ou un Hamlet, – 'un mythe'.[11]

Montherlant's apparent surprise at the import of what he himself had written is typically disingenuous. For in *Don Juan* nothing is clearer than the fact that the author is consciously reacting against the 'idées toutes faites' relating to the mythical Don Juan. Not only do we have the overtly satirical Act III, scene ii, with the three grotesque 'Penseurs-qui-ont-des-idées-sur-Don-Juan' producing theories about him which range from his being 'en quête de l'absolu, c'est-à-dire de Dieu' to his drama's being 'le drame même de l'artiste, qui n'arrive jamais à réaliser parfaitement ce qu'il imagine, comme Don Juan n'arrive jamais à réaliser l'amour'; the play also contains a number of scenes in which other people come out with equally false generalizations. Don Basile sees him, successively, as 'un rêveur, un cérébral' (24), 'un malade' (25), and 'un raté, un pauvre type' (26).[12] Le Commandeur believes that he is 'malheureux' (II, iv); and the Double Veuve encapsulates it all with the view that Don Juan 'a dépassé le stade de la personne pour accéder à celui du mythe' (127). As Don Juan himself says, in Act III, scene iv,

Ce que je suis mourra, non ce que je ne suis pas. Ce que je ne suis pas, tous le carillonnent, avec quelle outrecuidance! Don Basile, le Commandeur, la Veuve, les trois doctes. Les voilà, mes spectres, les spectres de ce que je ne suis pas. Ce sont eux qui me persécutent et m'écœurent, et qui me survivront. Ils vivront, car ils sont le mensonge.   (146–7)

By this reference back, at the end of the last act, to so many different scenes, Don Juan shows the extent to which the debate about the falsity of his 'myth' lies at the centre of the whole play. Is the play, therefore, *solely* caricatural? Such a negative interpretation could ease our way towards explaining why Montherlant had written such an 'untypical' drama. But there is surely more to it than that. After all, Montherlant said he had gone 'assez loin dans l'expression de la vérité' in this play. There is, we will find, a positive side to the play, which rests on the reality and 'vérité' of Don Juan himself, in contrast to the world around him.

In one of the speeches which Montherlant had originally written for the play, but then rejected, Don Juan says:

Quelquefois je me demande: est-ce moi, est-ce vraiment moi qui suis le lieu de ce drame? Ce drame me paraît tellement effrayant qu'il m'arrive de douter si c'est moi qui le contiens et le supporte.[13]

At the beginning of Act III, there is an equally significant exchange between Don Juan and Alcacer:

ALCACER   Quand je pense à tant de comédies où des fils usent de mille
              stratagèmes pour tirer quelques méchants écus de leur père!
DON JUAN   Oui, mais cette fois nous sommes dans une tragédie. (123)

In the old metaphor, life is a play. Most of us participate in it without perceiving its nature. Yet Don Juan is perpetually aware of it. Montherlant's play, by its self-conscious artificiality, stresses the artificiality of life. Don Juan, by his awareness, stands out from this unreal background, and proclaims his own reality.

The elements of parody add to the sense of the artificiality of the world around him. Themes from the Don Juan legend are deformed and ridiculed: the statue that arrives to dinner with Don Juan, for example, is a mock-up made of 'carton-pâte' and containing the three Carnavaliers. Similarly, themes from Molière are equally mocked. Giving, for example, a brooch to Linda, Don Juan says:

Tiens, va, prends-la. Je te la donne pour l'amour de . . . Non, je ne peux pas dire 'pour l'amour de Dieu'; Dieu, ce n'est pas sérieux. Pour l'amour de qui? Pour l'amour de moi? Bah! disons 'pour l'amour de toi', et qu'on n'en parle plus. (48)

There are other elements of parody, too, which relate to other authors. Barrès, for example; the Deuxième Carnavalier, commenting on the Carnavalier-chef's description of how, when he was burgling the Marquis's bedroom, the sleeping Marquis had '[lâché] un énorme pet', says: 'Il est des lieux où souffle l'esprit' (69).[14] Claudel, too, figures among those parodied: Don Juan's placing of the bouquet at the feet of the Virgin's statue, when he is departing, and the scene between La Double Veuve and Alcacer, are both reminiscent of scenes in *Le Soulier de satin*, as is Don Juan's 'C'est par ses passions qu'on est sauvé' (60), just before the placing of the bouquet (this typically Claudelian theme being completely transformed and mocked by the context).[15]

These parodies do not merely serve to highlight the artificiality of the play itself. The Claudel parodies (together with the numerous parodies of biblical and liturgical phraseology) illuminate one of the major themes of the play − Don Juan's attitude to religion. And the statue 'en carton-pâte' symbolizes not only, as Don Juan points out, 'toutes les impostures',[16] but also the unreality of the characters in the play itself. For it is not just the statue that is made of pasteboard: the Carnavalier-chef's first description of the Marquis de Ventras is 'On dirait tout à fait une de ces figures de Carnaval en carton-pâte, que nous fabriquons, et qu'on met sur les chars' (67).[17]

The characters are not merely unreal; they spend their time playacting. The Comtesse, we are told in Act II, scene iv, will soon be seen in her 'frémissement spécial'. We are treated, in the next scene, to a blatantly self-conscious *performance* by her, as the despairing widow on her husband's body. The Commandeur, planning his own tomb, arranges a 'performance' for posterity, in which all is false (110). Don Juan perpetually plays a part for others, too, so that all his attitudes come into question for us. When Alcacer criticizes his 'extravagante confiance' he admits: 'Je n'ai pas confiance, mais j'agis comme si j'avais confiance' (115). He appears vulgar, yet informs us at one point that that, too, is an act:

Et comme il n'y a qu'un seul moyen tout à fait sûr de plaire aux femmes, c'est la vulgarité, tu peux te dire aussi que depuis un demi-siècle je joue la comédie de la vulgarité. Ne t'étonne donc pas si j'ai des rides, comme tous les vieux acteurs.   (122–3)

But Don Juan *knows* he is acting various parts. Amid all the characters made of 'carton-pâte' he stands out as a real, and rounded, figure. He is real in that he does not conform to a pattern. As Montherlant himself said of him, 'Don Juan, dans ma pièce, est un personnage simple . . . Le trait essentiel de son tempérament, c'est la mobilité.' (So much could be said of most of Montherlant's heroes.) He conforms to Montherlant's theory of 'syncrétisme et alternance', whereby human beings are full of different tendencies, many of them opposed to each other, which in their natural state alternate, rather than attempting to conform to some kind of factitious pattern.

The Spanish race, in Montherlant's view, most evidently embodied these qualities, as he had pointed out in an article entitled 'Syncrétisme et alternance dans l'âme espagnole', written in the late twenties.[18] In it he quoted a number of other writers in support of this view. What he quoted from Unamuno, on Lope de Vega, is particularly relevant to his own theatre:

Chez Lope de Vega, certains personnages changent tout d'un coup, surtout à la fin de ses *comedias*, sans que rien le justifie. L'Allemand Schack écrit des Espagnols: 'Les sentiments les plus opposés naissent dans leur cœur, sans présenter les mêmes gradations que chez nous.'[19]

Later on in the same article he quoted from Barrès, in a passage which singles out Don Juan as a particular example:

De province à province, en outre, vous trouvez les plus violentes oppositions, et dans chaque être même. Je n'insiste par sur les biographies particulières. Séville nous donnerait Don Juan . . . Ces êtres doubles, pour nous énigmatiques, sont les produits naturels du sol.[20]

In other articles by Montherlant in the inter-war period, we find further comments which throw light on the later play's central character. In 'La Tragédie de l'Espagne', written in 1925,[21] he described 'le mysticisme et le sens jouisseur, qui forment le fond du caractère espagnol'. And, singling out yet again Seville and

Andalusia, he spoke of 'le génie andalou' in the following terms:

Il reste impossible de composer la palette espagnole en y omettant cette note si franche de sensualité et de facilité heureuse. (L'Andalou n'est pas triste. S'il aime la tristesse, c'est pour s'en enchanter . . . L'alegria, la sevillana, qui sont purement andalouses, sont gaies.)

This early fascination with the Spanish character was later to be echoed in *Don Juan*; note how similar Montherlant's remarks after the 1958 performance were to what he had been saying in 1925 (though, typically, by now he has complicated the picture by adding to the joy of the *sevillana* the 'alternate' characteristics of the *cuadro flamenco* − 'la douleur et la mort'):

Mon Don Juan est un Méridional . . . c'est un Sévillan blagueur et brûlé . . . 'pas sérieux' et tragique, en qui se succèdent, apparaissant et disparaissant avec la même rapidité, les visions obsessionnelles du plaisir et de ce qui l'entoure (la chasse, l'intrigue) et de la mort: tensions et détentes alternées et instantanées . . . Je répète que ce que je viens de décrire est typiquement sévillan. Le mot 'Séville' est d'abord synonyme de gaîté. La *sevillana* est une danse toute d'allégresse. Mais le *cuadro flamenco* sevillan n'est inspiré que par la douleur et la mort. Ce mélange du léger et du poignant c'est Séville, et c'est Don Juan, Sévillan.[22]

Montherlant's sixty-six-year-old Don Juan is obsessed with sensuality and with death. Like Montherlant's typical Spaniard, he is divided, too, between 'le mysticisme et le sens jouisseur'. Contradictory attitudes alternate in this impulsive figure, who by that very 'alternance' is *real*.

Death dominates this drama, and Don Juan's attitude to it at first seems clear. The word 'death' is continually on his lips. He puts on a mask in Act I: 'Comme cela, la mort ne me reconnaîtra pas!' (45). He asks his son Alcacer whether his face is marked by death (53). He needs 'la chasse' and its excitement to keep him alive. As he says in Act I, after listing the two rendezvous that have been arranged, 'J'ai une raison de vivre du moins jusqu'à après-demain. Deux jours de gagnés' (57). He needs, he says later, 'des preuves que j'existe', for 'tout ce qui ne me transporte pas me tue' (85). At the end of the play, after the scene with Ana, he strikes the same note:

Je n'ai pas osé lui dire ce qui me brûlait les lèvres: 'Je serai exact au rendez-vous de ce bonheur, car bientôt je vais cesser d'être.' L'atroce de n'exister plus dans peu de temps ne peut être adouci que par des joies intenses, et je suis capable de tout pour les obtenir. Je deviendrais fou si quelque chose devait m'échapper, avant que tout m'échappe. (167)

Yet it is amazing, given his 'crainte de la mort prochaine',[23] that there are moments when he appears actually to welcome death. In Act II, scene iv he tries to cut short the Commandeur's questions by telling him to get on and kill him: 'Tuez-moi, Commandeur, tuez-moi. Je suis fatigué des explications . . . Je veux être en une seconde dans le néant, et ne me sentir plus' (80). A similar weariness is to be found in Act III, scene iv, where he says to Alcacer: 'Quand on a eu une vie comme la mienne – cette danse perpétuelle sur des pointes d'épées – mourir est aussi la fin des risques et des appréhensions' (150–1). Then, as people arrive, and Alcacer tells him to hide, he replies calmly: 'Donc, la mort. Bon. Je l'attendais depuis si longtemps' (152).

The play is full of similar contradictions. Many stem clearly from 'alternance' in this extremely mobile character, and from his ability to say 'ce qui lui passe par la tête' (166). Others, possibly, from his perpetual ability to play a part. (When he has asked for death, the Commandeur spares him with the words 'Je ne te tuerai pas. Tu en as trop envie, si tu es sincère, mais il est probable que tu ne l'es pas' (80–1). His sincerity is always in doubt. It is clear that he pretends to be unhappy, in order to comfort the Commandeur (the stage direction says *contrefaisant*); yet most of the play seems to suggest that he is indeed basically unhappy. Conversely, the stage direction *très sincère* occurs when Don Juan has *imagined* himself into a situation where he had a daughter who had been seduced: '(*Très sincère*) Tudieu! Tripoter ma fille! Coquin! tu m'en rendras raison' (94). Small wonder that, after Don Juan's scene with Ana, Alcacer is uncertain: 'J'allais vous croire sincère avec le Commandeur, et il paraît que vous ne l'étiez pas. Etiez-vous sincère avec Ana de Ulloa?' (163). Montherlant's own later comment on the Don Juan–Ana scene throws into doubt the whole question of 'sincerity':

Ce qu'il dit n'est jamais pesé, fignolé, appuyé, *pensé*: cela est *jailli*. Ses paroles tendres à Ana proviennent d'une exaltation; elles sont sincères, mais de la sincérité d'une minute.[24]

Where Don Juan's 'mobility' is particularly in evidence is in relation to God. This atheist, for whom religion is 'quelque chose de comique', is nevertheless obsessed with it. His speech is filled with deformations of religious language, used in relation to sexuality: 'Le pavé me l'a donnée, le pavé me l'a reprise: que la volonté de Dieu soit faite' (71); 'Le monde est racheté par ce moment de la créature humaine où elle est désirable et où elle consent. C'est vraiment cela qui rachète tout' (16); 'C'est une des mystères de la passion' (164); 'Il [Ana's love] m'est une lumière au milieu de mes ténèbres' (95); 'En servant votre fille je lui ai fait honneur, et je nous ai fait plaisir. Gloire à Dieu au plus haut des cieux!' (92). He continually acts with bravado in relation to God, too: 'Je ne demanderai pardon à un Dieu qui n'existe pas pour des crimes qui n'existent pas' (79); 'Tuez-moi, Commandeur, pour l'amour de ce Dieu qui n'existe pas' (80). When the statue appears at the end, he cries: 'Même si tu es un spectre, ne pense pas que tu me fasses croire en Dieu. Les morts reviennent peut-être, mais cela ne prouve pas Dieu' (170). The discovery that it is a hoax reinforces him in these views.

All this appears to relate Montherlant's Don Juan to a traditional model, and particularly to Molière's. But all is not so simple. Don Juan's obsession with religion involves an attraction to it. He ends Act I by placing a bouquet at the feet of the Virgin. In Act III he vows to go in pilgrimage to Santiago if his life is saved. The vow is made in typically ambiguous terms, but it will be kept, he assures Alcacer (151–2). Later, he swears an oath to Ana, on the cross she is wearing (160); and after her departure, he thanks God for what has happened: 'Une fois de plus, Dieu m'a protégé dans ma guerre! Dieu m'a protégé! C'est lui qui l'a conduite vers moi sur un char de feu' (162). Alcace echoes the puzzlement of the audience when he says: 'Vous ne croyez pas en Dieu, et vous l'invoquez à chaque instant.' To this, Don Juan's response is a very telling one: 'Il y a en moi une exaltation et une passion qui ont besoin du recours à Dieu, même si je ne crois pas en Dieu' (163).

The complexity of Don Juan's attitude to religion matches Montherlant's own. This non-believer was obsessed by religion, to the extent that a large number of his plays deal with it. De Gaulle once aptly described him as 'longeant indéfiniment le bord de l'océan religieux, que son génie ne quitte pas des yeux, ni de l'âme, sans y pénétrer jamais'.[25]

Both *Pasiphaé* and *Don Juan* dealt in this way with themes close to Montherlant's own heart – in *Pasiphaé*, forbidden love, and one person standing out against the conventions of morality; in *Don Juan*, sexuality, religion, and the duality of the Spanish character as a prime example of 'alternance'. Perhaps, however, he felt that there was added 'truth' in these two plays because of their treatment of two themes which equally fascinated him, but which are not normally treated in the theatre: in *Pasiphaé* bestiality, of which he wrote, thirty-five years later, 'si j'avais consacré un peu plus de temps à mon œuvre', he would have written the definitive book on it, describing it as 'la bestialité . . . sujet qu'on n'évoque que de loin avec horreur, que les plus intelligents, les plus courageux et les mieux informés n'ont pas osé aborder, et sur lequel j'ai – ou ai eu – surtout par mes longs séjours en Afrique du Nord, une documentation que personne n'a';[26] in *Don Juan* 'la drague', so important in Montherlant's own life (as recent works have shown), and in his view of mankind. The figure of 'Don Juan', as a human type, had obsessed him for years.[27]

In his other writings on Don Juan, Montherlant had shown a surprising tendency to generalize. While reacting against Don Juan as a 'myth', he had nevertheless characterized him as a 'type'. Suggesting that those who insist that Don Juan must be 'malheureux' have got it wrong, he tended to go to the opposite extreme and insist that it was of the essence of Don Juan to be *happy*: 'Lorsqu'il chasse, Don Juan se réalise; il fait ce qu'il aime faire, et il est donc heureux.'[28]

In the play, however, as in all other plays by Montherlant, the desire to generalize has disappeared. Don Juan becomes a three-dimensional human being, neither a 'myth' nor a 'type'. It is impossible to say whether he is happy or unhappy, or when, or how. (Some of his clearest statements about this matter are made in the scene with the Commandeur, when his sincerity is in doubt.) This three-dimensional figure moves in a two-dimensional world. He is surrounded by 'fantoches' in a clearly 'dramatic performance' based on artificiality. For this most 'real' of characters Montherlant has created a, for him, new form of theatre on which to set off the unreality of myth, and the reality of man.

There remains one problem: the ending of the play. Don Juan, heading for Seville to continue 'la chasse', puts on a mask once more. But, though he thinks it is his usual one, this one is a death's head; and he finds it impossible to remove it: 'Il s'est incrusté dans mon visage, il s'est mélangé à ma chair.' Nevertheless he sets off on his wild search once more: 'Une tête de mort? A la bonne heure! En avant! Au galop pour Séville.'

This incursion of the supernatural, into a play which has denied it, is surprising. But so, too, are the overtones of 'myth' which this ending produces, and which Montherlant himself underlined in one of his comments on the play:

Ses dernières répliques, quand il part chasser à Séville . . . ont un caractère presque démentiel qui l'apparente aux héros légendaires obligés par le destin d'aller sans cesse de l'avant: le Juif errant, Io dans la tragédie d'Eschyle . . .[29]

It has been suggested that Montherlant here denies himself, and shows that his 'Don Juan' is as much a myth as anyone else's; one critic has commented: 'Voulu en opposition au "mythe" dont on se moque dans la scène des Penseurs, il devient, comme les autres, prisonnier du Mythe: il rentre dans le monde du Don Juan traditionnel.'[30] Yet this is a misunderstanding of what has happened. For the last scene should not be taken as providing truths about the play as a whole. The answer lies with Montherlant's own theories of the human character. He depicts his own psychology as being as 'alternate' as that of his characters.[31] His audience has been lulled into perceiving the supernatural of the legend as being explicable; the statue of the Commandeur has turned out to be the disguised Carnavaliers. Similarly, the audience has come to see Don Juan as a real man, and as the 'anti-myth'. In one fell swoop, in one minute of action, these presumptions are reversed − and the curtain falls.

Montherlant once described the famous bullfighter Manolete as finishing 'sa série de passes par une *manoletina*'.[32] His own form of *manoletina* was, he said, the way he finished his plays with an unexpected twist, the end of *Celles qu'on prend dans ses bras* being, in his view, 'une passe de ma marque, purissime . . .'. Ravier says one thing, and does the other. This is 'un principe qui m'est si personnel, et si dominant en moi'.[33] In *Don Juan*, the unexpected end is a *manoletina* of a different sort; it stresses that the author is as much a figure of 'alternance' as his hero.

NOTES

1 'Notes', in *La Mort qui fait le trottoir* (Paris, 1972), p. 165.
2 Though the text of this new edition is 'revu et corrigé', the main differences are of points of detail. Most additions are concerned with underlining traits which already exist in the 1958 Gallimard edition. It is to this 1958 edition that I shall be referring in this article (page numbers being quoted in brackets after quotations from the play). Any significant variants will be noted in notes.
3 'Notes', in *La Mort qui fait le trottoir*, p. 186.
4 Montherlant, introductory speech to *Pasiphaé* (1938) in Montherlant, *Théâtre* (Paris, 1958), p. 103.
5 *Les Crétois*, started in 1928, was abandoned shortly thereafter.

6 Introductory speech to *Pasiphaé*, in *Théâtre*, 1958, p. 104.
7 'En relisant *La Reine morte*' (1954), in *Théâtre*, p. 254.
8 Preface to *Fils de personne* (1943), in *Théâtre*, p. 272.
9 'Après relecture de *Demain il fera jour* en 1965', in *La Tragédie sans masque* (Paris, 1972), p. 101.
10 The writer of this article remembers attending *L'Impromptu de l'Alma* in 1956, and *Don Juan* in 1958, and being struck by the similarity between the two scenes.
11 'Notes sur Don Juan', in *Don Juan* (Paris, 1958), p. 177.
12 Echoing these 'petits ventrus' whom Montherlant described as professing that Don Juan was a 'raté', because humanity envies him and 'veut qu'il soit malheureux comme elle pour n'avoir plus à l'envier' (*Sur les femmes*, (Paris, 1958), p. 69).
13 *La Tragédie sans masque*, p. 188.
14 This is the first sentence of Barrès's *La Colline inspirée*.
15 Montherlant was familiar with Claudel's play, which he mentions in his *Carnets*, and which was, of course, the play which succeeded *La Reine morte* at the Comédie-Francaise in 1942.
16 The 1972 text includes the further phrase 'les divines et les humaines'.
17 In the 1972 text, the point is made even more clearly by the fact that it is the Commandeur who is thus described.
18 And reprinted in *Coups de soleil* (Paris, 1976), pp. 63–8.
19 *Ibid.*, p. 64.
20 *Ibid.*, p. 65.
21 And published in *La Revue de France* in 1929, then republished in *Service inutile* (Paris, 1936).
22 'Notes sur Don Juan', in *Don Juan*, pp. 178–9.
23 *Ibid.*, p. 180.
24 *Ibid.*, p. 178.
25 *La Tragédie sans masque*, p. 167.
26 *La Marée du soir (Carnets 1968–1971)* (Paris, 1972; année 1971), p. 122.
27 See, e.g., the section of *Sur les femmes* entitled 'Don Juan le satisfait'.
28 *Sur les femmes*, new edn (Paris, 1958), pp. 59–60.
29 'Notes sur Don Juan', in *Don Juan*, p. 180.
30 Fernande Ravoil, in *La Mort qui fait le trottoir*, p. 177.
31 It is worth noting that much of his writing about his own theatre seems self-consciously aimed at producing this vision of the creative artist.
32 Notes on *Celles qu'on prend dans ses bras*, in *Théâtre*, p. 839.
33 *Ibid.*, p. 839.

14

The myth of the theatre in the theatre of Anouilh: a personal impression*

DONALD WATSON

In his effort to understand himself, his life and the life around him, Anouilh the dramatist would appear to have sought an answer in the theatre itself. Always present in his work from the beginning has been the tendency to use the theatre as a metaphor for life; little by little this aspect of his work increased in prominence and passed from being a series of devices to becoming a major ingredient in his dramatic form.

At the end of his chapter on Anouilh in *Forces in Modern French Drama*,[1] W. D. Howarth, commenting on the dramatist hero of *La Grotte* (1961),[2] suggests that Anouilh 'has become the prisoner of his own imaginary world, living in a new intimacy with his created characters, who possess . . . a reality more real than that of the world itself'. And he wonders 'what new direction he takes to escape from it'. Perhaps one might now surmise that he has not escaped, but rather dug himself in so deep that he not only confirms a tendency already manifest, but almost comes to believe that the theatre is the only prison through whose windows the reality of the world can be glimpsed. Dare one go on to hint that Anouilh has finally conferred on the theatre the status of a myth?

Myth? The complexities involved in the interpretation of this word are such that it may be the simplest solution is to be preferred.

MYTH: 'a word introduced into the English language little more than a century ago as a name for a form of story characteristic of primitive people', so runs the definition in *O.E.D.*, 'a purely fictitious narrative usually involving supernatural persons, actions or events, and embodying some popular idea concerning natural or historical phenomena'; ' . . . today the meaning popularly attached to the word is little more than a tale devoid of truth or a non-existent person or thing, or event . . .', adds Fowler in his *Modern English Usage*.[3]

No one would deny that the stories of Anouilh's plays are 'purely

---

* Jean Anouilh died on 3 October 1987, while this book was in the press.

190

fictitious narratives', even if they may represent historical personages – such as Henry II, Joan of Arc, Robespierre or Napoleon[4] – and actions and events recorded in history. Unlike his much-admired Giraudoux, for example, Anouilh does not favour 'supernatural persons, actions or events', unless one accepts mythical figures such as Medea, Antigone or Orestes as being supernatural in the sense that they are 'out of this world'.

Yet all the characters mentioned could be said to embody 'some popular idea concerning natural or historical phenomena'.[5] But so too, in a broader sense, could many of the figures popularized by Anouilh: his Duchesses, his Servant Girls, his Generals, Doctors, Actors and Actresses, etc., even if this 'popular idea' is transmitted through familiar theatrical types.

The idea of myth today has clearly extended so widely that one is tempted to sense something 'mythical' about the whole of Anouilh's drama solely because it is so patently 'unreal'. But if a myth is 'little more than a tale devoid of truth or a non-existent person or thing or event', something 'imagined' or 'unreal', then it is reduced to meaning little more than 'a fiction'.

But in what sense are Anouilh's historical or mythological characters 'non-existent' or 'devoid of truth'?

While considering Anouilh's 'ludic approach to the theatre', H. G. McIntyre stresses that his use of well-known stories or characters (mythological or historical) underlines the artificial nature of the dramatic process:

The mythological characters of these plays . . . are by definition literary or dramatic fictions since each is an integral part of its own story and they exist in our mind *not as real people but as fictions. Their reality depends on the very fact that they do not have to try to be realistic.* (My italics.)[6]

They are not 'devoid of truth' or 'non-existent' in the usual sense; but their truth and their being depend upon the artificiality which governs their creation in a way peculiar to Anouilh. Mythical characters are essentially non-realistic. No wonder then that their lack of realism should be associated with their 'theatricality'.

Anouilh's treatment of figures drawn from Greek myths has been thoroughly covered, as recently by E. Freeman in his edition of *Eurydice* and *Médée*.[7] Few critics of Anouilh and his plays have failed to point out his continual, and some would say abusive use of 'theatre in the theatre' in his dramatic form and in the constant references made by his characters to the fact that they are

191

actors performing roles in this or that play and so by analogy in the theatre of life.[8]

Just as the mixture of illusion and reality is the essential subject of theatre, by making an audience fully conscious of the confusion Anouilh makes its members feel that this very mixture *is* the reality of life.

Such too is the nature of myth, neither real nor unreal, because it contains a truth about life that exists on so many levels that it conveys 'truths' rather than 'the truth' and offers no clear-cut solutions. So theatre is easily given a mythical value because it holds the key to an understanding of that balance between reality and unreality which constitutes our comprehension of life.

In his introduction, Freeman quotes T. S. Eliot's comments on the utility of classical myth as 'manipulating a continuous parallel between contemporaneity and antiquity . . . It is simply a way of controlling, or ordering, of giving a shape and significance to the immense panorama of futility and anarchy which is contemporary history.'[9]

The antique theatre was eminently responsible for keeping the old myths alive. Its history is essentially bound up with myth. Perhaps we should not be surprised if the mythical element should have rubbed off a little on the theatre itself. If antique myth provides a parallel with contemporary life, the whole history of Western theatre has produced examples of dramatists who have used theatrical analogies to illuminate our understanding of life. The theatre has acquired its own mythology. It can be a myth in itself.[10]

So if for Anouilh the theatre takes on a mythical meaning of its own, inherent in his own *sens de la vie*, this tendency is nourished and strengthened by his growing habit of identifying his central character with himself, sometimes in the shape of a writer/hero, who may even be a dramatist, and who is often endowed with a name that recalls that of the writer himself.

Just as Anouilh has assimilated mythological and historical figures to his own beliefs and purposes, so that they become actors in a play obviously concocted by the author,[11] his honest admission that his attraction to Molière resides principally in the latter's recognition of mankind's essential egoism should prepare us for his becoming the hero of his own dramas, and perhaps of his own personal drama. Can it be that in his effort to understand himself Anouilh has passed from the theatricalization to the mythologization of the self? For it is in the extent to which he has placed himself at the theatrical centre of his own work that one might be able to consider him to be creating his own myth of himself.

What of the man himself? Anouilh has of course in life always maintained his invisibility: 'Je n'ai pas de biographie et j'en suis content.'[12] But it is hard not to deduce some idea of the man from his plays, where the repetition of themes has constantly been noted − the fruitless search for the absolute in an absurd world, the clash of idealism and reality, the impossibility of love (or friendship), the failure of wealth (or poverty) to provide an answer, the nostalgia (or, later, revulsion) for childhood; repetition of characters too − the 'pure' young heroine (who tends gradually to disappear), the old childhood friends (who grow apart into betrayal), the uniformly detestable mother figures and the more ambiguous depiction of wives (at times viewed with some respect and compassion, at others seen as rapacious blood-suckers) and the gross and vulgar fathers (presented more sympathetically as Anouilh grows older), being much put upon by their families. His 'heroes' tend to fall into two major categories, the purely intransigent Alcestes or the mocking Don Juanesque cynics, though they blend at times into one character in varying proportions. But all of them in some sense play at living, escape into a dream world of the past or the future, into a world they create for themselves. Whether they be dreamers or artists or even generals, they live in a world of their own devising.[13] No wonder there are so many *metteurs-en-scène* disguised as characters in Anouilh's theatre.

Whereas the use of 'theatre in the theatre' or some kind of framing device is common from the start, several critics have noted the importance of his increasing reliance on farcical techniques, first clearly apparent in *Ardèle* (1948) and *La Valse des toréadors* (1951)[14] − under the influence of Roger Vitrac − where the central character first begins to coincide closely with the age and style of the author.

It is sometimes thought that this concentration on farce is a sign that Anouilh is side-stepping into facility, content with his oft-professed desire to be an entertainer. But here Anouilh is not only moving his plays more firmly into the tragi-comic mode (due perhaps to the impact of Absurdist drama?) but also, one suspects, experimenting in another variation of 'theatre in the theatre'. For no one takes farce realistically. It is as obviously unreal, with its familiar theatrical conventions, as exemplified by Feydeau, as is a subject drawn from myth or the distancing pretence at unreality of 'theatre in the theatre'.

Ornifle (1955) is one of the best examples of his use of farce. The writer/hero — combining the characteristics of Tigre and Héro in *La Répétition* (1950), frivolous *honnête homme* and bitter realist (locked in the usual contest of old boyhood friends) — is closely modelled, as is the whole play, on Molière's *Dom Juan*. Now Anouilh seems to be almost identifying himself with one of myth's greatest egoists in a play in which references to *l'âme* first become clearly apparent.

In the epilogue to Max Frisch's *Don Juan, or The Love of Gallantry* (1953)[15] the author makes a judgement on this legendary character which could, one feels, be applied to Anouilh himself:

Behind Don Juan stands boredom, even if it is outplayed [*sic*] with bravura, the boredom that does not yawn but makes faces, the boredom of a spirit that thirsts for the absolute and believes it has learnt that it will never find it; in short the great boredom of melancholy, the distress of a heart whose desires are dying, so that all it has left is wit. A Don Juan with no wit would hang himself.

After the failure of *La Valse des toréadors* in France,[16] Anouilh for various reasons changed tack for a time, without entirely abandoning farce.[17] The group of plays that followed, though successful, is rather a mixed bag, dominated by those with an historical background: *L'Alouette* (1952), *Pauvre Bitos* (1956) and *Becket* (1958), notable for their framing techniques, flashbacks, dream sequences and other technical devices, by which Anouilh heightens the mythical quality of Joan, the universalizing parallel between Bitos and Robespierre and the doomed and embittered friendship of Henry and Becket.

This is also the time when Anouilh's social and political views come to the fore. In *Ornifle* he ridicules French attitudes to literature. *Pauvre Bitos* enraged the Left, who took the play to be an attack on *them*, in spite of Anouilh's denial that it was a political play. It is perhaps better described as an anti-political play. But he seems to be extending his targets to include the whole political spectrum from Left to Right.

Two critics have in my view rightly seen the crucial importance of *La Grotte* (1960).[18] It introduces a whole group of plays extending through the *Nouvelles pièces grinçantes* and *Pièces baroques* to *Pièces secrètes*, in which the myth of the theatre is examined and tested again and again. If the theatre has been used up to now as a kind of metaphor for life, now we have a metaphor plus, in which life and the theatre become inextricably entangled. Already in *Colombe* (1950) the needle had veered from side to side in its effort to point to either the illusions of theatre or the illusions of life as holding the key to our understanding of reality.

There are too many of these plays for me even to hint at the full extent of the analogy. But most of them have a central character (usually an Antoine) who would appear to be our dramatist's stand-in, seeking to unravel the mystery of life.

La Grotte, the play its Auteur was unable to write, the most overtly Pirandellian of all Anouilh's plays, presents a parallel between the problems of a society governed by a well-ordered system on the verge of break-down and the problems of a dramatic author uncertain whether to write an out-of-date *pièce bien faite* or allow 'real life' to break through. Chaos versus order, life versus form, art versus life. There is no solution. The Inspecteur, a character intent on solving a crime, advises the Auteur to stick to a well-tried dramatic formula; the Maître d'Hôtel, dependent for his very existence on his one predestined role in drama, wants the Auteur to uphold the conventions of the old order. These attitudes are challenged by the Comtesse, who tries to break down the barriers of the class structure, thus completely disrupting her world; and by the young Séminariste,[19] who threatens to break out of his allotted role in order to oppose the social system, thus ruining the plans of the Auteur. If strict forms satisfy our need for order, vibrant life always breaks through and upsets the pattern. In an oddly moving ending the Auteur takes over a role in his disintegrating play; and as his favourite character, Marie-Jeanne the Cook, a Mother Earth symbol of indomitable life, lies dying, he steps up to her bedside to console her. The form of the play reflects the collapsing order of society and underlines the artist's failure to find a satisfying answer to a reality whose complexities escape him. Though criticized for setting the play in the early part of this century, Anouilh understandably chose a period that highlights social change.

Anouilh at the crossroads? In his social thinking and his craft? Once again the theatre is the filter through which Anouilh views the problems of life and art.

Now he really enjoys playing games with time, either by enlisting the fantasies of his characters (as in *Le Boulanger etc.* (1966) and

Les Poissons rouges (1968)) by a technique in which his dead Antoine looks back on his life with little respect for chronology (*Cher Antoine* (1967)) by bringing his unnamed hero on stage at three different ages simultaneously (*L'Arrestation*, 1971) or by combining a survey of the life of an *homme de théâtre* with the evocation of scenes by a number of playwrights from Shakespeare to Chekhov (*Ne réveillez pas Madame*, 1964).

As Mcintyre puts it:

The deliberately non-chronological and fragmented presentation of the action in many of these plays and the frequent use of flashbacks keep us standing on the bank of the river of time . . . We view our lives, forwards and backwards, from the present moment, but we need only step out of the flux of time to see that this is a false perspective . . . The time theme and the sense of life's essential immutability which lies behind it brings Anouilh to refine his ideas on the relationship of theatre and life.[20]

Through 'theatre in the theatre' and the variations he plays on it Anouilh creates a timelessness which is one of the universalizing characteristics of myth.

But here it is firmly anchored to Anouilh's *sens de la vie*. The *metteur-en-scène* figures, who first appeared in disguised form as Duchesses incorporated into the structure of the plot, have gradually grown into an Antoine de Saint-Flour or a Julien, coalescing into the hero–dramatist, theatre or opera director, professional man of letters. By placing himself at the centre of his mythological approach to theatre, Anouilh is creating a mythology for himself, of himself. The myth of the theatre gets absorbed into the myth of the dramatist.

The play he cannot write has been identified with the author–hero's failure to grasp reality. This is all well exemplified in *Cher Antoine*, where the hero's young mistress Maria appears in the 'real life' episodes only as a fleeting figure in the background; in the rehearsal scenes it is the actress who plays her part who reveals to us and to Antoine by some kind of theatrical osmosis with the character that she belongs to 'reality' and must leave him in his unreal world to go and play her part in 'real life'. The dramatist (Antoine and/or Anouilh) was able to create this 'real' character in his play only by a theatrical device.

Similarly Anouilh seems able to explore his mother–son obsession[21] only by reference to the theatre, by playing on the Hamlet–Gertrude scene in *Ne réveillez pas Madame*, where it is

linked to Oreste–Clytemnestre, a comparison followed up in *Tu
étais si gentil quand tu étais petit.*

In numerous plays of this period we reach a point where the
tenuous nature of our existence trembles on the brink of explicit
recognition, when a mystery seems about to be unveiled. Is this not
one of the prerogatives of myth?

Yet we hear more and more about his personal problems as he
begins to speak about the *pièce secrète* of life,[22] those hidden personal and family relationships that escape our full understanding.
Is he weakening his drama by overstressing the personal element?
Or is he reinforcing his belief that we are all so locked into our own
egoism that comprehension of reality is precluded?

At this moment Anouilh returns to the 'Léon' of the more farcical plays in his *Pièces farceuses.* It is no accident that this volume
contains *Episode de la vie d'un auteur*, first written in 1948.[23]

This gross impromptu starts in a way reminiscent of Henri
Becque's *La Parisienne*[24] and develops almost like one of
Ionesco's farces. Centred for the first time on a dramatist–hero,[25]
it portrays the absurd world of theatrical farce, even if at its serious
heart are glimpsed the problems of love and our essential solitude.
The hero is persecuted by a Romanian lady journalist, his mother,
his wife (this time called Ardèle), an envious cadging old friend (the
familiar La Surette), a writer friend jealous of his popular success,
another friend suicidal over a love affair, a housing inspector, a
pregnant maid, a lady who continually demands a Léon on the
telephone and plumbers, called to repair a leak, so inefficacious
that the ceiling collapses over the characters at the end of the play.

Its pertinence lies in the fact that Anouilh has taken it up to serve
as the *canevas* of *Le Nombril* (1981), one of his greatest recent suc-
cesses. But first a very brief word about *Chers Zoiseaux* (1977). Le
Chef, this time a successful writer of detective novels, has a family
of appalling daughters and lives in an atmosphere of *bourgeoisie
gauchiste.* Although, needless to say, the play was labelled ultra-
reactionary, its familiar themes have been better treated elsewhere.

La Culotte is a different matter. Centred on the much-humbled
phallus of today, it is not, Anouilh insists, an anti-feminist play.
By setting it in a France of the future chaotically ruled by women,
and by using the trial of the hero as a kind of play within the play
– during which one of the characters announces the interval –
Anouilh manages to cast over the proceedings a veil of unreality.
The writer–hero of this fantasy world of *gauloiserie* is again the still

lecherous Léon, ignoble yet honour-bound and ridiculously dignified. He needs to be, as he is tied to a stake, kept on a leash by the women of the family, accused of impregnating a former maid, who has just had a baby — which eventually turns out to be black — and given just enough freedom to write his regular article for *Le Figaro* in order to keep his family in funds. Refuting at the trial his defence lawyer's plea of impotence, Léon is condemned to lose his vitals and only saved by the new maid, who, as they escape to Switzerland, makes it very clear that rigorous wives are self-perpetuating.

Inadequate in the exercise of their new-found power, all the women are obnoxious — except Léon's little daughter, who refuses to betray him. But it is true that Anouilh lashes out all round him. Even perhaps mocking himself when he puts Hamlet's 'To be or not to be' soliloquy to good use. As Léon is under threat of castration, the word *sleep* conjures up in his mind the thought of anaesthesia before the operation.

Every critic of his latest group of plays has noted the element of personal confession — his obsessions, vulgarities, pet hatreds, regrets and nostalgia — what Philippe Sénart calls 'son impossible biographie' and André Alter 'la voix la plus authentique, la voix qui jaillit du plus secret d'un cœur'.[26]

Anouilh heads his introduction to *Le Nombril* 'Voyage autour de mon nombril'. Using *Episode* as his base, he develops his 'autobiographical' approach in a way no critics could fail to notice, invited as they were by the author himself to do so, in spite of his coy disclaimer: 'Ici l'auteur (celui qui est le héros de la comédie, pas moi — ne pas confondre), qui est en train d'écrire la pièce devant vous, en même temps qu'il la vit . . .'[27]

This, he claims, is an example of 'l'égocentrisme . . . la tarte à la crème de la littérature classique . . .' of which many were lucid observers, 'même Molière — notre tendre patron — dont pas un seul personnage n'en est exempt, même le soi-disant pur Alceste . . .'.

While hoping that he too shares in this lucidity, he admits that his hero has failed with regard to his 'vanité littéraire (maladie incurable et à l'issue toujours fatale de tous les gens de lettres)' though he has the excuse that 'il est entouré d'une jolie collection d'égocentristes . . . L'auteur (moi cette fois) espère qu'elle sera perceptible.' The critics responded unanimously, in praise this time, with:

The myth of the theatre in the theatre of Anouilh

Cette fois il [Anouilh] se met carrément en scène . . . il règle ses comptes . . . avec les siens — femmes, enfants, amis (même les détails autobiographiques y sont). Avec lui-même aussi — l'homme, le futur mort et l'auteur dramatique . . . (Gilles Sandier)

Tous les personnages de sa légende, toutes ses ombres, tous ses fantasmes sont là . . . l'auteur mieux que jamais et plus directement s'explique sur lui-même. (Philippe Tesson)

And this in spite of Anouilh's comment 'Au théâtre . . . on ne peut pas s'expliquer comme les romanciers.'

Jan Mara writes of 'Le canevas quasi-pirandellien de la pièce', and Guy Dumur notes that 'Anouilh a voulu résumer en une seule soirée *Le Misanthrope, Le Malade imaginaire, Les Femmes savantes* et *L'Ecole des femmes*. Il se met en scène lui-même . . .'

It would indeed appear that here Anouilh has not only staged himself as a dramatic author writing the very play we are witnessing, but has combined in the process a short summary of his work: the theatrical framework of farce,[28] the *dédoublement* of the hero in the two friends Gaston and Léon,[29] the absurdist device of the empty boxes brought on stage by the delivery men throughout the action,[30] the outrageous demands of the family and the interminable chatter in bed of his young mistress, the comments on the theatrical scene and the dramatist's reflection on his own work, the mockery of doctors and the realization of solitude, illness and death.

Has Anouilh at last succeeded through the theatre in tracking himself down?

At the end of *Episode* the Auteur indicates that he wants *all* the bad news: 'Je suis comme Oedipe, moi, maintenant. Je veux tout savoir.'

Perhaps the calamities of farce are not so far removed from those of tragedy after all.

It comes as no surprise that in 1986 — at last — La Table Ronde publishes Anouilh's *Oedipe, ou Le Roi boiteux*.

Here his treatment of Sophocles' play is not unlike the method he used in his *Antigone*. Again he uses a framing device. While the Choeur recounts the background, Oedipe and Jocaste are seated on a bench. When we reach the point in the story when the two first meet, they start reminiscing about the past, how Jocaste had observed his desire for her grow into something more pure, how Oedipe had revelled in his new power instead of being 'le petit

DONALD WATSON

boiteux d'autrefois dont ils se moquaient', and how now suddenly
all seemed vanity and his only consolation was the woman 'où je
n'avais plus peur – enfin!'. The Choeur continues with the story
of the plague: 'Et c'est ici que l'histoire commence . . .' Oedipe
assumes the people's sufferings: 'C'est mon rôle' and the Choeur
adds: 'Sauver la ville, c'était son métier de roi.'

Henceforth the action resumes its normal course, though
Anouilh tends to clarify and rationalize some of the happenings.
He deliberately adds details that remind us of his other works.
Tirésias, whom Oedipe treats violently, recalls Becket with his
'C'est un autre roi que je sers', Jocaste reminds us of some of his
other mothers, and he is at pains to prepare the ground for his own
earlier *Antigone*. References are dropped to Etéocle and Polynice
and Ismène; Créon insists that he was made king to 'retrousser mes
manches' or 'prendre la vie – leur vie – à pleines mains pour les
aider à vivre'. This time, however, somewhat oddly, Oedipe calls
Créon 'l'ami du premier jour', presumably to hint at the old theme
of betrayal (of a boyhood friendship?), and when they come to
blows Jocaste has to separate them like brawling schoolboys.

Anouilh has no fear of being accused of repeating himself; in
fact he seems to delight in familiar situations and phrases. When
Oedipe has rejected Tirésias and Créon, the Choeur continues:
'Voilà. Oedipe est prêt à jouer maintenant la pièce pour laquelle de
toute éternité, sans doute, il avait été créé. Il va aller jusqu'au
bout.' The idea of eternal repetition is part of his tragic vision, as
he also made clear in his treatment of the House of Atreus in *Tu
étais gentil . . .*, where the characters are condemned to perform
their tragedy night after night on stage.[31]

Rehearsal leads to performance, performance to repetition, and
it is repetition that creates the construction of myth and lends it
timelessness. So by repetition the theatre in its history has created
its own myths, its own archetypal situations and characters. Not
only does Anouilh remind us of those in the past, but in the totality
of his work by repetition he creates his own. His characters and
situations acquire a mythic status by the way they evoke the past
and repeat themselves from play to play.

His use of related intertextual levels make his plays sounding-
boards, resonant of Shakespeare and Molière, Marivaux and
Musset, Strindberg and Chekhov, Feydeau, Vitrac and Ionesco, an
echoing chamber of the timeless history of the theatre and its
endlessly repeated situations. So his heroes *se dédoublent* with

archetypes from the past, between themselves and within themselves; they multiply themselves.[32]

Gaston and Léon in *Le Nombril* are two sides of the same hero, both prey to literary envy and spite, with a shared and almost interchangeable past. They repeat all those other pairs of friends which have become so familiar to us. Oedipe and Créon are no different, recalling *La Répétition*'s Héro and Tigre or Julien and Armand in *Colombe*, Oedipe with his seriousness and flawed ambition being opposed to Créon, the *homme léger* and *corrompu* who hankers after *le bonheur*. Yet two halves of the same self. Half way through *Oedipe* the Choeur has a long monologue:

L'homme est un roi boiteux. Il va, un pied dans son ombre, un pied sur le chemin clair de sa raison, et il avance, sans trop savoir où. Sur la route de lumière il reconstruit orgueilleusement le monde et il peut tout – d'une jambe! Mais l'autre pied suit un sentier obscur et glissant au fond de la boue de son être. Et c'est pour cela qu'il boite, le malheureux! Parfois il croit avoir vécu comme un juste, mais il oublie la bête qui est en lui et qui va se venger, parfois il a vécu comme une bête cédant à tous ses désirs, mais il oublie le petit garçon pur qu'il a été autrefois et qui va le juger à son tour, jeune ange exterminateur. Car au plus haut de son triomphe l'homme est à l'affût de son remords. Etrange bête!

Thus Anouilh slots himself into the role of tragic hero, while at the same time putting into the mouth of the Chœur at the end of the play, when Oedipe has left for the mountains, his claim for the universality of the myth:

C'est fini pour cette fois . . . Quant à la peste . . . Cela sera un souvenir que les vieux raconteront aux enfants plus tard. Puis il y aura d'autres maladies . . . Et bon an mal an, il meurt toujours à peu près autant de monde . . . Le malheur, comme dans l'histoire d'Oedipe . . . n'est pas toujours exceptionnel . . .

As the girls say at the end of *L'Arrestation*:
LA FILLE: 'Merde! C'est pas gai la fin! . . .'
L'AUTRE FILLE: 'Non, mais c'est beau quand même . . . Et puis de toute façon, on sait que c'est pas vrai. C'est qu'une histoire . . . Dans la vie, ça ne se passe jamais comme ça.'

However universal he aims to be, Anouilh can never eclipse himself completely. He even takes over Oedipe when he expresses his social views in characteristic fashion: 'Ils font semblant de les haïr, mais au fond les pauvres adorent les riches: c'est leur théâtre.' And who can help being reminded of Anouilh's early plays, where money dictated to fate?

Can a writer create a private mythology about himself? A mythology has to be received and accepted, and partly created by others. At times methinks he protests too much. While he prides himself on being an entertainer, his very success seems to have denied him serious recognition in France, and this failure to win an official accolade from the people he constantly ridicules and mocks rankles so deeply that his Léons and Antoines collectively can be tiresome in their complaints. His lucid appraisal of this defect does not entirely excuse it.

But he has taught us one thing.

If the reality of the world about us is, as is often suggested, a collection of signs which we are conditioned in our own minds to interpret in a particular way by the customs and thought patterns of the age and society in which we live, then we are indeed the creators and directors of our own play, in which we always perform the leading part.

By delving into the theatre and its myths, by immersing himself so completely in its ambiguities, its archetypes and its mysteries, Anouilh has sought to uncover its multiple meanings and give us an insight into some of the ways it can help us to learn about ourselves and our destiny. If myth thrives on the fascination it evokes, then Anouilh has surely nurtured the myth of the theatre. And if not myth, what other word can one use?

NOTES

1 W. D. Howarth, *Forces in Modern French Drama* (London, 1972).
2 '. . . une pièce que je n'ai jamais pu écrire . . .' The play in which the author steps into the action to hold the hand of his dying heroine and expressly recalls Pirandello's 'theatrical trilogy' – and in particular *Six Characters in Search of an Author* – in which the reality of the world on stage is deliberately confused with the real life of actors and audience.

Both *La Grotte* and *Six Characters* exemplify their authors' problems in creating reality on stage through form.

In the first play, the Author falls too much in love with the reality of one character to be able to find a satisfactory form for the whole play; in the second, Pirandello's Author has failed altogether to embody his characters in a play, so that they seek to live their story out in performance with a company of actors. In both plays the 'reality' of death intervenes to underline the fact that, especially in the theatre, as the Japanese playwright Chikamatsu wrote, 'art lies in the slender margin between the real and the unreal'. Not unlike myth perhaps?

3 2nd edn. (London, 1965).

4 In *Becket, L'Alouette, Pauvre Bitos* and *La Foire d'Empoigne*. See W. D. Howarth's comment on the last play in the chapter already quoted, p. 103: 'History has now become theatre, and the only concern of kings and emperors is to play to the gallery.'

5 As notably in *Pauvre Bitos* and *Le Boulanger, la boulangère et le petit mitron*.

6 H. G. McIntyre, *The Theatre of Anouilh* (London, 1981), p. 44.

7 *'Eurydice' and 'Médée'*, ed. E. Freeman (Oxford, 1984), p. xiv.

8 Attention could be drawn in particular to J. Harvey's *Anouilh* (New Haven, 1964) and to the above-mentioned study by McIntyre.

9 *'Eurydice' and 'Médée'*, ed. Freeman, p. xiv.

10 Perhaps it is hardly necessary to mention names such as Rotrou, Corneille, Calderón, Molière, Shakespeare, Marivaux and, supremely in this century, Pirandello.

11 This is especially apparent in *Tu étais si gentil quand tu étais petit*.

12 In a letter to H. Gignoux published in 1946. Quoted on p. 10 of Thérèse Malachy's *J. Anouilh: Les problèmes de l'existence dans un théâtre de marionnettes* (Paris, 1978). But Anouilh is, it seems, about to disappoint himself. The autobiography of his early years is due to be published at any moment by La Table Ronde under a typically arresting title: *La Vicomtesse d'Eristal n'a pas recu son balai mécanique*.

13 Malachy's study is particularly good in her examination of Anouilh's characters.

14 See McIntyre, *Theatre of Anouilh*, and also J. Styan's *Dark Comedy* (Cambridge, 1968), and his *Elements of Drama* (Cambridge, 1967).

15 As quoted in the E.N.O. programme (1987) for Dargomyzhsky's opera *The Stone Guest*.

16 'Un de mes fours célèbres'. But not in England.

17 In *L'Hurluberlu* and, as we have seen, in *Ornifle*. See McIntyre, *Theatre of Anouilh*, ch. 6.

18 Paul Ginestier in his *Anouilh* (Paris, 1971), and McIntyre, *Theatre of Anouilh*, ch. 7.

19 Who becomes a Pirandellian 'Character' in Act II. See his speech in *La Grotte*, in the *Nouvelles Pièces Grinçantes* (Paris, 1970), p. 260.

20 McIntyre, *Theatre of Anouilh*, pp. 118, 119.

21 First strikingly apparent in the Gaston/Mme Renaud confrontation scene in *Le Voyageur sans bagage* (1936).

22 See *Cher Antoine*, Act I, in *Pièces baroques*, p. 47. See also McIntyre, *Theatre of Anouilh*, p. 119.

23 Whether this play was revised for publication in 1984 is not known to me.

24 'Ouvrez ce secrétaire et donnez-moi cette lettre.'
25 The other early Léons were Generals.
26 Both writing of *Le Scénario* (1974) as quoted in *Avant-Scène*, 15 Sept. 1977.
27 *Avant-Scène*, 1 Jan. 1983, contains all the following critical comments.
28 The whole family indulges in a slapping session.
29 Who both suffer from writers' vanity and envy.
30 Anouilh has often parodied Absurdist drama.
31 In all the plays that deal with characters touched by myth – *Antigone*, *Becket*, *L'Alouette*, for example – this idea has been present to suggest tragic inevitability and mythical timelessness.
32 Inspired perhaps by Alfred de Musset, especially in his *Lorenzaccio*?

15

'Entre le mythique et le quotidien': myth in the theatre of Michel Vinaver

DAVID BRADBY

'Pour qui ne fait pas profession d'étude de textes mais est conduit par un désir de mieux apprécier l'actualité à s'efforcer de saisir le passé de l'homme et de le comprendre et l'abolir dans l'exercice du quotidien, la lecture de la *Théogonie* d'Hésiode est difficile: glissante pour l'esprit qui dérape sur une succession de catalogues, qu'interrompt ça et là la relation d'une anecdote où l'on s'accroche, se crispe, et qui enfin élude toute prise, car ni le récit de la guerre des Titans ni celui de la castration de Ciel ne débouchent sur ce qu'obscurément on attend: l'éclatement du mythe en sa signification.'[1]

This Proustian sentence, published by Vinaver in 1955, the year he wrote his first play, can stand as a summary of the treatment of myth in all his subsequent work. It comes at the beginning of an article in which he reviewed a new translation of Hesiod, a review which was the occasion for a meditation on the use of myth in literature. The first half of the sentence contains a remarkably compact summary of the 'théâtre du quotidien' school of dramatic writing, which was not to establish itself in the public eye until the 1970s. The second half suggests an approach to myth in the theatre quite different from that current in the French theatre of the time, in which myths were invariably exploited for their ability to confer a general meaning on particular experience – a process well conveyed by Vinaver's last phrase, 'l'éclatement du mythe en sa signification'. Hesiod's particular method of composition appears to have had a profound influence on Vinaver, who acknowledged his debt by using the title of Hesiod's other major work for one of his own plays: *Les Travaux et les jours*.[2] In Hesiod he found a heightened experience of 'l'exercice du quotidien'.

The value to be attributed to 'le quotidien' is crucial to an understanding of Vinaver's work. By his own admission a particular relationship with the everyday lies at the origin of his creative life: 'Je crois bien qu'enfant j'étais étonné qu'on me

205

permette les choses les plus simples, comme de pousser une porte, de courir, de m'arrêter de courir, etc. J'étais étonné, émerveillé de ces droits qu'on me donnait, et j'étais toujours à craindre qu'on me les retire, qu'on me repousse dans la non-existence'. Because he had a sense of standing somehow *outside* reality, the act of writing became not an imitation of reality, but rather a constantly renewed attempt to capture or to penetrate something never perceived as given in advance: 'Toute mon activité d'écriture . . . est une tentative de pénétrer ce territoire, le quotidien, qui ne m'a jamais été *donné*, dont l'accès est toujours à découvrir, à forcer.'[3] One possible method of approach must have been suggested to the young Vinaver by the existentialist writings of Sartre and Camus. The insistence of Meursault (in *L'Etranger*) on the validity of the sensation of each fresh moment, divorced from concerns of past or present, would seem to offer a model for the experience of 'le quotidien'. But in the case of Meursault moment-by-moment existence is precisely that which is given, the primary experience which is then threatened by intrusions of different kinds. In Vinaver's early novels, as well as in some of his plays, he comes close to creating figures similar to Meursault: a conscientious objector in *L'Objecteur*, a drop-out in *Dissident, il va sans dire*. But they are not innocents whose instinctual approach to life is misunderstood by society with its categorical structures. Rather, they are people who, like Vinaver himself, have to struggle to penetrate the territory of the everyday.

Moreover, the vivid experience of the present moment does not, in Vinaver's work, involve being cut off from the past. Unlike many of Beckett's characters, for example, Vinaver's have not forgotten everything that went before. Instead, the experience of the present implies an effort to 'saisir le passé de l'homme et de le comprendre et l'abolir dans l'exercice du quotidien'. In Hesiod this takes the shape of a particular temporal framework: 'le Cosmos a eu une histoire. Cette histoire est terminée. Le futur ne s'entend que comme une réalisation toujours plus totale du présent.'[4] What has taken place in the past is not denied, but nor is it available to provide a ready explanation for the present moment. This must be created in and through the moment itself. For the writer with these convictions there is a major difficulty, one that has been faced by many twentieth-century authors: how to present banality without falling into the banal. It is a problem rephrased from the reader's point of view in Vinaver's opening sentence quoted above, where he writes of the mind sliding over successive events, grasping momentarily at one anecdote or another, but unable to find a unifying sense for the whole. In modern French theatre this unifying role has so frequently been performed by the imposition of myth that it comes as a considerable shock to find in Vinaver an author who uses myth quite differently: in a fragmentary, discontinuous manner that recalls the poetry of T. S. Eliot. In fact the difficulties facing both authors could be expressed in similar terms: how to make of a life 'measured out with coffee spoons' a drama as intense as that of the House of Atreus.

Vinaver himself attributes enormous importance to Eliot's poem *The Waste Land*: 'En tant qu'écrivain de théâtre la rencontre avec *The Waste Land* a été, je le sais aujourd'hui, fondatrice. Beaucoup plus qu'une influence.' He first read the poem while a student in America and spent the best part of 1946–7, when he was between 19 and 20, making a translation into French. For the last forty years Eliot's waste land has been the environment inhabited by Vinaver the author. The features he picks out to characterize Eliot's poem can be used equally well to particularize Vinaver's own plays:

c'est la primauté du rythme par lequel il y a poussée vers le sens; c'est le traitement contrapuntique d'une multiplicité de thèmes autonomes; c'est la prééminence des thèmes sur les éléments d'intrigue; c'est le mouvement donné aux thèmes pour qu'ils s'entrechoquent ou se frottent les uns aux autres jusqu'au point de fusion, plutôt qu'un mouvement d'enchaînement causal.[5]

From this list it is evident that for Vinaver considerations of rhythm, theme and language precede those of plot, character and meaning. Vinaver has commented that he would have felt more at ease as a painter or composer than as a writer.[6] In the above passage he uses terms such as 'rhythm' and 'theme' as a musician or painter might use them. For Vinaver, writing is not a means of expressing something already formulated, but rather a process of discovery, a journey starting from the attempt to penetrate 'le territoire du quotidien' and discovering along the way juxtapositions or points of articulation between experiences of different orders. By renouncing the attempt to impose a single, unified meaning, and by accepting a fragmentary method of composition, he is able, like Eliot, to achieve startling effects by the joining of disparate elements. He described this as 'le niveau moléculaire où la jointure se fait entre le plus universel et le plus trivial, entre le mythique et le quotidien, entre le plus ancien et l'absolument actuel – sans passage par la métaphore et encore moins par l'allégorie'.[7] This method results in dramas of multiple viewpoint having their own integrity, which is not to be judged by the traditional Aristotelian criteria. Eugène Vinaver (Michel's uncle) once suggested that in the Aristotelian perspective plays might be judged by how easily they submit to paraphrase. The most perfect example would be *Bérénice*, reduced by Racine himself to the phrase of Suetonius: 'Titus, reginam Berenicen . . . dimisit invitus invitam.' He set this in contrast to the methods of both medieval and modernist poets: 'No summary, no paraphrase can do justice to *The Waste Land* any more than to the *Song of Roland* or *Beowulf* or *Piers Plowman*.' In these works he detected a different kind of integrity: 'not the integrity of a pivotal centre, narrative or conceptual, but that of a close-knit fabric, the various strands of which are inseparable from one another, and yet not subordinate to any single one of them.'[8]

Because Vinaver's plays present a multiplicity of strands, they do not submit easily to paraphrase. This reflects his method of writing, never starting from a strong story-line: 'ce qui m'intéresse au départ se présente de façon très nébuleuse, ne s'oriente pas dans le sens d'une histoire, d'une fable. Je pars de ce qui est le contraire d'une histoire.'[9] As Sartre showed in *La Nausée*, the first line of a story already implies its ending and its meaning. The opposite of a story, for Vinaver, is 'le quotidien', seized in the vivid, undifferentiated intensity of its multiple experiences. This does not lead him to avoid the mythic dimension or to limit the field of experience. Most of his plays draw on events that have given rise to myth, whether ancient or modern. His first plays were concerned obliquely with the two major conflicts of the 1950s for France – the wars in the Far East and in Algeria. What interested Vinaver was the ways in which myth or symbol intersects with everyday existence: 'Notre existence quotidienne s'alimente de symboles, en est pétrie, c'est peut-être même ce qui la différencie des existences minérales et végétales. Que serions-nous sans les "mises en rapport", les "conjonctions" que nous effectuons, le sachant ou ne le sachant pas, comme nous respirons, sans relâche?'[10] In Vinaver's plays we find a constant emphasis on this 'mise en rapport'.

It was embodied in the very title of his first play: *Aujourd'hui, ou Les Coréens*, the effect of which was to question the accepted myths surrounding the French military presence in the Far East. It is set in Korea and follows a French soldier through the experience of becoming separated from his company, being taken in by villagers, and discovering a reality not accounted for in the propaganda of either side in the war. It seeks, through the experience of one man, to open out an experience of life in a Korean village unmediated by familiar preconceptions. It achieves what Roland Barthes called a kind of transparency in human relationships, escaping the hierarchies and values imposed by myths in the sense of ideological propaganda – the myth of colonialism as civilizing mission or the myth of revolution as ultimate liberation: '*Aujourd'hui*, comme son titre l'indique, donne le présent comme une matière *immédiatement* structurable et contredit le dogme traditionnel de la Révolution comme durée essentiellement eschatologique.'[11]

Although the subject-matter was contemporary, Vinaver chose to employ the structure of an initiation rite, making this explicit in his programme note: 'Il n'est pas indifférent que le théâtre grec ait pour origine les rites d'initiation au moyen desquels, dans les sociétés tribales, le passage se faisait de l'enfance à l'âge d'homme, de l'hiver au printemps, *d'une situation à une autre*.'[12] He pointed out how his French soldier went through a kind of initiation process, being lost, tested, and in some sense restored. But he was worried that this structure threatened to impose a univocal reading of the play and went on to explain that a performance should not place too much emphasis on the central character's rite of passage: 'C'est plutôt la pièce entière qui doit chercher à figurer dans son progrès l'avènement d'un "temps neuf", d'un monde délivré de tout procès, ouvert à tout mouvement.'[13] From this experience, he concluded that in the future his aim should be to subject his audiences to an experience similar to that of his protagonist in this play, and that this was the fundamental link between the theatre of Ancient Greece and his own: 'Dès son origine, le théâtre a pour usage d'émouvoir l'homme, c'est-à-dire de le faire bouger. Sa fonction est de bousculer le spectateur dans son ordre établi, de le mettre hors de lui, et sens dessus dessous. D'ouvrir un passage à une configuration nouvelle des idées, des sentiments, des valeurs.'[14]

It is perhaps ironic, in view of Vinaver's desire to represent 'un monde délivré de tout procès', that the play should have been banned by the Minister of Youth and Sports. Gabriel Monnet had planned to perform it with young people on a course sponsored by the Ministry. Needing something to replace the banned play, he commissioned Vinaver to write a new version of the *Antigone*. Vinaver chose to retain the standard French translation of Sophocles' play unchanged, but to rewrite the chorus passages in a modern idiom. The result is unusual. Most contemporary authors who have dramatized the Antigone story have used the chorus in order to generate sympathy for the protagonist. Anouilh's version is perhaps the most clear-cut example. In his *Antigone* (first performed in 1944), he reduced his chorus to a single voice, whose main function is to arouse the sympathies of the audience for Antigone's plight. The chorus passages written by Vinaver do just the opposite. They preserve, indeed emphasize, the multiplicity of different voices, and so present a response to the heroine which contains unresolved contradictions, now approving, now condemning her stand.

Vinaver was working towards a dramatic method in which elements quite different from one another, or even with no connection at all, would be juxtaposed, as in a montage, so as to create unexpected reverberations. This was taken one step further with his next play, *Les Huissiers*, an attempt to dramatize political events as they took place without the slightest chance to stand back or impose judgements gained from hindsight. As if to avoid the danger of creating something excessively rambling, Vinaver decided to employ the structure of an Ancient Greek play, Sophocles' *Oedipus at Colonus*, chosen as 'structure neutre à priori, sans rapport significatif avec la pièce quant au contenu'.[15] Thirty years later the play's central thrust emerges very clearly: as the politicians of the Fourth Republic play their interminable but ineffective power games, we realize that there is no real difference between them. The centre of interest is rather the chorus of ushers, people with a different set of priorities altogether, people who only occupy the position of go-between in the power games, but who will continue to occupy that position, whichever government is in power. Moreover, the passages in which they speak together, like a Greek chorus, preserve a multiplicity of different voices, not reducing the group to a single entity but validating different view-points. These passages achieve a poetic quality which recalls T. S. Eliot in *Sweeney Agonistes*: the ushers are no heroes − they are simply go-betweens, with only the most fragmentary awareness of the political struggles being fought out; yet theirs is a profound image of modern consciousness, while the concerns of the politicians seem almost irrelevant.

Myth in the theatre of Michel Vinaver

With *Iphigénie hôtel* (1959), Vinaver again attempted to open up an area lying in between daily experience and mythical events. The action takes place in a hotel near the ruins of Mycenae in Greece on the three days following the colonels' attempted putsch in Algeria on 13 May 1958. The different visitors and the hotel staff having to cope with them are sketched in realistic detail. All are conscious, to a greater or lesser extent, of the mythical events which took place in ancient times at Agamemnon's palace and of the sensational events taking place in Algeria. But neither is used as metaphor or allegory of the events in the hotel, where the conflicts between the guests and the power struggle amongst the staff provide the fabric of the play. Vinaver explained what he was trying to do by means of a musical image: 'Deux principales bandes d'harmoniques "courent" tout au long de l'histoire: celle de la Mycènes ancienne, celle de la France du 13 mai. Ce qui se passe dans l'hôtel ne *reflète* pas la Mycènes ancienne ou la France du 13 mai; mais ce qui se passe dans l'hôtel est enrichi, nourri, approfondi par la Mycènes ancienne, par la France du 13 mai.'[16] He was attempting to achieve the same effect as in his first play: to treat a politically sensational subject in such a way as to neutralize the ready-made response and to highlight the perception of the events of those caught up in them at the immediate moment.

This method could be defined as a withholding from the audience of familiar outlines and a recentring of their interest on everything that takes place *between* the occasional events that capture the headlines. The text of *Iphigénie hôtel* carries an epigraph by the painter Georges Braque explaining that for him the important thing about a picture is not the objects represented but the spaces between two objects: 'Cet "entre-deux" me parait un élément aussi capital que ce qu'ils appellent "l'objet". C'est justement le rapport de ces objets entre eux et de l'objet avec l'"entre-deux" qui constitue le sujet.'[17] The subject of Vinaver's plays was also to be the relationships between things rather than the things themselves. The quality of the dramatic text that results from this frame of mind is best described as open. Every action, every statement can be understood in a variety of different ways and in relation to different 'harmonics' or associations of ideas. The text is constructed so as to favour a multiplicity of reference, and indeed it makes a univocal rendering almost impossible.

This dramaturgical method reached its most complex realization in *Par-dessus bord*, written in 1969. In this play Vinaver interwove

211

half a dozen different actions so as to achieve that 'close-knit fabric, the various strands of which are inseparable from one another and yet not subordinate to any single one of them'.[18] Taking his cue from *The Waste Land*, Vinaver engineered a 'traitement contrapuntique d'une multiplicité de thèmes autonomes', and these different themes collide with one another, fuse and separate again with a minimum of emphasis on causal sequence of events. As well as its different themes, the play employs a wide variety of linguistic registers. Through the juxtaposition of these different themes and languages, Vinaver achieves a series of 'mises en rapport' provoking constant ironic commentary on the actions portrayed. The play's mythical reference-points are drawn from many different sources: from the Norse legends, from modern psychoanalysis, from the world of business and advertising, from European history. But more important than the play's use of existing myth is its analysis of how modern capitalism constantly secretes new myths, something that Vinaver was well placed to observe from his position as executive director of a multinational corporation.

The framework for the play is the life and times of Ravoire et Dehaze, an old-fashioned French family firm, manufacturers of toilet paper. Faced with the successful penetration of their traditional markets by the new American 'softies', the French firm decides to fight back using the enemy's own weapons. A couple of American marketing consultants are brought in and set in train a monstrous mythification of the everyday need for toilet paper. Quoting extravagantly from such authorities as St Augustine and Nietzsche, they elaborate a sales strategy depending on changing the associations habitually surrounding defecation: first they aim to remove the guilt induced by potty training and then persuade the customers that a new brand of luxury toilet paper will be the passport to guilt-free anal eroticism. Different registers of language collide with one another to Rabelaisian effect, especially in a scene depicting a brainstorming session, in which the executives have to practise free association to discover a new name for their product. The suggested names for the new paper include 'Gai Sourire, Doux Baiser, Chaud Baiser, Toison d'Or, Mon Plaisir, Sable d'Or, Vigne Vierge, Mousse et Bruyère'. The last is the one finally chosen for its ability to encapsulate the myth of cleanliness and release associated with nature.

The competition between the French and American firms becomes a fight to the death with no holds barred. The interests of the firm are identified with those of the nation, and the successful selling of toilet paper becomes a matter of defending the values enshrined in French culture and history. After titanic struggles, forcing painful upheavals in the lives of most of its staff, the French firm finally wins the battle for the market. But this victory is so complete that the Americans decide to abandon competition and instead buy it up as a profitable subsidiary; suddenly the battle-lines which had seemed so clearly defined disappear like smoke.

Other themes, events and characters impinge on this commercial world to set its events in startling perspective. A number of tales from the Old Norse sagas, for example, are expounded by a professor and set to music by a dance group. Without explaining the commercial struggle, these stories offer a different language and a different mythical form for conveying a power struggle which ends as unexpectedly as it had begun. At its most complex, the setting of different elements in juxtaposition can be seen in the party sequences, which are written in a manner similar to the choral passages of *Les Huissiers*. The lines of dialogue are arranged not sequentially, but in what at first appears to be random order. They give expression to attitudes often in direct contradiction to one another: for example, both loyalty to the firm and annoyance at being exploited by it. Such contradictions are not resolved but are allowed to remain in juxtaposition, setting up a multiplicity of response in the audience's mind. This resolved, fragmented viewpoint is both statement and formal device. It states the impossibility of ever reaching a simple, unified view of the events depicted and asserts that only *meanings*, not *meaning*, can be found. *Pardessus bord* illustrates more clearly than any other play Vinaver's strategy for avoiding the tendency of myth to solidify and impose a unified meaning on a play. The strategy is to multiply the mythical reference so that no single voice or interpretation emerges to dominate the whole.

The play marked a watershed for Vinaver. It came at the end of a decade when he had written almost nothing. It has been followed, over the last sixteen years, by eight more plays, almost all of which follow a similar method with regard to elements of myth. The myths that he dramatizes are often connected to the major fears and traumas of our time, both private and public: unemployment in *La Demande d'emploi*; drugs in *Dissident, il va sans dire*; cancer in *A la renverse*. But they are never tackled head-on. They are set in a rich texture of 'works and days', of everyday life dramatized with never-failing inventiveness, so that audiences find they are no longer confronted with the familiar outlines of a Major Problem but instead with a multi-faceted human reality. It is a reality hard to pin down, constantly open to change because of the way it is constituted by a ceaseless oscillation between the mythical and the everyday.

NOTES

1 M. Vinaver, 'Les mythes de la Grèce ancienne: une marche d'approche, I', *Critique*, XCIV (1955), 193.
2 M. Vinaver, *Les Travaux et les jours* (Paris, 1979). For a discussion of this play and of Vinaver's place in French theatre, see D. Bradby, *Modern French Drama 1940–80* (Cambridge, 1984).
3 'Pièce jointe', in *Les Travaux et les jours*, p. 73.
4 'Les mythes de la Grèce ancienne: une marche d'approche, II', *Critique*, XCV (1955), 212.
5 Vinaver's translation remained unpublished until it appeared, with a prefatory note, in *Poésie*, XXXI (1984), 4–19.
6 As n. 3, p. 74.
7 See n. 5.
8 Eugène Vinaver, 'Medieval poetry and the moderns', unpublished lecture. (Eugène Vinaver, uncle of the dramatist, was Professor of French at the University of Manchester, and a noted medieval and classical scholar.)
9 *Ecrits sur le théâtre* (Lausanne, 1982), p. 290.
10 *Ibid.*, p. 199.
11 Roland Barthes, 'Note sur aujourd'hui', *Travail théâtral*, XXX (1978), 59.
12 *Ecrits sur le théâtre*, p. 154.
13 *Ibid.*
14 *Ibid.*, p. 35.
15 *Ibid.*, p. 249.
16 *Ibid.*, pp. 198–9. For a fuller discussion of myth in *Iphigénie hôtel*, see Judith D. Suther, 'The medium is not the message: myth in Vinaver's *Iphigénie hôtel*', *The French Review*, XLV (1972), 1106–16.
17 *Théâtre I* (Arles, 1986), p. 277.).
18 See n. 8.